Praise for Mary Gerardy

"In this fine memoir, Mary Gerardy, educator, mentor to students, and citizen of the world, reflects on her extended volunteer service with the Missionaries of Charity community in Kolkata, India. Writing with insight, humor, humility, and an abiding sense of compassion, Dr. Gerardy documents her life-changing experiences, inviting us to share in the stories of those for whom she cared and who cared for her."

—Bill J. Leonard, Professor of Divinity Emeritus, Wake Forest University

"In *Pieces of My Heart*, Mary Gerardy provides a poignant and insightful account of her experiences working alongside the Missionaries of Charity in Kolkata, India. Her story is a testament to the difference that each of us can make in the lives of others and the complexities of international service. By allowing ourselves to be vulnerable, opening our hearts and our minds to different ways of doing things, and embracing, not just the good, but also the tough, challenging, and uncomfortable experiences, amazing things can happen. This book will take you to the heart and soul of the "City of Joy," which will always have a special place in my heart and where I had the pleasure of working with Mary many years ago. I am beyond pleased that Mary's Kolkata story did not end there and that it is available to all in this very readable, enjoyable and inspiring memoir!"

—Winston Tilghman

"There is a distinct badge that is worn by the odd few that choose to give themselves to the service of Calcutta. It is a badge of curiosity, love, kindness, and all of those virtuous qualities one would imagine when admiring the work of caring for the poorest of the poor. It is also; however, a badge that reflects a grief that is healing within. Everyone who serves long-term in Calcutta has this grief. It is a grief that they heal by giving themselves wholeheartedly to people they serve. In *Pieces of My Heart*, Mary Gerardy wears her badge gracefully and tells the tale of losing the love of her life and her ultimate renewal achieved by giving every inch of herself to the service of others, all while living the daily adventures of surviving Calcutta. For those of us who had the privilege of working alongside Mary, it was evident that she is a bright light that shines even in the darkest places. It was an honor to serve with her, and an even greater honor to relive her journey through the pages of *Pieces of My Heart*."

—Ana Paola Garcia Bocanegra

"*Pieces of My Heart* by Mary Gerardy is a wisdom-filled guide for anyone considering person-centered volunteer work, as well as a superb manual for adapting to another culture. She weaves important ideas and observations into colorful, sensuous descriptions and traces her own healing process of recovery from the death of her beloved husband through her Indian experiences and the people she meets along the way. As one who lived as an expat for nearly five years and taught prep and re-entry classes for study-abroad students at WFU, I think anyone considering this type of life experience or in need of deep healing would benefit from reading Dr. Gerardy's book."

—Helen Akinc, author of *The Praeger Handbook for College Parents* and *Turkish Family Favorites*; interculturalist and former Wake Forest University administrator.

"*In Pieces of My Heart*, Mary Gerardy shows us through her stories that the resolution of grief and the renewal of one's spirit are not found in focusing on oneself but in serving others. Her reflections on six months of volunteering in Kalighat, the home for the dying established by Mother Teresa in Kolkata, India, are extraordinary interesting and enlightening. She listens to herself and hears the needs of others as her external adventures lead to inner growth. This is a book about lessons in life that are universal in their impact."

—Samuel T. Gladding, Professor of Counseling, Wake Forest University

"Nirmal Hriday is perhaps the closest place to heaven, here on earth. If you feel the gentle whisper of God instructing you to go to Kolkata... If your heart is calling you to serve, by caring for the poorest of the poor, it isn't a question of if, but when. You will meet many of your soul friends while serving in Kolkata. Friendships are instantaneous, and easy because you automatically know another's person heart, their deep desire to alleviate pain and suffering, and to spread joy, mixed with God's love. Go to India and serve with the Missionaries of Charity. Allow yourself to be transformed by the experience, into a version of yourself that could only be born from traveling into the unknown. Your hands are ready, your heart is open... go."

—Dr. Kristin Best, Chiropractor

Pieces of My Heart

Pieces of My Heart

A Journey from Grief to Renewal in Service of India's Poor

MARY GERARDY

Library Partners Press
Winston-Salem, NC

This memoir is a work of nonfiction.
While the stories in this book are true,
some names and identifying details
have been changed to protect the
privacy of the people involved.

ISBN 978-1-61846-111-7

Book and cover design by: Celeste Holcomb

Produced and distributed by:

Library Partners Press
ZSR Library
Wake Forest University
1834 Wake Forest Road
Winston-Salem, North Carolina 27106

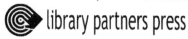 library partners press
a digital publishing imprint

www.librarypartnerspress.org

Manufactured in the United States of America

Table of Contents

In heartfelt appreciation,

Jessica Davey – Thank you for the inspiration!

Jeff Cain, Catherine Dyksterhouse, Laura Florio, Rich Galinski, Griff Gatewood, James Han, Katie McKenna, Holly Miller, Brittany Neal, Amanda Silva, Winston Tilghman, and Weston Willard – thanks for your service in India and for allowing me to accompany you in 1998. When we left India, I vowed that I would return; I just didn't know how long it would take. I hope that, over twenty years later, memories of Kolkata, the Missionaries of Charity, and those you served still resonate and feed your souls.

Oliver – When you were born, I fell in love instantly. In a world where you can be anything, choose to be kind! Your Mimi loves you and looks forward to sharing lots of adventures.

Prologue

On January 2, 2017, I woke up early, eager to start my new adventure. I confess that I lingered under the toasty sheets and blanket a bit longer than I'd planned to, but I wanted to soak up the joy of my blissfully comfortable bed for as long as possible. Finally, I got up and put on fresh new sheets so that when I returned in late June I could sleep in comfort. I checked each room of the house to ensure that everything that needed to be turned off was off and that everything that needed to be on was on. Although I haven't ironed in years, I checked twice to ensure that my iron was not magically plugged in. I also checked my steamer. Of course, it was off, but I needed to be able to remind myself that that was the case. My Chihuahuas, Chico and Carlos Santana, and my cat, Max, ran around clearly agitated. To them, suitcases mean disruption, but they had no idea just how much their routine was about to change.

After packing my car, I headed to my daughter's house in Raleigh, with both dogs in their crates. During the two-hour drive, I reminded myself that the next six months would be a great adventure, one that I had contemplated for a long time. Another confession: I was a little beyond terrified as well, as the "what ifs" took up precious space in my consciousness. My fur babies were hyper-ventilating during our drive, and I was doing the same. After I arrived at my daughter's house, we headed out for the biggest salads we could find. I didn't know how many raw vegetables I would be able to eat in India, my destination, so I wanted to load up! Our next stop was the airport. I gave my daughter a big, big hug, knowing how much I would miss her. Check-in and security went smoothly, and I headed to my gate. Soon it was time to board my flight to Newark – and nothing happened. I heard some muffled groans and looked up to see a sign notifying us that the flight would be delayed for 40 minutes – and then it was an hour – and then it was clear that I would miss my connection to New Delhi. When I got to the gate agent, she said I could fly to Newark and leave the next evening or she could rebook both flights for the next day. Sitting in Newark for nearly 24 hours sounded like a terrible plan. I opted to head back to my daughter's house for the night. The gate agent called, had my bags removed from the plane, and told me I could pick them up on baggage carousel 4. I went to baggage claim and waited and waited. I asked the United representative at baggage claim to check on the bags again and she too was assured that they would be on the baggage carousel within minutes. When I checked for the last time, I learned that while my bags HAD been taken off the plane, another baggage handler had found them and, thinking they had been left OFF the plane, put them back ON. While I was stuck in Raleigh, my bags were headed to Newark. As I headed back to my daughter's house, I wondered if this was a bad omen. Who has their bags "lost" before they even leave the airport? A new low in air travel!

The next morning, I woke up ready to start my adventure again, and hopefully more successfully than the day before. Fortunately, this time everything went smoothly. By that evening I was on my way to New Delhi. The long (15+ hours) flight gave me ample opportunity to reflect on how I arrived at this juncture in my story.

Before

CHAPTER I

The Beginning

My parents met at College of the Bible (now Lexington Theological Seminary) in Kentucky in the early 1950's. My father was preparing for full-time church ministry, and since women were not accepted as pastors at that time, my mother was earning her master's degree in religious education. My father's first pastorate was Midway Christian Church. The town was given its name because it was midway between Lexington and Frankfort. When I was born a month early, in 1954, my mother gave birth in Versailles (pronounced Ver-SAILS), as Midway was far too small to have a hospital. The census population in 1950 was a mere 950; the estimated population in 2016 had grown to a whopping 1,706. In the 1950 census, Versailles had a population of 2,760; today the estimated population is 9,270.

I have often told my three younger brothers that they should be grateful to me for "breaking in" our parents. Case in point: When I was only two years old, they told me that Santa didn't really exist. Santa represented the spirit of giving, blah, blah, blah. I was unhappy with such nonsense and told them that there was indeed a Santa Claus and never again to suggest otherwise. In their defense, they didn't want to lie to their child and were probably on the cutting edge for parents in the mid-1950's. I still believe in Santa though, and my brothers got to enjoy Christmas a bit longer! By the time I was ready for Kindergarten, I had two younger brothers (my youngest brother was arrived when I was in 1st grade). I was born with no spatial intelligence or sense of direction, and because my mother was always afraid that I would end up lost, she bundled up her little boys and walked me to and from school every day. We had moved to Erie, Pennsylvania, where my father had accepted a call to First Christian Church. The one memory of Erie that will never leave me is how very, very cold it was for eight months or so each year. I remember my father telling friends that in Erie we had winter and the 4th of July. My parents' first big test came when I entered first grade. I am a lefty all the way, and my teacher tried in vain to change my handedness. Perhaps as a result, I was slow to read and to write legibly. Our teacher named all the reading groups in the class. The top readers were the swans, which sounded lovely. The slow readers, where I ended up, were the monkeys, which felt like an insult. Today it is funny to me because I love primates of all kinds – and I am a voracious reader!

When we vacationed, we usually visited one set of grandparents or the other, or went camping, which was not my favorite thing. My brothers would go off and play together, and I often ended up reading by myself. Today, that sounds great, but back then I was lonely. The first time I ever left the United States was a family trip to the Canadian side of Niagara Falls. I was beyond excited to travel outside of the country.

While our Canadian trip was great, the first foreign country to truly capture my imagination was India. My mother's college roommate, Barbara Hoskin DeHaven, and her husband Tom, served as medical missionaries there. One year when they were home on furlough, they came to visit and made us the most delicious dinner I'd ever tasted. The curry spices smelled amazing and the poori was better than any other I'd tried before. My dad was a meat and potatoes guy and our dinners were usually meat, frozen or fresh vegetables, starch, bread, and salad. There was always dessert too. With the likely exception of Italian food, I hadn't eaten anything remotely "foreign" in my young life.

My first "celebrity" crush was on Paul McCartney, and I was one of the millions of young girls screaming in front of the (black and white) TV on February 9, 1964, when the Beatles first appeared on the *Ed Sullivan* show. My second crush was on an Indian actor, Sajid Khan, who starred with Jay North on the short-lived TV show, *Maya.* On the show, the American boy had arrived in India to live with his father and learned shortly thereafter that he was missing, likely killed by a tiger while big-game hunting. Raji (Khan) and his elephant, Maya, befriended the American boy and joined forces with him. When the show was cancelled after only 18 episodes, I was heartbroken.

I was always an avid reader, despite what my first-grade teacher thought of my intellectual capacity. My dad took me to the public library regularly, and I would check out the maximum number of books allowed. Several of those books piqued my interest in India once again. The most notable for me was *A Passage to India* by E.M. Forster. When I first read the book in junior high school, I didn't understand the issues around imperialism and colonization, but the tension in the book was palpable. My favorite book of all time, *Lost Horizon* by James Hilton (1933) told the story of a group of travelers whose plane crashed in what was likely modern-day Tibet (between China and India). The passengers were led to an untouched paradise called Shangri-La. I don't want to give away the plot, but I will admit that I have read the book at least ten times and still love it. I recently learned that such a kingdom first came to Western attention through a treasure map found nearly four hundred years ago. The map was later lost but was found again in Calcutta approximately one hundred years ago.

Michael Wood wrote this commentary about *Lost Horizon* for the BBC:

> *Shangri-La is a modern tale with a powerful appeal for to-day's world, but its roots lie deep in much older times. We*

live in a period where global problems threaten to over-whelm us and instill us with fear. The appeal of the tales of Shambala and Shangri-La lies in their connection with this fear – both recognizing it and alleviating it – and this appeal is universal. The stories reflect our desire that something of our world will survive, and that our connection with our past will not be entirely erased, even as we move faster and faster into an uncertain future. These are tales that we still need to believe in today.

CHAPTER II

High School and College

When I was in the seventh grade, my father accepted a call to become the Senior Minister of Third Christian Church in Philadelphia. Although I have lived in North Carolina since 1985 and love it, I still consider Philly to be my "hometown." Dad's church was in the Overbrook area in what was described as a "changing neighborhood." White residents had recently fled to the suburbs in large numbers, and the church mirrored the neighborhood situation. The white members, about fifteen percent of the congregation, were all over the age of sixty, which seemed ancient to me. When I read this to my mother to corroborate my memories, she said that she thought that the white members were even older. One year our parents went to a convention and left us in the care of a church member who was at least eighty-five. She frequently ran red lights while driving, scaring us to death when we were forced to have her take us anywhere.

Growing up in this multi-racial church environment was an education, to say the least. At times, I was in the minority, and I quickly learned that it was not a comfortable place to be. My experience was a teeny, tiny speck of what it must feel like to be marginalized or in the minority. We sang songs I'd never heard of before, and some church members encouraged my father with shouts and comments of affirmation throughout his sermons. My favorite person was the old man who sat a few rows behind us (my dad liked his family to be in the front pews). When the sermon started, he would begin rocking gently in his seat, while quietly chanting, "Well, well," over and over. On a more serious and important note, my brothers and I became very aware of issues involving the Civil Rights Movement that was taking place across the nation in the late 1960's. I'd never seen my father cry until the night that Martin Luther King Jr. was assassinated. My experiences growing up in this environment instilled in me a deep sense of compassion for the oppressed and truly marginalized. I was also moved by the stories that my mother, who directed a Head Start pre-school program, told us about her work and the children in her care.

The church wanted the minister's family to be "comfortable," so we lived in a parsonage in Drexel Hill, a west Philly suburb. In some ways, I wish that we had grown up near the church so that we had lived in the neighborhood and fully immersed ourselves in the culture. We all attended Upper Darby High School, a large and ethnically diverse institution. Todd Rundgren, Jim Croce, and Tina Fey are notable alums, although none of them were there when I was a student. It is said that Fey based some of her film, *Mean Girls,* on her own high school experience at Upper Darby. My friends were Greek, Black, Armenian, Italian, Puerto Rican, and more. I loved visiting their loud, lively families. My own meat-and-potatoes family felt just a little boring and I lived vicariously through my friends. Theater was my life then and the theater department was very active. I planned to study theater and French in college, and eventually make it to Broadway.

I headed off to Hiram College, my mother's alma mater, affiliated with the Christian Church (Disciples of Christ). Unfortunately, the theater crowd in college seemed "out of control" to me and I didn't fit in. The chair of the French department was critical of everyone and I did not enjoy my courses with her. Dismayed by the downfall of my fail-proof plan, I ended up majoring in Religion, with a teaching certificate in Educational Media. I was double majoring in English until a required course in creative writing coincided with the semester I had mononucleosis. I dragged myself to every class, but the 10-page writing assignment each week was too much for my foggy mind to handle. The class would not be offered again for three years, which was after my scheduled graduation.

In college I did venture abroad for the first time, studying at Balls Park Teacher Training College in Hertford, England. It was a wonderful experience and perfect for me because the faculty member leading our group, Dr. Fritzie Redmond, became my lifelong mentor. I miss her to this day and am incredibly grateful for her guidance. On one of our long weekends, I traveled to France, along with several friends. I quickly learned that my high school and college French did not serve me well. I was ill-equipped to speak or understand much and was mightily disappointed. I felt like a fish out of water, particularly in Paris. Every morning we were kicked out of our youth hostel by 9:00 and were not allowed to return until early evening. It was a very cold February, which intensified my unhappiness. I was awed by the sights: the Eiffel Tower, Notre Dame, Versailles, the Louvre, and more, but was put-off by what I perceived to be the arrogant French attitude toward foreigners. Even the small amount of French I knew and tried to use did not charm anyone. The food looked and smelled delicious, but on a very limited budget I couldn't try many of the dishes that appealed to me. I did begin my lifelong love of art on this trip. I walked through the Louvre and other museums reciting the names of artists I'd never heard of previously and feeling awed by the grand masterpieces in front of me. I did have a huge laugh at the pint-sized *Mona Lisa*. I hadn't expected that! Having travelled the world many times now, I would love to return to France, and particularly Paris, to see the city and the country with new eyes.

That trip was my last experience outside of the United States for many years. At twenty-one I accepted my first job, at my alma mater. I worked there for nine years as Director of the Kennedy Center (student center) and Student Activities. Working with students and planning weekly events on a shoestring budget became a passion for me. During this time, I also married and had two children, Jordan and Jenna. I quickly realized that I both loved and was good at my new job. I knew that if I wanted to advance in my career, I would need a master's degree in Higher Education. I received my MEd from Kent State University in December 1981, just a month after the birth of my son. Gradually, living in a town of less than 1,500 people became difficult for me. I needed MORE entertainment, restaurants, events, activity, and stimulation.

In 1985, I accepted a job at Wake Forest University in Winston-Salem, North Carolina, as Director of the College Union. I was busy with a demanding job and young children, and travel was pushed to the back of my mind. During this period, I finished an MBA, divorced my first husband, and was promoted at work. In 1992, I married Ben Gerardy, a minister in the Christian Church (DOC), despite my vow that one thing I would NEVER do would be to marry a minister. God laughs! When I chose religion as my major in college, I wasn't sure that I'd want to go to Divinity School. Despite that, my faith and denomination were and are incredibly important to me. When Ben and I started dating, we were amazed at all the Disciple connections we had. We knew many people in common, and held similar beliefs, particularly the relationship between faith and social justice.

CHAPTER III

City of Joy

Jessica Davey, a remarkable Wake Forest student, started writing to Mother Teresa when she was only twelve years old. She wanted to travel to Kolkata (also known as Calcutta) to serve with the Missionaries of Charity there. Mother Teresa responded and essentially told her to volunteer where she lived instead and that when she was ready, she could come to Kolkata. That time came after her sophomore year at Wake Forest. Jessica had a life-changing experience there and when she returned to school for her junior year, she lobbied the administration to start a service trip to Kolkata so that other students could have the same opportunity. We had many concerns about sending students to the other side of the world, but eventually our fears were allayed. The City of Joy program was born, and our first group of students traveled during winter break 1994-1995. When the students returned, I attended every presentation they gave. A quiet longing grew inside of me. I wanted to have this experience too.

A few years later, Winston Tilghman, who was the student leader for the 1998-1999 service trip, interviewed me to serve as trip advisor. I loved this model that provided such great leadership opportunities to students, while still allowing space for a faculty/staff advisor. I sweated it out as I waited for Winston to deliberate. Finally, he asked me to serve as the trip advisor. I was elated, as was Ben, who loved to travel and wanted me to have great travel experiences as well. It wasn't until about 2 weeks later that my excitement gave way to another feeling - abject panic! It had finally dawned on me that I would be responsible for 12 students from the time we left for India until we returned. I also had recurring nightmares about being unable to do the work myself. What if it was just too hard, physically, emotionally, or otherwise? I had never been in such a vulnerable position with students, and perhaps, with myself.

As it turned out, volunteering with the Missionaries of Charity was a wonderful experience. The work was indeed hard, and some days frustrating. To me, the way that the sisters did things was, well, strange. At the same time, I learned more than I ever could have imagined. One day, during my first week working at Shishu Bhavan, I was greeted by my "posse" of toddlers. I loved their smiles and greetings each morning, so I was beyond irked when one of the "massies" (paid workers) motioned to me to follow her. She walked into a small room, grabbed a big basket of wet laundry, and pointed to the roof. Once we were up there, she showed me how to hang laundry. I didn't think I needed that instruction, having dealt with laundry for most of my life. I noticed, however, that as I hung more laundry, she was sneaking up behind me to "fix" my work. Seriously? I didn't think that I was doing anything wrong. We replayed the same scene over and over for the next few days. Finally, one morning, I realized that I was on the roof alone with the laundry. I wandered over to the edge to look out at rows and rows of rooftops also adorned with colorful laundry swaying in the soft breeze. Then all the rooftops faded away as I stood there feeling "at one" with the universe. I felt so small, yet totally connected to humanity, and experienced God in a way I never had before. It was such a powerful moment and that kind of authentic experience that fills the soul. Several years later, I read the book, *After the Ecstasy, the Laundry: How the Heart Grows Wise on the Spiritual Path,* by Jack Kornfield. He described growth along the spiritual path, and how to sustain ourselves while still living our beautifully imperfect lives. I posed a different scenario. What if the laundry IS the ecstasy? In other words, what if the simplest of actions produce the most spiritual growth and learning? I think about the moments spent on a rooftop in Kolkata almost every day. If I returned to Shishu Bhavan and was called to hang laundry, I would pick up my basket and walk up the stairs with gratitude and love in my heart.

After we returned to Wake Forest, Winston asked us to write a reflection about our time in India. We had participated in reflection sessions most evenings while we were there, which was very helpful as each of us decompressed after our long and eventful days. I knew that this final reflection would also help me to put into words what had happened to me and through me in India.

Often in my life I have wished for revelation or insight to descend on my life like a thunderbolt from the sky. That is the kind of transformation experience that I expected in India; that is, something so powerful that it zapped me with its splendor. India was indeed a transforming experience for me – but it was more like a quiet whisper, a stirring in my soul, and a connection with all of humankind. My experience in India is one that I will never forget – the memories are something that I will cherish forever. India is with me every day and is quietly changing me from the inside out.

My favorite moments are simple ones; the faces of the precious children at Shishu Bhavan, particularly those in our "posses" when we would arrive in the morning; summoning the humility to do things "their way" and not "my way" (which I assumed to be better); Lucy at Kalighat, a rare long-term patient there, who would chide the volunteers for our stupidity on a regular basis; the desk workers at the YMCA (where we stayed), who always had a smile and a greeting for us; the streets, people and traffic (getting around in Kolkata); breakfast at the Mother House with other volunteers; my first taste of real "yummy" chai; and the occasional coke (nothing ever tasted as good as those cold cokes in India).

I was especially pleased with the "City of Joy Scholars." I was excited to have the opportunity to be part of such a talented group of students. Their dedication, enthusiasm, and spirit brought me immense joy. [I then shared with them individual events or snapshots that I would remember about each one of them.]

Before we left for India, I was excited about seeing the Taj Mahal. And, while it was a wonderful experience, I found it oddly disconcerting to feel like a tourist in a country that I had come to claim as my own. The most difficult part of the trip was leaving just as I was beginning to find my niche and feel really at home. I plan to go back some day!

I also hope to have a permanent part of India in my home. The adoption process is an arduous one, but my family is very excited about the possibility that we could have an Indian baby/child sharing our home and our life. I will keep you updated as the process continues. [2018 update – The cost of an international adoption was too high, and we were unable to make this dream a reality, although we remained champions of adoption.]

CHAPTER IV

Return to India

Three months before I traveled to India with my students, I took another big step and started a PhD program through the Fielding Institute in Santa Barbara, CA. (now Fielding Graduate University). Fielding was an incredible place, full of bright, interesting people. During our summer session in Washington, DC in 1999, I saw a sign on the bulletin board about a possible consulting trip to India – I was beyond interested! My rock star professor, Dr. Valerie Bentz, lived next door to a gentleman from Mizoram, the youngest state in India, who was looking for a team to study the state's existing infrastructure and make recommendations to the government. We would work side by side with Mizo partners. Ultimately, about 20 of us headed for Mizoram in April 2001. Mizoram was part of Assam until 1972, when it became a Union Territory. Fifteen years later, in 1987, it became the 23rd state of India.

We traveled from Los Angeles to Bangkok to Kolkata. It felt great to be in the city again, although there was no time for sightseeing. We stayed at Mizoram House in Salt Lake City, a planned satellite community designed in the late 1950's to handle the growing Kolkata population. While there, we finalized our consultation plans.

When we arrived at Lengpui airport in Mizoram, I felt like we had just landed in the middle of nowhere. As I walked from the tarmac to the airport building, I was surprised to see multiple soldiers with automatic rifles. I later learned that there was ongoing concern that drug-runners from Myanmar might try to hijack a plane. The small building that passed for an airport was full with our group of 20. At that time, there were very few "outside" visitors to Mizoram; the previous year there had been only 106.

The adventure truly began when we got in our jeeps and headed up the mountains to Aizawl, the capital city. We traversed narrow roads that looked like they could accommodate a car and a half. To make matters worse, there was no berm – it was simply the road and the abyss. We asked our driver if there were a lot of accidents in the area. I don't remember his answer and I am sure I've repressed it. Any accident, with a vehicle tumbling end over end, would certainly result in severe injury or, more likely, death. I recall trying to remain calm while secretly hyperventilating. At last we arrived at our government guest house in Aizawl. The next morning, I woke up at 4:30 am, a time that I understand exists, but that I rarely see. As a night owl, I am more likely to head to bed at 1:00 am than to get up before 7:00. Since I was up, I decided to go out for a walk. I was in awe of the houses built into the hillside. As I rounded a corner, heading up a mountain path, I came across a little boy wearing a University of North Carolina t-shirt and was immediately reminded that the world is actually very small! I would have been even more impressed if he had been wearing Wake Forest gear, but that didn't diminish the moment of realization.

For nearly two weeks, we worked in teams with our Mizo partners. I was on the education team and we visited schools, met parents, and talked with education leaders to offer the best possible advice for their situation. For us to visit one of the schools, the government had to create a road for us to traverse. During our stay, I learned so much from our partners. Parents, teachers, and school administrators all talked about making sure that Mizo children were prepared for the world they would inherit. And they had several concerns. First, jobs were hard to find. Some unemployed youth were disillusioned and had turned to drugs.

Recently, China had dumped a load of unsold play guns in Mizoram, which angered adults. Gun violence was virtually unheard of there and adults did not want toy guns in the hands of children. Improved technology and infrastructure had brought the *Cartoon Network* into homes. Children who had previously spent their time playing outdoors now wanted to stay inside and watch TV, to their parents' dismay.

During our stay in Mizoram I did not feel like we were in India at all. Mizo people were likely part of a migration from China beginning in the sixteenth century. Eventually, they settled in the area known as Mizoram today. Years before it achieved Indian statehood, Mizoram had suffered from a famine and rat infestation. Local leaders felt that the Indian government had let them down by not coming to their aid in a timely manner. For this reason, the people consider themselves Christians first, Mizos second, and Indians third. Mizoram is 87% Christian, one of the few states in India with a large Christian majority.

Our most frustrating experience came when it was time to return home. We were going to spend the night in Kolkata before heading to Bangkok, then back to the US. I was excited to share "my Kolkata" with our team. When we arrived at the Mizo airport we were hustled to the passenger "lounge." Our plane was "delayed." As we later learned, Indian pilots were unhappy about flying to Mizoram because it was the jhuming (slash and burn agriculture) season. The resulting smoke made landing precarious at the visual flight rules (VFR) only airport. The longer we waited, the more frustrated we became. The father of one of the women in our group was dying, and she desperately wanted to get home to say goodbye. We also began to realize that if our flight was not able to land, we might be in Mizoram for a few more days. At the time, there were only a few flights to the state per week. After hours of waiting, some strings were pulled, and our plane finally arrived! When we finally landed back in Kolkata, it was too late to do any sightseeing. Further, we were all exhausted after such a long day. The next day we flew to Bangkok and then back to the United States. I wouldn't set foot in India for over seventeen years. Sadly, our team member's father died shortly before she got home.

CHAPTER V

International Service

On September 11, 2001, shortly after my experience in Mizoram, the world changed dramatically. After 9/11 it was hard to imagine sending students to the other side of the world, which suddenly felt much more dangerous. Earlier that summer, the Director of Volunteer Services at Wake Forest had resigned to take a new job. I agreed to make all the arrangements for our City of Joy service trip until a new staff member was hired. I had no idea that there would be such a major complication. Early in October, the students who had been selected the previous spring to go to Kolkata asked if the trip would still happen. Frankly, less than a month after such a devastating act of terrorism against our country, we were reluctant to allow students to travel to India. Perhaps, our feelings of discomfort would ease some by the end of December. But the students wanted to know sooner rather than later. Their logic did make sense. If we waited until December to decide whether to let them travel, and the decision was negative, they wouldn't have time to create an alternative plan. Given our uneasiness at the time, we did say no, and the students began to research alternative service locations. Ultimately, we sent them to volunteer at Casa de Caridad, which is run by the Missionaries of Charity, in Mexico City.

While students were looking for potential places to serve, they also found possibilities in Vietnam, through Peacework, an organization that works with colleges and universities to develop and execute international service programs. While we wanted students to volunteer closer to home in 2001, I couldn't forget the Vietnam idea. As a child growing up in the 1960's-70's, I watched black and white images of the war on television each night. The older brothers of some of my classmates were drafted, but by the time I graduated from high school in 1972, the war was winding down, and none of my friends were sent to Southeast Asia. Like most Americans, I was puzzled about our role in the conflict. How and why did we end up in Vietnam? I remembered watching returning soldiers get spit on and called "baby killers." What a harsh and unjust homecoming! Ben, who served as an army combat chaplain, could never talk about coming home from the war and being treated so unfairly without crying.

I continued to think about a service program in Vietnam. I began by assessing student interest, which was high. In December 2002, we were prepped and ready to go. Having Ben with us was a bonus, as he could share his personal history at various places we visited. I loved the country from the moment we arrived. Given our mutual, painful history I didn't know how we would be treated, but the Vietnamese people were, and are, incredibly friendly and gracious. When I questioned my new friends, they voiced their surprise that Americans were still holding on to negativity around the "American" war. They reminded me that the Chinese invaded and ruled Vietnam for 1000 years, and the French were there for nearly 100 years. The United States – we were a blip on the collective radar screen! Everywhere we went, people wanted to meet us. I was surprised that the country was so beautiful; it was lush with greenery, beautiful mountains, and dazzling, white sand beaches. One of my favorite places on that first trip was Dalat, which is in the mountains and perpetually cooler than anywhere else in the country. It was enjoyed by the French as a summer getaway during their rule there.

We built two classrooms for a small, rural village in the Mekong Delta, not far from the busy seaport, Can Tho. The old school building, made of bamboo, was leaning to one side and in danger of falling down completely. We spent our days painting, carrying stones, and preparing cement, staining desks and chairs, and more. In the late afternoons, we visited families in the village and occasionally did some sightseeing. I thought my backside would never recover after a five-hour boat trip along tributaries of the Mekong. Since that first experience in 2002, I've been back in Vietnam nearly 20 times. It feels like a second home to me and I never grow tired of being there.

CHAPTER VI

My Love, My Heart

On the night that Ben and I were married in August 1992, he promised me 50 years of love, laughter, and companionship. Given that I was 37 and he was 50, I knew that this promise would probably not be fulfilled, but I hoped for as much time as possible with him. Like most couples, we had our share of ups and downs, but I loved him fiercely. My first warning bell that we wouldn't make those 50 years came in 2009. In June, Ben's annual check-up revealed a high prostate-specific antigen (PSA). A follow-up appointment with a world-renowned urologist confirmed a diagnosis of prostate cancer. The doctor appeared very casual about the diagnosis, noting that, "Every man, if he lives long enough, will end up with prostate cancer." Surgery was scheduled for the end of August, after we returned from a 3 ½ week Wake Forest program in Vietnam and Cambodia. We traveled with 14 students, two professors and their families, a videographer and his spouse, and our in-country program director and his fiancée. In addition to refurbishing a school in a small Vietnamese village, we toured both countries.

When we visited Cu Chi, a war memorial site, Ben told the group about Agent Orange, a defoliant manufactured by Monsanto and Dow and used by our army as an herbicide to clear out the jungle. Ben was an army combat chaplain during the war (1970-1971) and was stationed at Cu Chi, where he said, "Agent Orange fell like rain every day." And now the herbicide was correlated with prostate cancer. Ben's surgery seemed to go well, or so we were told. We had two friends who had received the same diagnosis earlier that summer; they both had Ben's surgeon and the same surgery and had recovered easily. Unfortunately, Ben's recovery never truly got off the ground and he was never quite the same again. In 2012, he had follow-up surgery that helped some, but he soon began to complain about a variety of strange symptoms.

In May 2013, I accompanied a group of students and another staff member to Rwanda for a 2-week service trip experience. The day I returned to work Ben picked me up for lunch. On the way to the restaurant I'd selected, he mentioned three times that his chest felt heavy, like he was having a heart attack. The first two times that I suggested we head to the emergency room he said "no," but the third time he agreed. That made me nervous, as Ben hated going to doctors and hospitals. Yet, in the emergency room the doctors found no evidence of a heart attack and planned to release him until I noticed that one of his legs was hot and swollen. Instantaneously the room became a hive of activity, as the medical team began solving a new problem. It turned out that Ben's entire leg was a giant blood clot. He was in the hospital for five days, as doctors tried various medications to dissolve the clot. Ben was weak, although he rallied to attend our niece's wedding in July.

Throughout that summer Ben complained about two things — he felt like there was a constant lump in his throat that made it hard to swallow AND the actual, growing lump on his neck. He had a doctor's appointment scheduled for early September; that morning he asked me if I were prepared for what the doctor might say. The truth is that you can't really be prepared for the worst possible news — Stage 4 esophageal cancer with advanced metastasis.

A few days after Ben's diagnosis, when we were coming out of a shock-filled haze, we talked about what we wanted the next weeks and months to look like — no matter what happened! Ben wanted to ensure that we made lots of new memories, and we both realized that crying and sadness, while at times unavoidable, would only detract from the limited time we had left. We vowed to be honest with each other every step of the way, and I made sure that Ben's desires regarding treatment were met.

For eight months, we experienced the ups and downs of chemotherapy, radiation, feeding tubes (ugh), pneumonia, painful rashes that looked like major burns, and differing opinions from the doctors. But in early May, Ben's oncologist told us that the chemotherapy wasn't working. He gave Ben the option of trying yet another protocol, but Ben was exhausted and ready to stop. We called hospice the next day.

I can't say enough praise about in-home Hospice care. Every team member treated us with dignity, respect, and compassion. Our home began to feel like holy ground. It felt even more sacred when friends and family came to visit, and there were blessings for us every day. My colleagues brought us dinner nightly; I was reminded once again of the abiding compassion that is a part of the Wake Forest ethos.

On one of those last precious days, Ben commented with wonderment that, "It's so pretty." When we asked him what he was talking about, he said with conviction, "Heaven – It's so pretty." I urged him to tell us more and he said that it was "a multiplicity of colors." This is not something that Ben would have said previously, as it was not the exact vision of heaven that he held, so it was very affirming to us. We asked him to tell us more, but he moved back into a deep sleep very quickly.

Our Chihuahua, Chico, loved Ben and was his constant companion throughout his illness. During the last week, he desperately wanted to be in Ben's hospital bed, but I would not put him there, as I wanted Ben to be as comfortable as possible. But finally, on the last day, I knew that Ben was in a deep coma and Chico would not bother him. Chico took his place at Ben's feet, but regularly came up to do "breathing checks" before moving back down to the foot of the bed. One moment before Ben's last breath at 7:00 pm, Chico went into an absolute frenzy. He jumped off the bed and ran to the door, barking, twirling, and going nuts. I believe that he saw, heard, or felt something coming or going. This was another re-minder that we were truly on holy ground. There was no one out on the street and no traffic; in other words, there was no external noise that would cause this reaction. An hour later, I tried to put Chico on Ben's bed to say goodbye before the funeral home came to remove his body. When I picked Chico up, he resisted. When I dropped him on the bed, he refused to look at Ben and jumped down immediately. He knew, of course, that his "daddy" was gone.

CHAPTER VII

After Ben's Death

When Ben was sick, I avoided crying in front of him, per his request that we not wallow in pity or sorrow. I worked hard at "keeping it all together," and I did so throughout his illness and the funeral. A few months after he died, I had a simple, yet brutal, revelation while walking from my office to my car at the end of the workday. It was a beautiful late September afternoon with just a tinge of fall in the air. Students were hanging out by their residence halls or sitting on the grass reading. The band was practicing outside (Go Deacs!), and the chapel bells were ringing. I stopped to take it all in and realized that everything was just the way that it was supposed to be. I'd passed similar scenes countless times in nearly 40 years working as a student affairs professional. But one thing WAS different – me! My life was forever changed, and I felt lost and disconnected from the identities and things that had grounded me throughout my adult life.

No matter how hard I tried, I couldn't find my way back into loving my work. What had once held incredible meaning and joy now seemed empty. By February 2016, I was in full-on crisis mode. I was exhausted and depressed and had to force myself to get up in the morning. I often came home and went straight to bed, which made me feel even worse. The first weekend in March, I took a life-changing meditation class. The energy in the small group was positive and loving, and I was grateful for the support. Despite this awakening, I hit a true low point a few days later. It was spring break for students, and I had taken off a few days to rejuvenate and prepare for the last half of spring semester. On my first morning off, I woke up and reached for my phone to see what time it was. When I almost had it in hand, I accidently bumped it off the nightstand and it landed on the floor. I leaned over to pick it up and fell out of bed, hitting the hard floor beneath me. In that moment, one thought came to me, unbidden and unwelcome, "I. AM. BROKEN." And I had no idea how to "fix" what was wrong.

Nights were torture. At the very time I needed sleep the most, it was elusive. So many random thoughts ran through my head as I struggled to rest. Several times I found myself thinking about one of my favorite hymns, *Here I Am Lord*. I will never forget the first time I heard the song, sung by the choir at First Christian Church in Winston-Salem. I was immediately drawn to the lyrics, taken from Isaiah and Samuel.

Here I am Lord, Is it I, Lord? I have heard you calling in the night. I will go Lord, if you lead me. I will hold your people in my heart.

Now, every time I thought about the song, my eyes filled with tears. I finally realized that I was responding to the unanswered call - the knowledge that I hadn't been listening (or listening but not responding) to a path that had been set before me. My work had been a place where I had sought to heed the call in the night and my students had been the most important part of that work. Now, I was called to a new path, as a long-term volunteer. As I thought, prayed, and meditated, my plan began to solidify. I would retire in December 2016 and leave for six months in India a few days later. This was completion of the promise I'd made when I left India in January 1999. I knew that I had the perfect window to do this – my daughter and her husband were planning a family and I did not want to be away when she was pregnant. My mom was a healthy eight-six and had just moved to a wonderful senior living center in Lynchburg, Virginia. I knew that I would hate being out of the country if she had serious health issues.

Once I'd made my decision, I shared my plans with family and a few friends. I'd tell my colleagues months later. I booked my flight and found a great apartment in Kolkata on Airbnb. While moving forward, I alternated between excitement and terror. I imagine that I might have changed my plans, if given the chance.

Throughout the nine months before I left for India, I spent time thinking about my hopes and dreams for the future. It felt at times as if I were birthing a new me. To prove to myself that I could travel alone, I took a 10-day trip to Peru to fulfil a lifelong dream to visit Machu Picchu, and it was as magnificent as I'd imagined. The moment I saw the ruins that I'd seen only in photographs, I was on my knees in tears. The day after I returned home, I woke up unable to get out of bed without screaming in pain. After five days of crawling around the house, I finally went to the emergency room, where I was diagnosed with sciatica. For the next few weeks, it took me 20 minutes to walk to my office from the parking lot, a trip that normally took less than 5 minutes. Now I felt broken in both spirit AND body. Despite my loss of joy and purpose, I wasn't sure that I was ready to "retire." Would I find enough to do when I returned after six months in India? I understood that I was about to find out a lot about myself and prayed that I would like what I found.

CHAPTER VIII

New Beginnings

I arrived in Delhi on the evening of January 4th. Of course, all my careful planning was out the window. Months earlier, I'd reserved a room at an in-airport hotel so that I could get 5-6 hours of sleep before my flight to Kolkata the next morning. I'd emailed the hotel to let them know that my journey had been delayed but, when I made it to the hotel, I learned that, just as I'd feared, there were no rooms left. I prepared to "tough it out" on a stuffed chair in the small lobby, along with some weary fellow travelers.

While sitting there, half awake, I thought about my travel day and the interesting people I'd met. At the Raleigh-Durham airport, I'd started up a conversation with a young Indian guy who was headed to Delhi to visit with family. He told me that he was Indian-American and serving in the US Army, and I told him that I was going to Kolkata to volunteer with the Missionaries of Charity. We laughed at the symmetry of our travels. I met another interesting guy in the French restaurant at the Newark airport. He sat at the table next to mine and told me his life story. His father had died two months earlier, and he'd just gotten back from a visit to his mother. Ten minutes earlier he had received the news that his mother had died shortly after he left. He was a former New York police officer, injured in the line of duty. He was scheduled for surgery the next day but that would have to be postponed as he was headed back to bury his mom. I hadn't flown through the Newark airport in many years and had to wonder when it became so cool. My last memory was less pleasant –

hanging out for three days during a blizzard when no flights were coming or going. I loved the iPads and docking stations everywhere, as well as the nice restaurants. At the French restaurant I had the best croissant and French onion soup I've ever eaten outside of Paris!

I was delighted when I got on the plane that the ONLY empty seat was next to me. The audio didn't work on my individual screen, so I tried my best to sleep. I am always frustrated when I see people who "go out" soon after the first meal is served and wake up an hour or so before we land. How do they do it? I struggle for even a few hours of restless sleep. This time; however, I did sleep, and it was glorious! Despite that, I was tired and out of sorts when I arrived in New Delhi. While I waited in the hotel lobby, I talked with an Indian woman who works for a children's health NGO. I was really impressed with the work that they are doing. I also met a man from Charlotte, North Carolina, who works in Nepal. He and his wife invited me to "come up and visit them" sometime. These conversations kept me going while I waited. An hour or so after I arrived, the hotel staff let me know that a "napping room" was available. Closet would be a much better description of this teeny-tiny room with a bed and a nightstand. But it was all I needed. My wake-up "call" came with tea and delicious, spicy cookies.

I headed to the domestic terminal for the last leg of my journey. I asked several security guards which entrance I should head toward and got conflicting responses. Finally, I was pointed toward a customer service station where five different men looked at my reservation for ten minutes or so before saying anything to me. I was ready to "freak out." What was wrong with my reservation? Did I have an ongoing ticket or not? Finally, one man printed a ticket and handed it to me.

It was a relief to see my luggage on the carousel when I arrived at the terminal in Kolkata. I gathered my bags and headed out of the airport, looking for a sign with my name on it. Ananda Mitra, a Wake Forest colleague who grew up in Kolkata, had given me the name of a gentleman who made arrangements for his summer programs in India. Mr. Basu agreed to pick me up at the airport and take me to my apartment. It took a while, but I finally found a sign with my name scribbled on it. I shook hands with the man holding the sign. He wasn't Mr. Basu or his driver, but rather a runner, sent to find me. Mr. Basu and his driver were waiting for me in the huge parking lot. As I walked to the car, I was reminded of the first time I arrived in India. I have never been particularly conscious of the air around me, but in Kolkata the air has real weight. Now, it felt as if I could reach out and grab a huge chunk of pollution. The ride from the airport was interesting and I looked around at my new home with rabid curiosity. As we got closer to the heart of the city, I grew less comfortable. Everything looked dumpy and dirty.

We arrived on Rawdon Street and my heart sank even more. This did not look like the neighborhood I'd envisioned. Eventually we pulled up to a gate and drove through what looked like an alley. We'd entered my apartment complex. The apartments were painted a very light blue, although they needed a touch-up job. My apartment was on the ground floor. When the door was opened, my first thought was that artful photography can make anything look good. While the house looked like the photos on Airbnb, it also seemed cheaper and less inviting. I'd been told by the "host" that I could choose the room with the best mattress. Two of the bedrooms had very thin mattresses, so I selected the third bedroom and knew my back and I would be happiest there. Anyone staying for a shorter time could manage one of the thinner mattresses. Mr. Basu bid me farewell, and I was on my own, feeling the weight of being alone and far, far away from home. I unpacked my suitcases and the small treasures and mementos that friends and colleagues had given me before I left to let me know that I was not alone, and that love and good wishes had accompanied me on my journey.

I was grateful to my friend and fellow traveler, Maria Henson, who reminded me before I left North Carolina that I could give myself some grace and not rush off to volunteer the day after I arrived in India. I took her advice and began with a slower pace. Given my lack of spatial intelligence, I decided to spend a few days getting to know my new neighborhood. Each day, I set off in a different direction to discover what was in that area. There are lots of private schools within a few blocks of my apartment, and I enjoyed watching the young boys heading to and from school in their white shirts, pants, and blue blazers with the school emblems on the pockets.

I was really surprised each day, as many people spoke to me during my walks. One man shook my hand, practiced a little English, and thanked me for being in Kolkata. Another man looked surprised and said, "It's wonderful to see you again after so many years." In my head, I calculated that it had been at least 62 years. I'd never laid eyes on this man and wondered who my doppelganger might be. He asked me how things had been going in Australia and invited me to have tea. I'd just had tea at home before I started I out, so I told him I'd have tea on another day. I had an odd feeling that I'd see him again, but I never did. My third conversation was the most interesting and I was a little surprised that **it only took one day to come up**. An older woman with just three discernible teeth stopped me and asked where I was from. When I told her the US, her next question was surprising and immediate - "Who did you vote for?" I told her and she shook her head, "The Democrats should have run Bernie against Trump because he would have provided the change people wanted." She also said that she thinks Americans are in for a challenging time. We talked for 10 minutes or so, and I was blown away by her knowledge of the election and US politics. The lesson I took away from our conversation was that the world does indeed watch what happens in the US.

The most frustrating situation during those first few days was trying to get an Indian SIM card for the phone I was using as a GPS and, as it turned out, a way to request Uber and/or OLA drivers. It used to frustrate and amaze me, as someone without the spatial intelligence gene, that Ben could go somewhere once, and would never need to use a map or GPS again to return to that spot. My housekeeper took me to a small phone store, and they directed us to Vodaphone, the second largest carrier in the world in terms of overall connections. Trying to get my phone set up was like buying a new car; it went on forever. I had to produce multiple pictures of myself and my passport, references, etc. I was then sent home and told that my phone would be activated after 10:00 pm. At that point, my phone was supposed to cue me to put in the SIM card and... it didn't work. The next morning, I woke up and went back to the Vodaphone store, feeling much less patient. I was told that before my phone was fully activated, the company would have to confirm that I lived where I said I lived. Sure enough, that afternoon a man appeared at the door and asked me numerous questions. I thought all was good until a second man showed up hours later and asked me all the same questions again. Once my phone started working, I had to go back to Vodaphone again because, for some reason, the language on my phone was set to Spanish. Since I don't know Spanish, I couldn't figure out how to switch the language back to English. After consulting with most of the staff in the store, I finally had a fully functioning phone. I was relieved but it seemed like a lot of fuss for a phone that was going to cost me a pre-paid $15/month.

The other difficulty was trying to communicate with the housekeeper, Brindaban, who spoke about ten words of English, which was better than my five words of Bengali. One morning I showed him Google pictures of eggs and toast, and he made some for me. Hot peppers in the eggs rocked my world a bit, but I got used to the heat. I also realized that I could use the English-to-Bengali translator on Google to communicate with him, and I showed him the Bengali-to-English reverse. He was delighted with this and began showing me new phrases! I believe that there is an innate desire within all of us to communicate with others.

That first year I took students to Vietnam, we were frustrated with the communication barriers we faced. We loved spending time with the children from the village, but all of us wanted to learn more about each other. One day after school, the children came running to us with immense joy. They showed us that they had written their names on their hands, so that we could read them (we'd had a lot of difficulty trying to learn their names). They urged us to do the same and we wrote our names on our hands too. Just knowing each other's names was the begin-ning of greater communication and illustrated their longing to know us better. I've never forgotten that day!

Each day I walked further. One afternoon I walked to the Mother House for the Missionaries of Charity and was pleased to find that it was only a 15-minute walk from my apartment. On my way home, a young man walked with me for a while. He asked me what I was doing in his city and if I liked being there. I said I did like the city. He nodded assent and then said very thoughtfully, "Kolkata is a very good city, and a bad one too!" I told him that the same can be said about most places. He thought about it and agreed! He wanted to have lunch, but I'd already eaten... Perhaps another day...

One night that first week I made a rookie mistake. To have warm wa-ter for my shower, I had to flip a switch in my bedroom. The water heater, known as a geyser (but pronounced like an old man), is to be turned on 10 minutes before use, then turned off to save money. I forgot to turn it off, and when I went to the bathroom in the middle of the night and then attempted to wash my hands, what came out was black, hot, burnt-up water. Lesson learned.

I made some other rookie mistakes as well. One day, Brindaban made lunch for me, in addition to breakfast. He first brought in a plate of rice, followed by a large bowl of chicken curry and a small bowl of dal. I poured the curry over the rice and started eating (It was delicious). He came in a few minutes later with a puzzled look on his face and pointed to the bowl — "It's soup." I can say, however, that it tasted delicious over rice too! Another lesson learned...

At night, we attempted to watch TV together. First, a movie with universal themes. I had no idea what the actors were saying, but the plot was crystal clear. We also enjoyed watching the grand finale of DANCE BANGLA DANCE, JR. The children were great dancers and I loved watching the classical art form.

If I could describe what I learned the first week in Kolkata, there would only be one truly appropriate word – patience! Yes, it's a virtue, but it is one I've always struggled with. I have generally been patient with students and others, but less patient with myself. The hassles of travel also provoke my impatient ire. During the fiasco of the delayed flight and lost luggage in Raleigh, I jokingly asked the gate agent to find me a seat with no one next to me for the long flight. I was thrilled to see that she'd done just that. Losing my airport hotel room in Delhi meant that I met interesting people and had some great conversations. Seeking ways to communicate with the housekeeper caused me to think creatively about how to do that. He began teaching me Bengali every day and I taught him some English. We made slow progress. Giving myself a few days to get to know Kolkata and feel more comfortable on the streets was a great plan. I also worked on having a bit more patience with our spotty Wi-Fi. Some-times it worked and, well, sometimes it didn't. Despite promises that it would be fixed soon, that didn't happen during my stay.

Diary

CHAPTER IX

January

Every year, hundreds, perhaps thousands, of volunteers show up in Kolkata to volunteer with the Missionaries of Charity. No reservation is required or even expected. At times, especially in December, January, July, and August, there are many volunteers; at other times the numbers vary. New volunteers must register on Monday, Wednesday, or Friday, at 3:00 pm at Shishu Bhavan, an orphanage run by the Sisters. The alternative is to show up at the Mother House in the morning at volunteer breakfast and receive a day-pass. So, like thousands before me, I headed to Shishu Bhavan, which is about two long blocks away from the Mother House on A.J.C. Bose Road. When I got there, I saw a small hand-printed sign that said registration was cancelled for the afternoon and that new volunteers should come to breakfast in the morning. I headed home, eager to start!

I woke up at 5:45 and was ready to set out for the Mother House by 6:30. The streets were quiet – for India that is — giving the city a mystical quality. Many of the market sellers along the way were still sleeping on top of their displays. When I arrived at the Mother House, mass was just ending, and I was surprised to see so many volunteers. We all gathered in a small room to eat a simple breakfast of white bread, bananas, and chai. I realized that I would probably need to supplement this breakfast by eating at my apartment. Bananas were the first food I was fed as a baby after milk and cereal. My reaction was not what my mother had expected – I spit that terrible stuff right out and have never eaten an entire banana in one sitting in my life. It must be the texture, because I love banana muffins, bread, and other versions of the fruit. The chai was delicious, but very sweet and I didn't know if the small slices of bread (think "Wonder Bread") would keep me full until our morning tea break. I am very introverted, although I often function as an extrovert; I just feel exhausted after being in a crowd of people. So, walking into the gathering area was scary. Fortunately, a friendly seminarian from Minnesota started talking with me. His group was leaving for Darjeeling the next day and then back home to the US.

I spoke with Sister MM, who oversees volunteers. She knew previous Wake Forest groups and leaders and she asked me how they were doing. When she asked me where I'd like to work, something surprising and unexpected came out of my mouth. I'd planned to work at Shishu Bhavan with the toddlers, so when I said I'd like to work at Kalighat Home for the Dying, I was floored. Sister MM assigned me there, at least for two days, until I could formally register. The seminarians offered me a ride to Kalighat, and I happily accepted. The full name of Kalighat is *Nirmal Hriday, Home of the Pure Heart*. This was the name given to the house by Mother Teresa when she founded it in 1952. It is often said that Nirmal Hriday was Mother's first love. It is a home for the dying destitute with one side for men and the other for women. At one time, before the building was purchased by Mother Teresa, it was an abandoned temple for the Hindu goddess Kali, and the building is next to the Kalighat Kali Temple. When we arrived at the facility, we had to show our volunteering cards for entrance. The man who checked our cards also wrote our names in his book. He was rocking a poncho and a fur hat and looked like a boss. In January, the weather was still a bit cool in the mornings before warming up in the afternoon, so this clothing choice made sense.

We entered the building and walked to the lockers upstairs to store our things. Laundry was "all hands on deck," so I put on an apron and walked over to the wash tubs. I was in the second rinse and wring group. Clothes, bedding, blankets, towels, knit caps, and more were washed. Every time I thought we were done, the first wash and rinse group would dump a new basket of wet items into our tank. At times we would use our "fishing pole" to locate and retrieve things that had sunk to the bottom of the pool. Everything that we rinsed and wrung out was placed in the high-speed dryer and then taken up to the roof to dry.

When laundry was done, a party broke out. Several of the seminarians had brought their guitars and drums and played songs for the residents, including "Country Roads." I will forever be a John Denver fan (#taken-toosoon) and even so, I am always amazed at the powerful reach of this song. I've heard it in the Vietnamese jungle and atop a mountain in the Philippines, among other places. It resonates with all of us who long for home. Some of the female residents demonstrated great dance moves and I was impressed. Other women were oblivious to the fact that music and dancing were going on. During the music, I sat on the steps, smiled, and clapped. I admired the volunteers who were on the floor and interacting with the residents. I felt overwhelmed watching it all, and I couldn't yet see myself interacting in that way. One woman was frustrated because her sweater kept coming unbuttoned. I fixed it several times but one of the buttonholes was too big. Clearly a company had donated excess purple sweaters to the sisters because that was the "outfit of the day." I'd seen something similar when I'd volunteered at Shishu Bhavan years ago. Another company had given the sisters a load of the ugliest baby/toddler rompers I'd ever seen. Despite their ugliness, they kept the children clothed and comfortable, which was what mattered. Another woman kept losing the blanket on her lap, so I replaced it every 5 minutes or so.

After the volunteer break at 10:30, it was "all hands on deck" once again to feed the women in our care. A few ate with hearty appetites, while others barely touched their food. One of the women clearly did not like fish, as she kept throwing it on the floor. Another woman screamed when I set down her plate. Although I was taken aback, apparently this was her MO, as no one else seemed to react. I noticed that some women were being fed by other volunteers or the massies, who are paid workers.

From my first experience in India, I'd learned that occasionally there are culture clashes between volunteers and massies. Volunteers come motived by love and a desire to serve. While most volunteers come to Kolkata for a short time, massies are there for the long term. After a few months at Kalighat, I learned how little the massies make for the very hard work they do. It's true that they can sometimes appear gruff, but I believe that they usually have the best interests of the residents at heart.

When I worked at Kalighat in 1998, there was a female resident who spoke English and yelled at volunteers all the time about everything she thought we were doing wrong. I wondered if one of the current residents might be "Lucy," the woman I remembered. The voice and face were similar. When Lucy was scolding us, she would always comment that we were stupid. The woman who may or may not be "Lucy" is called the "big boss" by everyone at Kalighat. I saw her shake her head in frustration at volunteer actions several times and tried hard to suppress a smile.

After lunch, we started moving women to their beds. We pushed or pulled most of them in their plastic chairs. The first woman I helped got to her bed and did not like the fact that her gown was wet from lunch. She had it off and was sitting there in her glorious birthday suit before I could stop her! I quickly got her changed and provided a dry, warm blanket. She settled herself quickly after that.

Soon after, I joined the dish-washing team as the first-rinse person. When we were done, it was time to go. A group of volunteers from Chile invited me to go with them to a Spanish restaurant on Sudder Street, a busy road where many volunteers and backpackers stay. I ordered enchiladas verdes, which were neither enchiladas nor green for that matter. But they tasted like good chicken calzones. To my delight, it was right next to Sunshine, a store where numerous Wake Forest students and staff have shopped in the past and befriended the owners. I only had to drop the names of some colleagues and I was "in." I walked the half hour back to my apartment, got home around 3:00, and fell into bed for a long nap.

That night, I spent some time reflecting on the vagaries of memory. Kalighat didn't look at all like I remembered it. In my mind it was much smaller and darker. I also remembered that some of the women's beds were on raised platforms instead of the level floor. I later learned that the floors had indeed been raised for many years due to poor drainage issues throughout the city. During the monsoon season, water would come flooding into the sleeping area, creating havoc. Now, with better drainage, the platforms had been removed. I could only imagine the accidents that occurred in the past with women falling off the platforms. Getting them into bed would also have been a massive challenge.

I also recalled a very narrow, dark street in front of the home. I couldn't have been more wrong. Kalighat is on a very busy street. The area in front of Nirmal Hriday and the Kali Temple is closed to cars. On some days, throngs of visitors line up outside of the temple. There is a marketplace that extends for about two blocks, providing everything the faithful need for their visit, along with some tourist items. On the other side of Kalighat is a fruit and vegetable "market." Men and women sit on the edges of the road, selling their produce, making travel by car slow and treacherous.

The doorman determines whether you will be permitted to enter Nirmal Hriday. On your first day of volunteering, he writes your name very, very carefully in his book, which seems to be organized by country. Every day, volunteers must show their card to be re-admitted. After I'd volunteered for a few months, he got to the point of just waving me inside, checking me off when he had more time. When you walk in the door, the men's sleeping area is to your left. On your right is an open space where mass is held on Sundays. On my first day, I noticed that a few men were on their beds resting, instead of sitting with the others in a large area behind the stairs.

The stairs are in front of you as you enter the Kalighat. The volunteer area is up the first flight. Here there are lockers for backpacks, water bottles, and whatever volunteers bring. There is a long wooden table where the volunteers eat together at snack time. Behind the table is an old treadle Singer sewing machine, which is used to make and mend garments and bedding. On the other side of the table is the kitchen, where the cooks make three meals every day and provide a variety of snacks for both residents and volunteers. You can feel the heat as soon as you walk in the door. That said, most volunteers never cross the kitchen threshold, as scolding is possible. The cooks are very picky about their workspace. Across the way is the area where the sisters live. This is closed off to volunteers and when someone needs to speak to one of the sisters, they ring the doorbell and wait. Next to the living area is a small chapel where sisters, volunteers, and others pray. There is also an outdoor balcony on the second floor. Most volunteers go out there daily, as there is a sink and a daily morsel of soap, where everyone can wash their hands before eating snacks and drinking chai. Sometimes, volunteers hang out on the balcony and watch the crowds waiting to get into the Kali Temple. There is an additional flight of stairs that leads to the roof, where laundry is hung to dry.

When you go back down the stairs, heading away from the entrance, you walk into the women's area of Kalighat. I often paused about halfway down the stairs to watch the women before they saw me, gauging the mood of the day. At the bottom of the stairs, you can turn left into the laundry room and dish-washing area, or straight into the women's sitting area. The women's beds are to the left, off the main sitting area, with the bathroom at the back and to the left.

When new volunteers come to registration, Sister MM describes what they will be expected to do. "Imagine," she says, "that you have a family member who requires care at home. You might help them bathe, brush their teeth, give them their necessary medications, feed them snacks and meals, help them to bed to rest, talk with them, sit by them, rub their back or shoulders, put lotion on their dry skin, and other simple activities." At the homes it is a bit more complex than that because no one really tells you what to do. New volunteers need to observe and listen. Sometimes they can look to long-term volunteers to get ideas about needed tasks. Eventually, it is easy to understand the regular routine, while being aware that what worked yesterday might be different today. I always kept sister MM's words in mind as I went about my daily tasks. I tried to treat each woman as a beloved family member.

☾

My second day at Kalighat was even more intense. I started the day at the Mother House. To be honest, I didn't really care for the breakfast. Eventually, I would stop for croissants or just-made luchi (fried flatbread) along the way. The best part of breakfast wasn't the food, but rather the opportunity to meet other volunteers and listen to the daily announcements. The Missionaries of Charity operate six homes in Kolkata, so volunteers are scattered in many places. I wanted to get to know as many as possible, and breakfast was the place to make that happen. After breakfast, prayer, singing, and announcements, volunteers who were serving for their last day were always invited into the center of the circle, and we sang them goodbye with gratitude and love. On my second volunteering day it seemed like a third of the group was leaving, including the Minnesota seminarians and a group of students from Fordham University.

I took the bus from Mother House to Kalighat with a group of about ten volunteers. The morning began with never-ending laundry. After what felt like at least an hour of wringing out wet clothes and other items, I checked the clock and saw that it was only 9:15. My back was really hurting, and I was soaking wet. Soon laundry was done, and I walked into the women's ward. It was not a joyful scene. Many of the women were sleeping in their seats, wrapped up in warm shawls. There was a lot of complaining about the cold – it was about 68 degrees Fahrenheit outside, and, for India, it was indeed chilly. One woman started asking me when lunch would be served. The first time she asked, it was 9:30, so she had a long wait. It reminded me of the familiar vacation refrain, "Are we there yet?"

After lunch, we helped the women settle into their beds for the afternoon rest period. I drew bedpan duty, which was humbling. I need to stop right here and thank every nurse and caregiver out there. What you do is so important, not always "fun," and generally thankless. I am inspired by your dedication and service to others. One woman kissed me on the cheek as I was tucking her into bed, and that was all the thanks that I needed. As we left, we saw a crowd gathered in front of the Kali Temple. We stopped to see what was happening and were confronted with a snake charmer, bending a cobra to his will. Trust me when I say that I stayed as far away as possible. Snakes freak me out and I had no desire to be anywhere near this spectacle, no matter how compelling and exotic it appeared to be.

☾

The next day was Thursday, our volunteering day off. A day off should be relaxing, right? Well, this one was and it wasn't. My back was really hurting from the travel, adjusting to my new bed, and bending over the laundry tub. I went to a spa near my apartment and had a deep tissue massage. It hurt so much, but I could tell that it was exactly what I needed. Afterward Visakha, my property manager, took me to New Market. It's difficult to describe the scene there. It's like being at the mall with 20,000 of your closest friends – times one thousand! It's a bit overwhelming, to say the least. I bought a few tunics for times when I wanted to look nice. Indian women's street style is beautiful, and I had been feeling decidedly underdressed since I'd arrived. My clothing was perfect for volunteering, but I didn't realize when I was packing that I'd want nicer clothes to go out in. The best part of New Market today was the Jewish bakery. I got and promptly ate some delicious sweet bread, along with a brownie for later. Next time, the plum cake… That night, I made a surprising decision. I planned to tell Sister MM that I wanted to work at

Kalighat for the next few months. It had been tougher than working with the children, but after just two days, I didn't want to leave "my" women and I found the work very rewarding. The volunteers clearly had a tight bond and I wanted to be part of that as well.

☾

On Friday morning, I woke up miserable, after doing the "Kolkata Trot" most of the night. It's not a race nor is it fun! This is the Kolkata version of Montezuma's Revenge. I did get up and head to Kalighat, knowing that my misery was not contagious. It was gratifying to get more kisses and hugs from the women I put into bed for their afternoon rest. I didn't eat and took a long nap after volunteering. Later in the afternoon, I headed to Shishu Bhavan (the orphanage run by the Missionaries of Charity) to officially register with Sister MM after having day passes all week. I did indeed tell her that I wanted to work at Kalighat. In just a few days, I had come to love the women and the routine there. I was also learning so much about myself through each new challenge. I told sister that my back might give out before my love did. She gave me some good pointers about how to lift the residents without twisting or pulling my muscles. Her tips helped me to realize that this experience would require radical self-care, and I pledged to keep that in mind as I did my small part in Kolkata. While at registration, I also agreed to do volunteer orientation in English on Monday, Wednesday, and Friday afternoons.

☾

Unfortunately, I felt no better the following day and decided that it would be smarter to stay home and recover from whatever it was that my system was fighting. I was hopeful that the medicines would knock it out soon. Before I left for India, I bought a *Time* magazine special edition reissue that was on the newsstands during fall 2016, at the time Mother Teresa was canonized. I wanted to learn as much as I could about the founder of the Missionaries of Charity. Since I was spending the day at home, I began reading about Mother Teresa's life. She was born *Anjeze Gonxhe Bojaxhiu* in 1910 in Skopje, Albania. Her family was relatively rich, cultured, and active in the community. Her father was a merchant and her mother's family were landowners. Her outgoing father was known for his generosity of spirit; her mother was known for her deep piety. The family was committed to helping the poor and even adopted several orphans.

As a child, she went by her middle name of Gonxhe (spelling differs). She loved to attend church, sang in the choir, played the mandolin, and loved to write. She was described as social, dependable, and a leader. When she was only eight, her father died, leaving the family in dire straits for a few years, until her mother established a new rug making business.

A new priest at the family parish enthusiastically preached the Jesuit theology of godly action in everyday life. He discussed frequently the efforts of a group of Croatians who had been sent to Bengal, in India. His words and deeds moved Gonxhe, and she decided that she wanted to become a missionary as well. She wrote to the Loreto Sisters working in Bengal and they accepted her. Gonxhe left home for India in 1928. On the boat to India, a seven-week journey, she wrote this: "Goodbye, O mother dear. May God be with you all. A higher power compels me toward torrid India...

—from the TIME Magazine issue *Mother Teresa at 100: The Life and Works of a Modern Saint* (2010)

☾

Although I hated taking the day off, I was glad that I did. The next morning, I felt much better and ready to go back to Nirmal Hriday. Throughout the day I thought a lot about the importance of touch. Some people haven't had loving touch in so long that it may scare them, while others absolutely crave it. One of the female residents LOVED to have her back scratched over her gown and purple sweater. I watched one of the volunteers start her day by scratching this woman's back for at least ten minutes. When she left to help another woman, I was commandeered to commence with more scratching. I was on duty for about ten minutes, and then I pulled another volunteer over to take her turn. I believed our resident would be happy if we rubbed her back and scratched every itchy spot all day long. Ironically, she frequently sat next to a woman who yelled at any volunteer who even tried to touch her, let alone give her a light shoulder or back rub.

Most days we spent some time rubbing cream on the very dry arms and legs of the women in our care. Some wanted a dab of cream on their hands that they could apply to their faces. One woman wasted no time my first day showing me EXACTLY how she wanted her legs rubbed – she wanted much more pressure than most of the other women could tolerate. She smacked another volunteer out of the way today and insisted that I rub her legs vigorously.

Some of the women like volunteers to sit with them and hold their hands. One of my favorite women shook all the time, but whenever I saw her waving her hands, I knew that she was looking for me to have some conversation and contact. I sat with her and at 9:30 she started asking me, again, when it would be time for lunch. I told her that it would be a little while, but I doubt that she was truly satisfied with my answer.

The male volunteers had a difficult day because one of the male residents died while they were working. Honestly, I thought that two of the female residents might not make it to the end of the week either, as both were nothing but skin and bones. During lunch, one of the women was being fed by a volunteer and she clearly didn't want to eat – period! If I'd been feeding her, I would have stopped then, but one of the sisters continued to feed her, noting that she had to keep up her strength. I had to smile and breathe deeply, remembering when I faced this hurdle with

Ben. He didn't want to eat during his last few months, but we continued feeding him a little at a time. I asked him one day about ten days before he died, if he wanted us to stop, and his answer was a resounding yes. The other woman who seemed to be actively dying was clearly in pain. She was shivering (it was in the 70's), couldn't hold her head up, and seemed to suffer deeply if we touched her even briefly. I began praying for the women of Kalighat every night and these two women were at the top of my first list.

Laundry is one of the constants at Kalighat, and it was how some of us began each morning. We first washed gowns, shirts, pants, bibs, and other small items. The last things we washed were the fleece blankets, bedsheets, and other items that absorb lots of water and are hard to wring out. It seemed like the massies changed up how we did laundry every day. Some days we didn't even try to wring out the water, throwing the heavy items over one of the sinks until they were taken to the roof to dry. There were several bamboo poles that volunteers used to fish items out of the bottom of the tub. It got harder to see the bottom as the water became dirtier. As it turned out, these fishing rods were useful tools. On a morning in late January one of the massies decided to extend a "fishing pole" from one laundry tub to the other and have us throw the wet, heavy items over it. The volunteers were looking at each other with raised eyebrows because we could all see that the pole would break very, very soon. Someone muttered quietly, "Are we taking bets?" Just a minute or two later the pole snapped, and Julio, a volunteer from Spain with a great sense of humor said (dryly), "Well, who could have seen that coming?" We all ended up laughing hard, both volunteers and massies. I loved the sense of camaraderie we all felt.

This camaraderie was present as we worked side by side and during our morning break time. As we drank chai and ate fortified biscuits, we learned each unique story. One of my favorites so far was the story of Jacques and Michelle, a young couple who left on a 13-month honeymoon around the world just a few weeks after their wedding, volunteering with the Missionaries of Charity at each destination. When they returned home, they wrote a book about their grand adventure.

☾

One of our female residents was considerably younger than the rest of the group. Most of the women at Kalighat are in their 50's – 90's, and she is a teenager. When I brought apple slices to her at snack time, she threw them on the floor and smacked me. I held her wrist, looked into her eyes, and told her that was NOT okay. I don't know if she speaks any English, but I do know that she understood exactly what I was saying. She needs to learn that hitting others and throwing things are not acceptable behaviors, but her story broke my heart. Four men "did things to her" (I can easily picture this scenario in my head) and she "lost her mind." One massie said it was very sad, and of course, she was right. She wanted to go home to her mother. She had given the social workers her address but when they went there to check it out, no one claimed to know her.

☾

Each day I realized even more how important it was for me to actually SEE the women I was serving. It would have been easy to lump them together as a bunch of frail, old women to whom the world has not been kind. I worked very hard to learn their names and something about each one of them. This was a bit tricky since many of the massies don't speak much English, but I tried to find ways to connect more deeply.

Soon it was Marcus' birthday. At break time we sang "Happy Birthday" to him in English, French, Italian, Japanese, Bengali, and Hindi. Everyone was excited to see how many languages we could manage! Because one of the male volunteers from Spain would be celebrating his birthday a few days later, I decided to sing the Vietnamese version from now on to add to the "language count."

One of the women refused to eat. I whispered to her before my shift was over that it was okay to leave if she was tired. She seemed to be in so much pain. One of the other women was mad today because someone stole her water bottle. She always wants it beside her bed. I think the massies take it away because they think she'll drink it and then clamor to be taken to the bathroom so that she can pee. I'm not sure she could open the bottle if she tried. I realized after listening to her cry for a while that it's really her security blanket. Two of us found a water bottle and gave it to her before we left, and she settled down immediately.

☾

During my second week in Kolkata, my key takeaway was the importance of self-care. I'd really appreciated Wake Forest's campus wellbeing program, THRIVE, that was instituted a few years ago. Through the program I joined a walking group, took meditation and yoga classes, learned about the benefits of aromatherapy, and much more. But, as I told my first-year students during fall semester 2016, it is easy to practice wellbeing when, in fact, all is well. When things get tougher, and exactly when we need wellbeing practices the most, we sometimes forget to be good to ourselves.

Before I arrived in Kolkata, I imagined that I would volunteer both morning and afternoon, every day. I soon realized that that program was too ambitious and unwise; most volunteers work either morning or afternoon shifts. When volunteers come for a brief stint, they often want to spend as much time as possible in the homes, choosing to work two shifts each day. As a seasoned volunteer explained to me, they are running a sprint. On the other hand, long-term volunteers are running a marathon, which requires more pacing. The reality is that working mornings at Kalighat is like working an eight-hour day. By the end of a shift, most of us (even the 20-something volunteers) were completely exhausted.

When my back and legs were hurting, I had a Thai massage at a spa down the street and I felt like a new woman when I walked home. The therapist (deep tissue) was excellent and found all the achy places, along with a few I hadn't yet discovered. I'd also treated myself to food that soothed body and soul, from tea and mango ice cream at Flurys, to soup and sandwiches at Au Bon Pain, to amazing Chinese food at BAR-B-Q. I'd eaten with volunteers at an excellent Spanish restaurant on Sudder Street. My self-care had not included eating street food (at least not yet) that looked and smelled good, but which might make me sick. I gave myself permission to stay home when my stomach/intestinal issues arose. I realized that if I had been traveling with students I might have "soldiered on," but was relieved that now I could rest. My housekeeper made me toast and tea for two days and it was exactly what I needed. I took a taxi one day when I still had a half hour walk home and my legs were saying "no way." Since then, I'd been getting stronger. Overall, I walked 1-2 hours every day and had already been thinking about how I would keep this up when I returned home in late June. I'd also been getting as much sleep as possible. As a "night owl," I'd reluctantly adjusted to an early to bed, early to rise lifestyle.

At the end of my second week of volunteering, we said goodbye to Jose and Maria from Spain. She didn't speak English, but we were able to communicate and worked very well together. Jose also had a very kind heart. I understood that there would be a constant stream of volunteers leaving, even as new volunteers arrived, yet it was still hard to see them go. When I was in Kolkata with students, I hung out with them and didn't recall this kind of camaraderie with the larger group. The volunteers at Kalighat were very close, and we relied on each other as we navigated each day.

Ryan (Ireland) and I treated Pierre, a new volunteer from France, to lunch at Blue Sky Café on Sudder Street. The café offers a wide variety of foods at reasonable prices and has been open for many years. When lunch was over, I teased Ryan, noting that Pierre and I were cheap dates.

The total bill for three people was about $11.00. When I was in Kolkata with students, I learned to sit with my back to the door, as the beggars with dirty babies and empty bottles would target me (a mom), motioning that they wanted food. The reality is that the beggars around Sutter Street are professionals and, in fact, may not even be the mothers of the babies they are holding.

We also said goodbye and hello to our residents. The woman I said my final goodbye to did die that night. I will always remember her, as I'd never seen anyone who fit the description of "skin and bones" so aptly. The next morning, just as our shift was ending, a new woman arrived, and I've realized that it will always be this way.

I began working with the physical therapist and really loved this activity. I encouraged women to move, even just a little bit more. One woman started crying during her therapy session, and I was afraid that we might be pushing her too far. That wasn't her issue; rather, she was worried because she didn't have enough money to pay us. When we told her that we were happy to do this for her; she gave me a hug and squeezed my hand. Before I left, I made sure that my woman who MUST have her water bottle had it right by her side when she went down for her afternoon rest. She was unusually calm. The young teen who was so abused called me over at rest time, told me she loved me, and gave me a kiss on the forehead. She didn't see my tears.

☾

On Thursday, my day off, I enjoyed having time to "wander." I started my morning with monkey bread and a latte. So. Very. Delicious. It was nice to sit, people watch, and enjoy my new community. People in the neighborhood recognized me now and greeted me warmly. One of the things I love about Park Street is the presence of bookstores and booksellers everywhere. I decided to spend some time in the Oxford Bookstore. I took time finding a few books by Indian authors. Since I wanted to absorb as much Indian culture as possible, I decided to read only books about India or written by Indian authors while in the country. In this bookstore, there are books in English, Bengali, and French, and lots to choose from. I also loved window shopping. The sarees, salwars, and other beautiful women's clothes are bright and colorful. I thought that in such a large city, more women would wear western clothing, as is the case in Vietnam. Not here – most women I see are dressed in traditional clothing of all colors and fabrics. On school days, most students in my area attend private schools and wear a variety of uniforms. After school is out, some teenagers re-emerge wearing jeans. One of them accidentally ran into me – he was texting, of course! Some things are the same wherever you go!

January 26th, our day off, was also Republic Day in India. On this day in 1950, India established itself as a sovereign state. The day honors the Constitution and its implementation. There are parades in all major cities, like the types of events that take place in the United States on the 4th of July. There are also traditional and cultural programs performed by professionals from different states to celebrate the many faces of India. President Obama was the "chief guest" in 2015. The day before, Sister MM had urged all volunteers to be safe and aware when we were out and about, as the streets were likely to be crowded with revelers.

I opted for a more low-key day with a trip to a nearby salon for a pedicure. My feet tend to become alligator-like, hard, and scaly. In India, they had been worse than usual! The woman doing my pedicure sighed often as she worked hard to scrape away all the dead skin. I have to say that the bottoms of my feet had never felt so soft. As she massaged my legs, she commented that I should really be moisturizing every day. And she wondered why my fingernails were not polished ("You should really do that"). When she was done with all the creams, oils, and lotions, my first thought was that my legs/feet had never looked so white. I think there might have been some whitening cream in the products used.

There are so many subtle and not-so-subtle messages here, and throughout Asia, that promote lightness. I know that many others experience this on a regular, if not daily, basis. I can't really walk in their shoes because of the white privilege I carry with me. In Vietnam I was always acutely aware of my light skin color. From the first day I was there, people stared at me wherever I went — I understood that the pale skin/red hair combination was rare, particularly in rural areas. I felt discomfort when Vietnamese would comment on the beauty of my pale skin. One day, two women stopped me on a path in their village. They grabbed my arm and ran their hands up and down it, saying *dep*, or beautiful, in Vietnamese. I struggled to tell them that I, like many other women in America, long for darker skin, and that the tanning industry is hugely popular, even though excessive tanning can cause cancer. That I don't want to be admired for THAT. Tonight, I am even lighter because in India that is the "gold standard" apparently….

☾

The theme for my third week in India was letting go. If we are honest, we let go of things all the time, whether we want to or not. The most succinct way to describe Buddhism is this – "Everything changes." And indeed, that is true, even if it is not easy.

During my third week I had to let go of new friends, as volunteers I'd enjoyed working beside were gone. The hardest goodbye was to my friend Ryan from Ireland. I enjoyed our lunches very much, as well as every minute I spent in his company. He is such a caring person, and it was a delight to talk with him about all things Irish. It was also fun to help him pick out souvenirs for his relatives.

During a morning shift this week, one of our women died. She was certainly ill but didn't seem to be in critical condition when we left the day before. When we arrived in the morning, she was on an IV drip and we could tell that it was bad. One of the volunteers sat with her until she drew her last breath. After she died, we asked Father Bob from the US to come in and pray for her, for all our women, for the sisters, the massies, and the volunteers. In January we lost two women and I had no idea how many more would die before I left in June. This death reminded me to be fully present each moment I was here with each precious soul.

It was also illuminating to let go of parts of my identity. If other volunteers asked what I did for a living, I told them, but at Kalighat all pretense is stripped away. Truthfully, it wasn't as hard as I thought it might be to just "be" here. I'd also been working hard to let go of ego and frustration around the "right way" to do things. For example, one of the massies asked me to feed a woman who had trouble eating. It was certainly expedient to feed her, but when Sister A explained to me that this woman needed to keep using her hands and feeding herself was one of the ways that she can do that, I understood. For as those who have traveled this road before know, the rules can change many times – even during a single shift. There is a time and a place for anger and frustration, but it is not here. This place is about humble acts of service. To facilitate my own service, I tried to enter the building each morning with a beginner's mind, as well as fervent prayers. I can't totally explain it, but I felt a certain peace when I walked through the doors of Nirmal Hriday. I'd also been letting go of some of my ideas about what India is and is not. This was an unfolding awareness that would emerge fully with time.

☾

As much as I had been trying to truly see people, I made an assumption one morning that landed me in hot, errrr, cold water. On my way to the Mother House each day I passed many beggars sitting on the sidewalks with their hands out, pleading for money. This particular morning, one of them, an old man, started shouting at me as I passed him. I was frustrated that he seemed to be escalating his daily request. Usually beggars stop at some point, but he kept on yelling at me. After I passed him, just as I reached the curb, I noticed that the sidewalk was broken into pieces and there was a bit of standing water I had to traverse before crossing the street. I had two options: I could walk through the water or backtrack past the beggar and then walk in the street. Oh, my – I was so embarrassed that my pride wouldn't allow me to walk past the beggar again, and I decided that walking through the water wouldn't be so bad. It appeared to be no higher than ankle deep. Imagine my surprise when, after stepping forward, I was submerged knee deep in cold, muddy water. I smacked my forehead as I realized that the beggar, who I refused to see because I thought he was asking for money, was trying to warn me instead. Talking about challenging assumptions! My situation reminded me of one of Ben's favorite sermon illustrations. Perhaps you have heard it before.

Autobiography in Five Chapters by Portia Nelson

I.   *I walk down the street. There is a deep hole in the sidewalk, and I fall in. I am lost, I am hopeless. It isn't my fault. It takes forever to find a way out.*

II. *I walk down the same street. There is a deep hole in the sidewalk. I pretend I don't see it. I fall in again. I can't believe I'm in the same place. But it isn't my fault. It still takes a long time to get out.*

III. *I walk down the same street. There is a deep hole in the sidewalk. I see it is there. I fall in…it's a habit. My eyes are open; I know where I am; It is my fault. I get out immediately.*

IV. *I walk down the same street. There is still a deep hole in the sidewalk. I walk around it.*

V.   *I walk down a different street.*

For me, a lesson learned. And you know what they say about assumptions….

☾

From the beginning, I loved feeding our residents. I was often called upon to feed Parul. Of all the women at Kalighat, she seemed to be the oldest and one of the most fragile. Her wrists were about the size of a toddler's wrists, and her legs were very thin. As you can imagine, she was always cold. Whenever I fed her, I went really slow, because she seemed to have trouble chewing and swallowing. One day, several massies came over while I was feeding her; because it was taking so long, they assumed that she wasn't eating. I'd seen others feeding her before, and they just kept shoveling food down her throat. It had to be scary to keep eating if you felt like you were choking. Even though it took us forty minutes, Parul ate every single bit of her meal and we were both satisfied.

After our shift, a group of Kalighat volunteers headed to Blue Sky, where I learned an important truth. "No, ma'am, it's not spicy," provides no useful information about the true "heat index" of the food you are ordering. I had Tom Yum soup, which was too spicy to finish, and green Thai curry which was also blisteringly hot. At least my rice and butter naan helped to bring down the heat. Later, Ryan and I wandered down Park Street, where he was looking for family gifts. In one store window, he found a cool piece of art and had to decide if the wood carving would make it home with him. Ironically, the shipping cost was three times the price of the art, so the carving went as carry-on luggage on his flight home.

☾

On another late January morning, I wondered what it would be like to have multiples (twins, triplets, or more). What would you do when your babies were all crying at once? If it's anything like Kalighat was on this day, it would be a challenge. To start, I was helping the physical therapist with one of our women. I worried about her because she seemed sad most of the time. Her hand/arm is curled into a tight fist. I don't know her backstory, so this may have been congenital, or the result of an accident or illness later in life. She is very, very protective of that hand. She did not like therapy even a little bit, and as the session went on, she was already crying softly. She hated it when the therapist flattened out her fingers. I'm sure the pain was intense. At the end of the session the therapist put a brace on her arm and hand to straighten her fingers and improve her ability to use that hand. At this point, she started crying in earnest! I moved her back to the sitting room and she immediately let everyone around her know how bad off she was. Silent crying became sobbing, which became yelling, which became wailing! Every time a volunteer stopped to offer comfort, her crying increased ten-fold. The women around her were sympathetic, but I could tell that some of them had had enough. I needed to get out of the room to sit and breathe, so I walked back to the sleeping area. What did I find? Another woman crying that she was having chest pains. Kaitlyn, an American volunteer, listened with her stethoscope and said that the woman's chest sounds were normal. She calmed down very quickly, which was good. I must admit that it was a challenging day indeed!

☾

I'd been struggling to describe what my early mornings were like as I headed from my apartment to the Mother House. Here's a look inside of my head on a typical morning:

Walk to the entrance of my "court." "Nomoshkar" (Namaste in Bengali) to each security guard for my apartment complex. Turn left. Watch out for the big crack in the sidewalk. Don't slip on that banana peel... Wave to the guy who rides his bike down Rawdon Street every morning. Why isn't the tea wallah open this early (sometimes I prefer a good cup of black tea to chai)? Stand at the corner trying to figure out when it might be safe to cross. Okay, that car is waay down the road, do NOT speed up, as I don't want to play chicken today. Phew, made it across the street with no issues. Smile at children and parents arriving at private school on my route. Begin walking through market stalls... Look down or only glance briefly at men in the market. Step off curb. Yikes, remember that cars are coming from the "wrong direction." Walk around 5 auto rickshaws...Make sure the drivers notice that I'm crossing. Move out of the way of the spittle that just landed at my feet (likely unintentional). Avoid getting hit by the tires being tossed out of storage areas to be stacked on the sidewalk. Hello, goat! Smile at more parents and children arriving at a different school...Nod to beggar, keep moving...Sidewalk is crooked, be careful. How much longer to the Mother House? Shut out incessant beeping of car horns as much as possible. Hold my nose (pee, poop, or fetid garage)? Oh no, stopped holding breath too soon. Ugh!! Pass another beggar, nomoshkar, *and keep on moving...Think twice before stepping off the curb. Glare at driver who doesn't care. Look away from the sidewalk where 8-10 men are brushing their teeth, bathing, and whatever else they do to begin the day. Smell luchi (flatbread, a little sweet) from the street vendor. Watch out for the dog poop on the sidewalk...Shake head at Mother Teresa souvenir store (really?). Stop in small store to buy bottle of water (I drink massive amounts of water daily). Turn in to the Mother House door, passing last beggar...say hello to the sister sitting by the door...walk down the hall to the gathering room.*

All of this before 7:00 am. India is just a lot. At the Mother House, we spent about 45 minutes eating, talking with other volunteers, praying, singing, and listening to announcements. After that, the Kalighat volunteers crossed the street to catch the bus. It took us 20-30 minutes to get to Kalighat, depending on traffic. We then walked about ¼ mile to the home past the large crowds waiting to enter the Kali Temple.

☾

As it turns out, difficult Mondays are a thing around the world. We had it all on the women's ward on the last Monday in January. First, one of our young volunteers fainted. She was in the wound-dressing room.

Perhaps she was watching a dressing change, but I wasn't sure. In any case, down she went. She was able to continue working after a brief rest, but she looked pale all morning and I kept a close eye on her. Next, there was a heated discussion between the massies and sisters over which type of cream or lotion should be used for massages. Either would have been fine, so this felt like a power play. I was massaging Aama's legs when my favorite massie whispered in my ear that she was switching the massage oil I was using. As she left, she gave me a shoulder pat and a smile. Soon after, one of our residents began choking on her morning snack (papaya). She recovered but started yelling at everyone. She must have been scared, as I'd never heard her make a sound before. So, everything seemed a little off. One of the massies shrugged her shoulders, "It's Monday," and we smiled ruefully at each other. Yes, it's Monday!

After lunch, I was walking down Park Street and heard "North Carolina" shouted. It was my Indian friend who thought that the Democrats would have won with Bernie Sanders. "What about the marches?" she asked. We talked about seeing women marching all over the world and how empowering it felt. She added (randomly) that she liked everything about the marches except for Madonna's remarks. To this day I have no idea what Madonna said, but my friend believed that her comments did not help the cause. She also told me to go home and brush my teeth because there was food stuck between them and if I didn't brush, I might end up with tartar build-up, which could cause me to lose teeth. She added that she smoked for too many years, which turned her teeth dark brown.

☽

One day near the end of January, I had what I could only describe as a really sh*tty day! It was Jan's last day of volunteering after five months in Kolkata, and I could tell that she was already feeling the loss. We worked together to pick up a woman from the lunch table to take her to the toilet and then on to bed. We were just a little bit too late and suddenly Jan was completely decorated in caca. Oh yeah, that is the perfect ending to a day of volunteering, yet it wasn't the end. Why in the world was it caca day for so many of the residents? Suffice it to say that I washed my hands over, and over, and over, all day long.

I was beginning to know the women of Nirmal Hriday better. Ananya and Pari were among our most mobile residents. They were always the first to greet me each day. Every morning they cut and folded gauze into squares to be used for the endless dressings our women required. It was a pleasure to sit and work with them in a comfortable, companionable silence. Their smiles lit up their soft, round faces completely. I did notice that, like the massie at Shishu Bhavan years earlier, they surreptitiously corrected all my mistakes, until one day when Ananya gave me a thumbs up with a big smile!

As the days went on, Diya's face looked more and more pained. Every morning, as soon as she saw me, she would ask to be taken to the bathroom. Sometimes she was there for thirty minutes or more. Soon after she returned to the sitting area, she would grab another volunteer with the same urgent request and no discernable results. Ben used to remind me that I was not "that kind of doctor;" however, I have a pretty good track record. I was willing to bet that Diya had a UTI, a bladder disease, or was diabetic. I hoped that the doctor would check this soon. Usually I got kisses when I put her to bed, but on her bad days she would pinch me instead because she was mad at all of us. Diya spoke Hindi rather than Bengali, so she was in a tricky situation. Few massies, sisters, or volunteers could understand her requests. It must be difficult when you think no one is paying attention to you when you are hurting!

Jayanti always had a big smile, with dreamy eyes. She liked to nap in the morning, and I wished we could keep her busier. Her age was somewhere between and 14 and 17 and she probably needed more activities. Sister A hoped to send her to another to another home that would be better suited for her, with more residents and activities for her age group.

Karima's face revealed little, and it would be easy to think that she was not all there. And THAT would be a huge mistake! She knew exactly what was going on, and if a volunteer didn't understand, she simply increased the volume of her many requests.

Aama and Prisha both had very patrician features. Every morning, Prisha sat with her glasses perched at the end of her nose and read the newspaper. As the "big boss" she always felt free to tell or show volunteers what needed to be done, or how to fix what they were likely doing wrong. Aama was darker and had an air of mystery around her. I saw her lips move with the slightest of smiles when I first called her by name as if to say, "Of course!" Shivani's face often looked lonely, and her movements reinforced that image. She tapped on her bed, motioning that you needed to SIT DOWN until she was ready to let go of you, which could be a long wait.

One of our residents loved to color every day. I think coloring was a calming activity for her. I love doing paint-by-number canvases, so I understood. I'd say that her coloring worked, as she was the most chill woman in our care. She never asked for anything and moved around eas-ily with her walker. There were several other women who chose to color occasionally, but she was the most consistent. Anjali's face never revealed much unless she was in pain. I wonder if she learned this on the street in order to protect herself.

Another woman I adored looked like she should have been on a 1960's sitcom as the friendly neighbor or visiting aunt. She always had a smile on her face. She never wanted much for herself, but her bed was next to "the scratcher's" bed (Scratching "the scratcher's" back 24/7 will never be enough). The scratcher requested constant attention, and this smiling neighbor was quick to unselfishly pull in volunteers for scratching duty.

Although this may sound strange, there was one woman, Deepika, whose face reminded me of Ben. From my first day at Kalighat she looked at me deeply as if trying to see my soul. Whenever I looked into her big, brown eyes, I felt that Ben was with me. It was surreal… Unfortunately, she began to look more and more confused every day, as if she had landed in an odd dream and had no idea where she was. I learned that she had arrived at Kalighat only days before I did. Her constant request was simple – she wanted to go home. She smiled at me wistfully at rest time and thanked me for taking care of her.

☾

A group of American volunteers arrived at the end of January. It was great to see some of them at Kalighat on January 31st, the next morning. Sister MM always tried to place larger volunteer groups in multiple locations. She worked hard to ensure that every house had volunteers from many different countries. I loved my fellow volunteers, but it was great to talk with other Americans. They were loving, compassionate people, and I looked forward to more conversations with them during their stay in Kolkata.

In contrast, I was not looking forward to more "tour groups" walking through Kalighat. They came regularly to "look around" and learn about the work of the Missionaries of Charity. Groups had come from numerous countries and various places in India. Perhaps they wanted to make donations or to work at Kalighat at some point in the future. That would be the "up" side of their visits. One group came in late January right as lunch was ending and we were getting all the women in bed for an afternoon rest. To someone walking in without a context, it probably looked like chaos. I commented to several members of an English-speaking group that this was the busiest, most hectic time of the day. Group members walked through the women's side with their heads down, as though seeing the women, their physical conditions, and the overall place, was difficult. Some men from one of the groups wandered in the direction of the women's bathroom before one of the sisters stopped them. What I'd seen on many of their faces was pity. What I wanted to say to them was:

"Do NOT stare or gawk at these women. Each one of them has a beautiful soul and a difficult backstory and they do not need or want your pity. They are lovely and they are not a sideshow or the zoo. The volunteers who work with them are lucky to have this precious opportunity to serve. We choose to be here, and we are grateful."

☾

I continued to enjoy getting to know Kolkata. One day I got off at the right metro stop but left from the wrong gate. I came up the steps with the feeling that something was "off." I was across the street from my normal exit. But this error allowed me to see an interesting statue on the other side of Park Street. Do you remember the Nehru jacket, an iconic trend in the late 1960's — early 1970's? The jacket is hip length, with a mandarin collar, with the front based on the Indian achkan or sherwani, which was worn by Nehru, the Prime Minister of India from 1947-1964. Ironically, Jawaharlal Nehru never actually wore his namesake Nehru jacket. This statue is Nehru, in his longer sherwani.

By the end of January my frequent sleep issues had returned. It was so frustrating to lie in bed, tired AND wide-awake at the same time. When my alarm went off, though, I'd jump up and prepare for my day. I began to really enjoy my walk to the Mother House and could tell that all the walking I'd been doing was paying off. At the same time, my Kolkata diet was not what I'd hoped for given the white bread, chai, and bananas at the Mother House, along with our break time chai and biscuits (fortified crackers). At lunch I often had soup, lentils, or fried/breaded food. I missed fresh vegetables so much that I finally decided I couldn't take it anymore and needed to just bite the bullet, or lettuce! I picked a restaurant with purified water and realized that after lunch I'd either be happy and satisfied or totally miserable. As it turned out, the salad – a chicken Caesar – was delicious, albeit floating in about a pint of mayonnaise. I had a few cramps later, but my lunch was worth it! And for the best chai in Kolkata, I only had to go home. My housekeepers made the best chai I'd ever had.

I'd been healthy since that nasty round of traveler's diarrhea, but finally at the end of January, the pollution felt oppressive. My throat felt scratchy and my eyes felt grainy. I was grateful for the friend who sent me to Kolkata with lozenges that kept me from coughing and gagging all day long.

CHAPTER X

February

Lightning fast, it was February. The 1st was Basant Panchami, a day that marks the end of winter and the approaching spring. The festival also marks the birthday of the Goddess Saraswati. I was excited to learn that Saraswati is the goddess of learning, wisdom, knowledge, fine arts, refinement, science, and technology. The holiday is treated by celebrants as Saraswati's birthday. On this day, people petition the Goddess to attain enlightenment through knowledge and to rid themselves of lethargy, sluggishness, and ignorance. On the puja day, statues of Saraswati are draped in yellow and worshipped. In some temples, homes, and schools, children are taught to write their first words on this auspicious day. Idols of Saraswati are taken on procession and immersed in the holy river Ganga. This puja day is also ideal for inaugurating new training institutes and schools. Mustard flower blooms are yellow, and celebrants often wear yellow garments. Saraswati is portrayed wearing a yellow dress, and sweet saffron rice and yellow sweets are consumed at family meals. I was invited to a Saraswati puja event by Mr. Basu, who had picked me up at the airport when I arrived. The family lives in Salt Lake, a Kolkata suburb, about a 30-40-minute drive from my apartment, depending on traffic.

It was wonderful to talk with the women who were present, including one couple from Kolkata who had lived in Brooklyn for 17 years They were back in India to celebrate their daughter's wedding with local relatives. I had both breakfast and lunch there, eating with just my right hand, as is Indian custom. The left hand is reserved for bathroom cleaning! I am left-handed and can't do much with my right hand, so this was challenging. I knew that they would understand if I used utensils or picked up food with my left hand, but when in Kolkata... The food was delicious and much of it (veggies, fried food, bread, and sweets) was indeed colored yellow.

☾

Since Thursday was our day off, I had big plans for February 2nd. Not long after I arrived in Kolkata, my landlord invited me to visit the school where he served as headmaster. We'd settled on February 2nd, and early in the morning Visakha and I took an Uber across town. I was incredibly impressed with the Christian school, which is an NGO, serving poor children. In their own words, the school is "the modest dream of a small team of educationists who thrive on the philosophy of 'the freedom to dare, the freedom to dream, and the freedom to explore' that is practiced when dealing with children."

I loved the holistic model espoused by the school. "Education not only prepares a child in multitudes of disciplines, but also instills in them confidence, poise, and a belief that everything is possible. Not only does it teach one to construct a good life for oneself but also the zeal to help others in their times of need. The aim of the institution is to train the students to become responsible citizens of their motherland and to inculcate in them the habits of piety, virtue, discipline, and self-efficiency. The school functions keeping in mind that extracurricular activities are for the well-rounded development of students. Today's students have scores of things to do with very little time available to them. Therefore, it becomes a challenge for the students and their parents as well to strike the right balance between education and extracurricular activities to avoid stress and burnout. St. Stephen's strictly maintains an equal balance between the two." The extracurricular activities promoted are dance and music, creative writing, sports, nature club, yoga class, karate class, and the annual concert.

The school has students from toddlers through class 12. February 2ⁿᵈ was a bittersweet day, as it was the last day for students in class 12. For the next few weeks they would be studying for their national board exams. It was very nice to meet and talk with them. Some were very emotional, as this was the only school they'd ever attended. They wanted to go to college; some wanted to be teachers, some wanted to own businesses, and others wanted to be fashion designers. It was clear to me that St. Stephen's has indeed created both hope and opportunity for students.

After we returned home, Visakha (my property manager), Sunaina (her friend who works with her), Brindaban (the housekeeper), and Sukumar (the new second housekeeper), and I, ordered in Biryani for lunch. Mutton for 2 of us, chicken for the others. We also had chicken and cheese kebabs. I was expecting paneer as the cheese, but it tasted like Swiss. It was **amazing** and I quickly added the restaurant and dishes to my "order again" list. The Swiggy app in Kolkata delivers food from hundreds of restaurants with only a small delivery charge. I loved it!

In the afternoon, I continued my neighborhood exploration. I found two new bakeries and a coffee shop! It was so exciting to keep expanding the boundaries of the area I was getting to know very well. When I was out exploring, I saw a man with two monkeys. I have a love/hate, but mostly loving, relationship with monkeys and I really wanted to watch them. I hid around a corner because the man would probably have asked me for money otherwise.

By the first week of February, I was the most senior volunteer at Kalighat on the women's side. Jan left for home, followed the next day by Jacques and Michelle. All three of them had been wonderful role models for me as I found my way at Kalighat. I began talking more with Gitta, an older female volunteer from Germany, whose gentleness and kindness to our residents were beautiful to observe.

There were always reasons to laugh, either out and about in Kolkata or as we worked at Kalighat. One morning my friend Kaitlyn was walking the two blocks from the Baptist Missionary Society to the Mother House, when a rat fell from the sky at her feet. "It's raining rats" is not a phrase I'd ever heard or imagined. Apparently, a large bird had grabbed breakfast or lunch and then accidentally dropped it at her feet. Kaitlyn was just as thrilled as I would have been (not). Another day, three children approached me with their adorable pet monkey. They had taught the monkey all kinds of cute tricks. Despite my love of primates, I wasn't going to get too close to this one. A bad monkey encounter in Vietnam that led to me taking a student to Ho Chi Minh City for rabies shots had impressed on me the importance of keeping my distance. Still, I did love watching the little capuchin play.

After nearly a month of volunteering, I was in awe of Sister A, who oversees the women's ward at Kalighat. When she asks a volunteer to do something, she tells you why. One day when I was doing simple movement exercises with one of the residents, at the direction of the physical therapist, I realized that we were headed for a standoff. She was in pain and was not having any of it. Sister A explained to me that she had been a beggar all her life and had spent most of her days sitting on the sidewalk. "She needs to work on straightening her legs, although she doesn't want to," she said. When I understood more clearly why it was important for our resident to move her limbs, I renewed my work with her. The two of us made peace and she did a fantastic job of pulling up to a standing position and holding it.

☾

I found myself wondering more and more about the lives of the women I was serving at Kalighat. Sister A told me that she brought in many of the women off the streets herself. Some were beggars, and because they sat on the street or sidewalk all day for years, their muscles had atrophied. For many reasons, their families were unable to care for them long-term.

What must these women be thinking when they arrive at Kalighat? In many cases their hair was cut or shaved off to prevent lice or other infestations. Do they feel like their identities are being shaved away? Some arrive very ill, while others don't **seem** as sick, yet their apparent good health may be deceptive. Several women who look healthy have cancers that will continue to grow and eventually kill them.

What must it be like to have women taking care of them who don't speak the same language? How frustrating must it be when your caretakers don't understand your needs or requests? When dozens of voices are calling out, "Auntie, Auntie," how do you make sure that your voice is heard? Perhaps a caretaker does, in fact, understand your needs and for a week or a month she takes exceptional care of you. Then, with little warning, she is gone, and new women are asking you the same questions.

How does it feel to sleep in a warm bed, in a safe environment? How does it feel to eat three nourishing meals every day that meet your personal needs (vegetarian, non-vegetarian, special diets)? How does it feel to sit with other women every day? What does it feel like to have the staff members tell you that they love and care about you? How does it feel to have clean clothes? What do the women wish they could tell us? I imagined that I would ask myself these questions as long as I was here and even after I returned home. As hard as I tried, I could not truly imagine the lives some of my women had led.

I realized that I was settling in. I thought often about my first morning at Kalighat, remembering that for long chunks of time it felt like there was nothing to do. I wondered then if I could truly be of service. During my first days, I would ask the massies, sisters, and other volunteers for "jobs," and they would merely motion for me to sit and relax. That only exacerbated my sense of uselessness. Now, weeks later, it seemed like there was never a free second. The busyness made me happy and I tried to care for new volunteers who were experiencing the same emotions I'd felt.

☾

Every day at Kalighat was different. One morning I began by shelling peas with Steve, who is an Indian volunteer/staff member, and a French woman whose husband had died a few years ago. She comes to Kolkata and volunteers for 4-5 weeks every year, "always to Kalighat." Of course, I understood the story and the pull to this place. My years of high school and college French started coming back to me as I spoke with her and other French volunteers. All of us worked hard to understand each other. I'd been wondering about Steve's story, and I learned that it was very intriguing. When he was 12, the local priest came to his mother to ask if Steve might be interested in the priesthood. His mother encouraged him to think about it and make his decision carefully. Ultimately, he decided against the priesthood, later choosing a career as a crew member on cargo ships. He told me about visiting Liverpool, England, when the Beatles were popular, and about passing through the Panama Canal, among other things. This conversation would serve as an opening to other rich discussions. Steve had so much wisdom, born of 75 years of life experience.

☾

Now, when I walked into the women's ward, there were cries of "Auntie, Auntie," from all quarters. I was immediately busy with bathroom visits, gown changes, sips of water, conversations, and more requests that were all part of our day. On the one-month anniversary of my first day at Kalighat, I realized that so much was different. The fear and uncertainty I'd felt on my first day were gone and had been replaced by a sense of true purpose. The residents, massies, and sisters trusted me. That didn't mean that I received more glamorous jobs, as if those exist in this place. Instead, I ended up doing jobs that the massies often did themselves. So, I was occasionally sent to the rooftop to fold clothing and bring it downstairs, or to the second floor to carry down big pots and pans of food to be served at lunch. Despite the language barriers, I was beginning to understand their pantomimes and knew what their usual requests meant.

☾

One early February morning I was surprised to see Aama, who usually sat in the same place in the main gathering area, in bed. She had "loose motions," which probably sounds better than diarrhea. The same morning, Shivani hobbled back to her bed as soon as she could, and Karima asked me to put her on the floor so that she could crawl to the bathroom by herself. Although it took her a long time, she needed the exercise. I began asking myself more often if a resident's request was necessary, or if it would be better for her to "do it herself." We tried to encourage the women to be as independent as they could possibly be. I was newly conscious of the fact that I was now talking about what "we" do and not what "they" (the Missionaries of Charity) do.

Sometimes I felt that, when I spoke with residents, they understood me, and I understood them in return, even though we were speaking two different languages. In early February I began having long "conversations" with one of our new residents. I had no idea what she was talking about and she did not understand me, but we wanted to be together. She gripped my hands in an iron vice so that I wouldn't leave. I nodded as I listened to her stories as though I understood every word. She was quite a character and I enjoyed our chats. On the other hand, Deepika, the woman whose eyes reminded me of Ben, appeared to be losing strength every day. It was not a dramatic decline, but it hurt me to see it. Indeed, some of our sickest residents hung on day after day by just a thread.

I was settling in at home too. My housekeepers and I found common ground as we watched Animal Planet, America's Funniest Home Videos, or Bollywood movies. My "big chai" came every night at 6:30. My first full sentence in Bengali was "I would like a large mug of chai." The housekeepers took note of what cookies and biscuits I'd eaten most quickly, and those seemed to come more and more often. One night I asked one of the housekeepers for more toilet paper and he handed me two thin rolls and said with a grin, "long time." "We'll see," I responded! Fortunately, the little store across the street from Blue Sky always had TP, and I would purchase a roll or two when I needed it.

☾

One crazy morning in early February helped me realize that "Dear God" can be the most fervent of prayers. We started off with a new resident who was the living definition of skin and bones. She reminded me of a graphic picture of Biafran orphans during the famine there. Her family had been caring for her but didn't have the resources to continue doing so. We were told that she had large bedsores that could lead to a deadly infection. I sat and talked with her for a while, took her hand, and told her she was safe. I thought she could have been 40-60 years old; I later learned that she was 28, a young mother with two small children. No wonder she was so scared. I don't think anyone believed that she would still be alive the next morning. We learned later that the MC Brothers worked with her family and that they brought her to Nirmal Hriday to have a safe and comfortable place to die.

We received another new patient the same morning. Her body was covered in large, raised bumps. Kaitlyn (US friend and chiropractor) and I wondered what the diagnosis might be. We agreed to ask one of the sisters as soon as possible, but before we could do that, two volunteers went over to sit with her and hold or massage her arm (they were wearing gloves). We asked and were told that she was indeed contagious. One of the younger sisters said that it could be severe scabies, but when I Googled images of scabies, they didn't match her strange-looking bumps. In any case, the gloves and anything else that the volunteers touched had to be thrown away. It didn't feel good at all to have to offer comfort and support from a distance. The woman had a lovely smile and we all wanted to reassure her — but we would need to wait.

☾

The men's side of Kalighat was experiencing a lot of sickness, and we hoped that it wouldn't travel to the women's ward. Despite our hopes, there was a lot of "loose motion" in early February, and it felt like a real caca storm. One woman was sitting on a bench sleeping and apparently pooping at the same time. One of the massies called to me to help her put the woman in a chair to take her to the bathroom to be fully washed. We put her in a chair, and she was completely limp. The massie said to me, "Auntie, she DIE." So, we hurried the woman off to the bathroom. Sister A ran in and we got the woman to a bed. Sister did CPR and the woman was "back". I don't know if her heart had stopped beating, but her breathing was very shallow. We cleaned her off completely, changed her gown, and put her in bed. She was shaking like a leaf, so I covered her with two blankets. We asked if she wanted lunch, but she rejected it. In the middle of this activity, one of our patients who had been refusing to eat, finished her entire lunch! Just another morning…

After our shift was over, I decided to eat at McDonald's. I know, I know…. I knew that they would not be serving beef or pork, but I was hoping for a good chicken sandwich. As you would likely expect, I was bitterly disappointed. The sandwich filling did not have the consistency of chicken and may or may not have been tofu; those who have traveled with me know that I despise tofu passionately. Ugh!! The fries were good, but there are good fries all over India. Suffice it to say that this would be my one and only foray into McDonalds while living in India.

☾

The next morning, I was surprised to find that our new resident was still alive. I didn't have to get any further than the last step before I was certain of this; her wailing pierced my ears immediately! I learned from the very tired massies that she had cried most of the night and was clearly still struggling. Some of her tears were not for herself but were out of concern for her children, particularly what would happen to her five-year-old daughter if she died. She was completely distraught.

Later, Shivani called out for me to come and visit, because she liked to have company all the time. When I got to her bed, I saw that she was crying. I asked if she was okay and she nodded that she was. She then motioned to our new patient and indicated that she was very sad about her story. It was stunning to see the empathy that she displayed toward another resident in a place where everyone has their own physical and/or mental health challenges. I'd seen this before from the resident who never asked for anything for herself, but always made sure that the less able woman who slept/sat next to her had a blanket, a snack, or whatever was being handed out. Not everyone was so empathetic about our new resident's struggles. Another resident had been so unhappy about the non-stop wailing that she had started kicking beds and hitting random women in the middle of the night.

There were many tears running down the faces of volunteers as we tried to comfort our sick and suffering resident. It seemed doubtful that she would recover, but I'd learned that you never really know. The woman who we thought was dead or dying the day before slept all morning, but I was able to rouse her and get her to eat about ten bites of lunch before she'd had enough and drifted off to sleep. The resident with the contagious skin lesions was sent to a local hospital for more critical care, which seemed like a good decision. Any contagious illness could create havoc here.

I went to Flury's for lunch and ended up sitting next to an Indian man. He asked where I was from and what I was doing in India. It turned out that he was a retired Associate VP at Virginia Tech, just two hours from my home in North Carolina. His family was in town for a wedding. We had a great, wide-ranging talk, and I was sorry to see him leave. I love random meetings like this one. I ordered a ham croissant, and it tasted like a supreme pizza. I walked home tired but with a heart full of gratitude.

☾

After a few days our young mom became feistier and more challenging. This meant that all of us had to dig deeper into the well of compassion to show love to her. When she had the dressings on her bedsores changed, the level of wailing increased dramatically. My friend Kaitlyn, who was in the room, said that the bedsores were large and deep. Any infection could travel through her system quickly, shutting down her organs and leading to death. When her dressings were all changed, Sister A put her in a wheelchair, just a bit apart from the other women. One of the social workers came to see her, and she began crying again about the fate of her family. Then the phlebotomist came from an outside lab to draw blood. He had a terrible time trying to find a vein and stuck her unsuccessfully five times. He was finally able to extract a small amount of blood. I was holding her hand and trying to distract her, but the sobbing started again during this procedure. Afterward, all she wanted to do was to go back to bed. Sister A felt that it was important to keep her sitting up for a while to relieve some of the pressure on the bed sores. I got up when several other residents called out to me, but as I as was walking away, she began slipping down in her chair. I immediately realized that she was doing this on purpose and was willing to face plant on the hard floor just to earn a quick trip back to bed. I sat her back up in her chair, but thirty seconds later she tried the same move again. One of the sisters or massies tied her into the wheelchair to keep her from falling, but she was having none of it. Since she was completely skin and bones, she managed to wriggle herself down under the ties five or six times. I was worried that she would accidentally strangle herself. It was lunchtime, so I encouraged her to eat a little lunch, but she was having none of that either. Finally, three of us put her back in bed, just a few minutes before the rest of our residents settled in.

On my first day of volunteering, the first person who spoke to me during breakfast at the Mother House was Dylan from Great Britain. He and his wife, June, were leaving for Thailand in a few days, and they invited me out for dinner at a fancy restaurant, Oh, Calcutta! How apt! Of course, the name took me back to the 1969 Off-Broadway musical review. The food was spectacular and the jaggery ice cream (non-centrifugal cane sugar) was delicious. I was reminded again just how fortunate I was to meet so many interesting and compassionate people.

☾

Given the late night, I knew I'd be tired in the morning, but the truth is that I was exhausted by 10:00 am. It seemed like our tea break would never come. I had really tried to get as much sleep as possible, because when I was depleted, compassion fatigue was that much more real, making it difficult to be fully present.

Before I started volunteering at Kalighat, I thought that the only way our residents left here was by death. I had a vague memory of reading that 80% of the men and women who came to Kalighat died in the first week. That may have been true at some time (I don't know), but it is not at all true now. In fact, some women go to the hospital, while others are sent to care facilities where their individual issues can be treated best. Others get to go home or to stay with relatives. In early February, both Ananya and Pari went home. Ananya had worked for the Missionaries of Charity for twenty-six years, until she injured her leg. She had been recuperating at Kalighat for nine months and was beyond eager to return home. She cried on my shoulder one morning when she found out that her homecoming would be delayed by a day. I was relieved to have the chance to say goodbye to her, as she was gone the next morning.

The day after the phlebotomist visit, our young mother wouldn't get out of bed. When I saw him arrive again, I mentally prepared myself for more crying and pain. The results were no better than the day before, as finding a good vein was nearly impossible. Sister A was eventually able to find a viable vein and I was relieved. After lunch, Sister set up an airbed for her, which would hopefully relieve the pressure on and pain from her bed sores. After lunch, she started crying again, and I sang her to sleep. I am guessing that sleep was the best defense she could muster against my terrible singing voice. I just hoped she could feel the love pouring out in her direction.

☾

On my next day off, I caught up on my much-needed sleep and it felt so good. My housekeeper made me eggs, toast, and chai, which counted as a perfect breakfast! Later, I headed off to one of the salon/spas near me for a shampoo and blowout. It felt wonderful to walk away with clean, styled hair. I didn't even bring my hair dryer to India with me. Most days, I just pulled my hair back and put on a wide headband or bandanna. When I was volunteering, I just didn't want to be bothered with serious grooming. The reason I did this was to (hopefully) prevent lice. I had brought home the nasty little critters the first time I volunteered in India and I wanted to avoid a repeat performance, if possible.

Later that afternoon, I got dressed up in my first formal Indian clothing for the Annual Function of Khalsa High School (a Sikh-run school in Kolkata). My landlord, who is a well-loved community leader, invited me to be an honored guest for the event. While the event was sponsored by the high school, there were children receiving awards from the earliest grades on. My favorite part of the evening was the cultural dancing, especially the boys. Several of them were excellent dancers, and it looked like they were having a wonderful time. In some ways the night reminded me of the dance recitals I'd attended in the US that were up to four hours long. I was invited up on the stage to receive a plaque and roses. All in all, a very nice evening.

☾

Throughout December and January (as well as summer), there is usually an abundance of volunteers at the homes, as many use vacation days to come to India. Most of the volunteers I met fell into two categories: college students and other young people who wanted to travel the world and serve others, or retired men and women who had the time. Even so, there were volunteers of all ages. By early February there were some days when only three or four volunteers were on the floor. This was especially difficult on Fridays, which were our super-cleaning days (Saturdays for the men)! Every Friday, all beds are cleaned and stacked up, along with the mattresses, which are scrubbed down. Next, the floors are mopped thoroughly. Beds and mattresses are put back in place, and finally, a sheet and a rubber mat are put on, followed by a draw sheet. Each woman has a pillow, and a soft, warm blanket during the months when it is needed. As a minister's daughter, and later a minister's wife, I'd visited many nursing homes in the United States and at times the smell of urine and other odors can be quite strong. There were moments at Kalighat when odors were unpleasant, but overall I found it cleaner than many senior centers in the United States. Most Fridays in February, my back hurt unmercifully.

☾

On February 10th, we worked as hard and fast as we could, even borrowing some volunteers from the men's side to help us with the moving of beds and mattresses. Despite the help, it took us a long time to get everything done. The massies typically took their break at 10:00 am, and the volunteers followed at 10:30. On this day; however, the massies were still on the floor at 10:30. We all got just enough time to chug hot chai and grab some fortified biscuits. A new, young volunteer, Valentina, started on this crazy day – and she was a trooper! I developed incredible admiration for the young volunteers I served with. I am nearly certain that I could not have been as calm and collected in my twenties. I did not know it on her first day at Kalighat, but Valentina was to become my closest volunteering friend.

By 11:15, we were just starting to hand out lunch, and that meant that it was really late by the time that we had everyone settled into bed. Gitta, Valentina, and I walked up to the volunteer room at 12:30 and just collapsed there for a few minutes before gathering the energy to head out for the day. Our 28-year-old mom had a big breakfast, then rejected lunch. Only after the food was gone and the plates cleared, did she decide that she might be hungry again. When Gitta and I said goodbye for the day, she held on to us so tightly that we were unable to break free. We looked at each other, then sat back down and talked with her for a few more minutes.

Before I left for Kolkata, one of my friends had told me to be sure to eat at Peter Cat. After a rough morning, I thought it might be the perfect afternoon for a satisfying meal. I was intrigued by a dish named Harem's Joy. If I had been part of a harem (or not), I would have expressed absolute joy at this incredibly flavored chicken and tomato treat. It was flavorful without being spicy hot, which is rare in India. And the best hot weather thirst quencher in the world (non-alcoholic) just might be fresh lime soda, which comes salty or sweet, and occasionally both (the salty and sweet version is horrible). I liked it sweet, and Peter Cat's version was my favorite so far.

After leaving the restaurant, I stopped into a pop-up Kashmiri market, looking at beautiful scarves, rugs, and other handmade items. I did not know that cashmere is an old spelling of the Kashmir region or that garments made from cashmere provide three times the insulation of sheep's wool. The young store owner had me feel different pieces of fabric to see how soft they were. It probably comes as no surprise that the softer the wool, the higher the price. I bought a few things that caught my eye. I'd pick them up a week later, giving him time to alter them to fit me perfectly.

((

I was starting to discover things that I didn't like about India. Instead of feeling concerned about this, I was relieved. If you travel and fall completely in love with a "perfect place," I doubt that you are very discerning. There is little in life that is all good or all bad. I suspect that anyone who has been to Kolkata has hated, or at the very least, been annoyed by the items on my *Ten Things I Hate About You – Kolkata Version* list.

1. **The incessant beeping/honking of car horns** — For the love of God, please STOP! I seriously believe that future generations of Bengalis will go deaf very early in life. The noise pollution all over the city is intense. Since many Indian drivers beep constantly, what good does it really do? I get that there is no such thing as a traffic lane here, but does your beeping cause other cars to get out of your way? I'm not sure there's a solution except for personal ear plugs.

2. **Playing Chicken with Pedestrians** — I know that there are 1.34 billion people in India (compared with 316.5 million in the United States) in an area that is just slightly more than one-third the size of the US, and that driving on over-crowded roads can be frustrating. Traffic jams are frequent, especially at peak hours of the day. This leads to unhappiness when you are supposed to be somewhere at a particular time, and you are stuck. This DOES NOT give you permission to SPEED UP in front of pedestrians! At least you are equal-opportunity players though; I've seen Indian men and women forced to scramble back to the curb too.

3. **Buses** — People should not have to get on or off a **moving bus.**
   And what about SHOCK ABSORBERS? Please get some! My
   back has been re-adjusted nearly every day on the city buses of
   Kolkata.

4. **TRASH** — One of the things that I associate most strongly with
   Kolkata is trash. I remember vividly walking past a huge mound
   of trash every morning on my first trip to Kolkata and watching
   people and animals pick through it for food. While huge piles of
   trash are picked up every day, the city is very dirty. More than
   once I have walked over a mile with trash in my hands and NOT
   ONE TRASH CAN to be found. If there were trash cans on every
   block, perhaps a city-wide clean-up campaign could begin. Even
   so, while I'm sure the problem seems intractable, I believe it can
   be solved. The first time I was in Rwanda, I was amazed at the
   cleanliness of Kigali, the capital city, and the entire country. Less
   than twenty-five years after a horrific genocide, the country,
   sometimes called "the shining star of Africa," is on the way back.
   President Kagame rightly understood that cleanliness could be a
   point of pride for the nation. No plastic bags are allowed in the
   country and the last Saturday of every month is *umuganda,*
   "coming together in common purpose to achieve an outcome."
   On umuganda, from 8:00 am to 11:00 am, everyone is expected
   to clean up and no driving is allowed without a special permit.
   Something to think about...

5. **Spitting** — Have you seen the ubiquitous signs that say NO
   SPITTING? Hum, perhaps there is a reason that the government
   is trying to stop this habit. There's nothing like having a big lugie
   land at your feet while you are walking down the sidewalk.

6. **Public Urination** — Turning your back to others and peeing on
   a wall in front of you doesn't make you invisible. We can SEE
   you. Nothing says Kolkata quite as much as getting hit with the

strong smell of urine, or feces for that matter, when you turn a corner and the wind wafts in your direction.

7. **Crowds of Men Harassing Women** — No one says this better than Indian author, Twinkle Khanna, in *Mrs. Funnybones.* "This is a peculiar Indian habit, see a woman alone anywhere and our men must harass her even if she has a moustache thicker than theirs, is eighty-three years old, or has a massive mole on her nose with three strands of hair sprouting through; basically they will revel in hounding any creature that vaguely has two X chromosomes lurking anywhere inside." Yep!

8. **Sizes** — Since when is a large cup of tea five tiny sips worth. At my apartment, I learned to ask my housekeepers for "big chai" and not the equivalent of a demitasse cup.

9. **Demonetization** — In November 2016, the government announced the demonetization of all 500 and 1,000-rupee notes (cash) of the Gandhi series. This action was taken to curtail the shadow economy and crack down on counterfeit cash. For weeks there was a cash shortage, which caused disruption. Demonetization was announced at 8:00 pm and took effect at 11:00 the same evening, creating widespread panic. While the government needed to take steps to improve the economy, it was frustrating to be given bills at some retail stores and restaurants that no other businesses would accept. We learned to study our change before leaving any establishment to ensure that it could be used elsewhere.

10. **The 5-Person Rule** — This isn't exactly a rule, but it can take hours to complete simple business transactions in India. If money is involved, at least five people must be consulted. It took two days and at least five Vodaphone employees to set up my $15/month account. Of course, two employees had to come to my apartment to ensure that I lived where I said I lived. I guess

that by requiring so many people to handle transactions – from hairdressers to restaurants to shops to businesses – there is more job security. Never mind the complexity of simple transactions.

Of all these irritations, my least favorite was the unwanted male attention, particularly on A.J.C. Bose Road, where the Mother House and Shishu Bhavan are located. Mornings had a mystical quality, as parents walked their children to school, men stood and sipped tea, the barber gave haircuts on the sidewalk, the street restaurant cook sat and made luchis (puffed bread), employees rolled tires out to the edge of a sidewalk for display, and people washed up, preparing for the day. In the afternoon, the same street was very different. It felt like "guy land." Being stared at, followed, and touched was creepy, especially when the men who were the most vocal could have been my grandsons. Ugh! I decided that on the afternoons I worked at volunteer registration I would Uber from either Sudder or Park streets, the two areas where I generally ate lunch. It felt good to find a way around this difficult and unpleasant situation.

During the first week of February, a group of American VIPs came to visit the Mother House. The day before, Sister MM asked for several American volunteers to greet the group and talk about their experiences with the Missionaries of Charity and in India. One of my young volunteering friends, Kelly, and a new volunteer from Colorado, Jon, were part of the greeters. I was working at orientation and could not participate. The next day at breakfast Kelly asked me to go on a city tour with herself and Jon the following day. Our host and tour guide would be Robert, an Indian man who worked at the US Consulate in Kolkata, and who had accompanied the visiting Americans earlier. I said yes and was glad I did. My favorite part of the tour was visiting an area of the city where sculptures/statues are made for pujas and other ceremonies. These creations begin with tying grass or straw together to form the needed shapes. Next, clay is used for the outside covering and to fine-tune the features of the statue. Finally, the statues are air-brushed or painted. When the festivals for which the statues have been created are completed, they are dumped in the river. When the clay wears off, the grass/straw rises to the surface and is collected, then dried and used again. We talked with an older gentleman as he manipulated clay around bundles of straw. He noted sadly that he was the last member of his family who knew how to do this. I enjoyed watching the process so much and hope that the art form will not be lost.

Because it was Kelly's twentieth birthday, we went to Peter Cat to celebrate. Robert suggested that we try the Chelo Kebabs, a favorite Bengali meal. They were delicious. Feeling the need for something sweet to end our meal, we went around the corner to Flury's for a variety of treats. In the afternoon we took a walk along the Ganga River, which was very, very pleasant. We encountered many families doing the same thing. We ended our afternoon with ice cream cones and conversation overlooking the river. It was simply a perfect day – interesting company, new knowledge about Kolkata, outstanding food and sweets, and a nice walk. I'd seen so many areas of Kolkata. What I still needed was to see exactly how they were all connected. One step at a time...

☾

On Monday, we learned the name of our 28-year-old resident – Aisha. One of the social workers brought Aisha's husband and children to Kalighat to see her. The children are a 2 ½-year-old boy and a five-year-old girl, and they were both precious, although a bit confused. Her husband seemed nice as well. The family came during volunteer tea break, and when I came back downstairs, they had just left. Sister A grabbed my hand and ran outside with me so that I could meet them. As we were coming back inside Kalighat, Sister A said that Aisha would probably be sad that her family had left and asked me to comfort her. I went to her bed and told her I'd met her beautiful children. This was the first time I'd seen her smile. A week earlier she was on the brink of death, and now she was beginning to feel better. I didn't know if this recovery would last, but I felt like we were witnesses to a miracle.

One of the massies was sitting with Aisha when I came back in from meeting her family. The massie was crying and crying and told me that her own mother had died when she was only five, the same age as Aisha's daughter. Her deep emotion moved me to tears as well. Here we sat, a massie, a volunteer, and a resident, all crying over the painful realities of life and death. When lunch was brought to her, Aisha said she didn't want to eat. I was surprised, because we'd been telling her that if she wanted to go home, she needed to get stronger. A little later she asked for just rice and dal. I couldn't be sure, but I wondered if these foods were all her family could afford to eat at home. Were these her comfort foods? We knew that her family was in dire straits. She finished the rice and dal and even asked for a second portion, along with a glass of milk. A while later she started crying softly and said that she was eating well in our care, but her family had nothing to eat. I was heartbroken as she poured out her pain. Her family's visit had brought her a new sense of hope and purpose – important ingredients for healing.

Valentine's Day arrived and was celebrated just like it is in the United States. Archie's, the Indian equivalent of Hallmark stores, had been deco-rated with red, pink, and white hearts for several weeks in advance. The shelves were lined with cards, teddy bears, flowers, and expensive im-ported chocolates. A bag of Hershey's kisses costs way more in Kolkata than in the US, and it tastes like heaven. Since Ben's death in 2014, Val-entine's Day had been a difficult reminder of my loss. Ben always gave me flowers, chocolates, and heartfelt cards, and we loved to have Valen-tine's Day (or week) dinner at The Melting Pot. Nothing says "celebrate" like fondue (she said longingly). I missed *eros* love in my life and sharing each day with a caring partner.

As I sat with my jumbled feelings on Valentine's Day, I realized that despite loss, I do have an abundance of love in my life. Another Greek word for love is *storge,* or family and friendship love. My family and extended family are SO important to me, as are my friends and former colleagues. *Phileo,* which is warm and tender platonic love, is also a deep and rich part of my life. I was also extremely grateful to have *agape* love that sees beyond the outer surface and unconditionally accepts the beloved. I love the women of Kalighat; their health and happiness are important to me. I don't know or care what caste they come from, whether they were begging on the streets, or other details of their lives. Love is a verb and every morning when I wake up, I pray that I will act only in loving ways toward them. Several volunteers have told me that "love radiates from my heart." I hope this is true! On this February 14th, I was the only volunteer in the women's section for much of the morning. Valentina was not feeling well, and the other female volunteers were hanging/folding laundry on the roof. I was running from one resident to the next, reminding myself of my desire to be present for each woman. Before I left for the day I whispered in all their ears that I loved them.

While *A Chorus Line* was my biggest Broadway disappointment, I resonate with the song, *What I Did for Love.* Of course, in the musical the singers are sharing their passion for dance, despite knowing that at any moment they could have a career-ending injury. In the end, they would still choose to dance. What I did for love was to come to Kolkata to share my heart in a small way with the dying destitute. My six months in India were a sacrifice in some ways, yet they were also filled with joy. The hardest part of the experience might be leaving India and not knowing the fate of the women I served and loved with all my heart. Even so, I won't regret the time that we spent together. After my Valentine's Day shift, I treated myself to a good lunch. I ran into some volunteer friends, a married couple, on the street, and they gave me a heart-shaped balloon that I kept in my bedroom until I left Kolkata!

☾

The next day at Kalighat was crazy. When I walked in and went upstairs to the locker area, I saw that someone else had put their things where I usually left mine and taken my apron. You might not even own an apron if you are a neat cook, but they are essential in the MC homes. I'd heard our female residents scold new volunteers because they were NOT wearing aprons. I didn't care so much about the apron, as there are many for volunteers to choose from, but I really wanted the items in the pockets – a squished roll of toilet paper, my Purell, and some massage lotion. So, I went back downstairs to find the volunteer who was wearing my apron. After looking around, I found a new volunteer in the men's ward from Korea and tried to explain that he took my apron. This took time, charades, and the help of a Japanese volunteer. I showed him where to find an apron and took mine back. Guess what – When I felt in the pockets there were earbuds and latex gloves. NOT. MY. APRON. So, I went back upstairs, searched through lockers, found my apron, and left the other green apron in the locker where I found mine. Ten minutes later, one of the Italian volunteers who only speaks broken English came to me, pointed, and said, "My apron." I grabbed him by the hand, ran upstairs with him, and got his apron. Then I explained, with some words and a few charades, what had happened. We cracked up and then went back to work. And the squished TP? Toilet paper is not provided everywhere, as many people simply use their left hand for bathroom chores. That's why many Indians eat with their right hand only! As for me, I was happy to have my squished roll in case of emergencies.

Even residents who were generally mild-mannered had their days. On this day, it was Shivani. I was helping the physical therapist prepare for his next therapy session by moving our resident from her chair to a bed. When we are doing physical therapy that involves the legs, we put shorts on the women to keep their private parts private. From day one at Kalighat, I understood the importance of maintaining the worth and dignity of each resident. So, I brought a pair of shorts (like bloomers) from the cupboard to put on Anjali. Shivani stopped me though – she really wanted those shorts, so I let her have them. I went to get another pair of shorts but got called away before I could put them on Anjali. I came back and they were missing. I could see that Shivani had them mostly hidden under her pillow. When I tried to retrieve them, she started to cry. I went off to get another pair, and the same thing happened again. I finally got a pair of shorts on Anjali, and Shivani had a few pairs under her pillow. She told another volunteer that she was going home, although this was wishful thinking. In any case, she must have had shorts on her mental packing list.

Jayanti, our teenager, wanted to go home too. We had to watch her carefully, because she was starting to roam when we turned our backs. This was a constant and heartbreaking theme at Kalighat. Many of the women who begged to go home didn't have a home to go to. Aisha, who does have a home, wanted nothing to do with any of us this morning. She pushed our hands away when we tried to help her. She was in constant pain, both physical (stomach issues and bed sores) and emotional (missing home and family). I worried that her stubbornness could sabotage her recovery, but maybe her feistiness would help her in the long run, as she fought to get better. On this crazy tilt-a-whirl day, I was exhausted by noon. Happily, a tuna sandwich and chips revived me for the afternoon.

When I got home, completely exhausted, I learned that my landlord was having a birthday party for a good friend in the beautiful backyard and that I was invited. I was exhausted but got dressed in another nice Indian salwar kameez (top, pants, scarf) and was ready to party. The guest list was incredible. I met several staff members from the US Consulate and many other guests who worked for the consulates of other countries. Passed hours d'oeuvres, wine, a late dinner, birthday wishes, cake, and stimulating conversations made for a delightful evening. I understood the next morning that the party continued past midnight, but I went to bed much earlier, as I could feel a cold coming on.

☾

The next morning my cold hit with a vengeance. My throat was so sore that I could hardly talk. Fortunately, it was our day off, so I didn't have to get up at the crack of dawn. I headed down Park Street for a muffin and hot chocolate to ease the pain a little. My throat felt a little bit better as I walked to the Indian Museum to meet my friends, Sara and Valentina. The museum was interesting. While we looked at artifacts, I asked my friends what they thought it might be like to participate in an archeological dig. I know that I would have loved it. Who knows? Perhaps such an adventure awaits in the future! We spent several hours at the museum until our backs and legs hurt. We saw artifacts that were thousands of years old, and I loved the depictions of ancient life. We also saw beautiful Bengali paintings in many styles. There was an Egyptology room that I couldn't quite figure out, as the exhibits had no apparent relationship to India. The featured exhibit was about the Naga tribes that live in the Nagaland, Manipur, Assam, and Arunachal Pradesh states of India, and in Myanmar. Their sculptures, artwork, weapons, and personal effects were fascinating. When we left the museum, we met up with Kaitlyn and headed to Sudder street to eat at the Spanish café. My throat was sore again, so I also ordered a fresh honey, lemon, and ginger tea that soothed the pain for a while.

☾

Although my throat felt like it was full of Kolkata "crud," I woke up the next morning feeling pretty good and headed to the Mother House. We had a large group of new volunteers headed to Kalighat. I had to laugh at myself as a tour guide, given my general lack of directional knowledge. When we walked into the door of Kalighat, my heart sank when I saw on the statistics board that one woman had died. After putting on my apron, I quickly ran downstairs to check on the women. Fortunately, the board was incorrect – no one had died overnight.

We did learn about a near runaway. Jayanti had tried to escape twice the day before. One of the massies was leaving for the day when she saw Jayanti several blocks away and had to run after her and bring her back. It's clearer now that she doesn't know where she lives. Sister A told me that before Jayanti could be returned home, if a correct address and family was found, they would make sure she was going back into a positive and safe environment. If that was not the case, she would likely be moved to a place that would be a more positive and stimulating environment for a teenager. Just before lunch, Jayanti tried to break out again. I cornered her this time, and she tried to push me out of her way. She knew I wouldn't put up with that, so she apologized quickly. I became very concerned for her safety on the streets of Kolkata.

Aisha, on the other hand, was happy to see us. She gave me a big smile when I came downstairs. I asked Sister A if she would be able to recover enough to go home in the future. Sister said that she thought Aisha just might recover enough to go home. Of course, the family is so poor that they often do not eat. But Sister A told me that the Missionaries of Charity help many very poor families by providing food staples every month. I didn't know that and was glad to hear it.

Several of us asked Sister A what it was like to work alongside Mother Teresa. She told us a few anecdotes about her compassion. The statement that resonated most strongly for me was this: The poor helped and supported the rich for so long (as housekeepers, servants, cooks, etc.) that it was time for someone to support the poor. Mother's words and actions are still felt strongly by the sisters.

I spent a large part of the morning giving hair and scalp massages. I love hair/scalp massages when I have my hair done, and when I have a massage myself. It feels so good, and clearly our women thought so too. They were not at all shy to ask for more, more, more!

During my Kolkata experience, I sometimes had to deal with my own cultural hang-ups. The previous week we had a large group of Japanese students arrive, and several them were volunteering at Kalighat. From my work in Vietnam, I knew that medical face masks were used throughout Asia to prevent sunburn and to avoid fumes and pollution. It bothered me that they chose to wear their masks and gloves around the residents at Nirmal Hriday. My bias suggested that this felt too cold and clinical, and I realized that I needed to work on my own reaction.

During the afternoon volunteer orientation for English speakers, my voice gave out again. By the time I got home, I could no longer deny that I was sick. It felt like the severe pollution in the city had made a home in my throat. After I finished my chai, I had a sneezing spell. Imagine how surprised I was when a large projectile came flying out of my mouth and landed on the coffee table. I quickly grabbed some toilet paper and scooped it up. It was a tan and gray gelatinous goo, and yes, it was gross. But I had felt for days that a little piece of Kolkata had been living inside of me, and now it wasn't. My sleep was restless, as I had a deep and constant cough for most of the night.

☾

In the morning I got up and got dressed. I sat down on the bed for a few minutes to gain some strength and tried again. I finally recognized that I wasn't in any shape to volunteer, and that I didn't want to give my crud to the women of Kalighat, the volunteers, and the sisters. So, I went back to bed and slept all morning. I read for a while during the afternoon, but it was hard to focus. I hoped to go to Kalighat the next day but thought that plan was likely unrealistic.

By the end of six weeks in India, I had learned a lot about presence and flow, as well as the need for restorative sleep. During 2016, I had developed a strong meditation practice, that allowed me to stay grounded in the middle of tricky situations. I'd tried meditation previously, but it had seemed excruciatingly slow and of little use. In 2016 I committed to 40 minutes a day (in 2 20-minute blocks of time) for one month.

Honestly, it was easy after that, especially after I stopped judging myself so harshly for those times when my attention wandered. What I discovered was that every session was different, rather than better or worse. Some days I was completely present and other days I seemed to be controlled by my wandering "monkey mind." It is what it is! I knew that I felt infinitely better and calmer at the end of twenty minutes than I did at the beginning. My work at Kalighat had a similar feel. Some days, and especially when I was tired, I noticed that my mind wandered during my work. Whenever I realized this was happening, I tried to come back to the present moment and to send positive energy and love to the woman who was occupying my attention at that time – even if it was the 5th time she asked for water or the 10th time I'd taken her to the bathroom that morning.

The days I loved most were those when I felt very, very present and the work went by quickly. I'd look up and couldn't believe that it was teatime already. That's what FLOW is like. I appreciate the work of Mihaly Csikszentmihalyi, the author of *Flow: The Psychology of Optimal Experience*. If you are wondering how to pronounce the name, my Wake Forest colleague, Dr. Sam Gladding, taught me that it is "*chick sent me high.*" Csikszentmihalyi says that people are happiest when they are in a state of flow, which is concentration or complete absorption with the activity at hand and situation. Time flies and actions follow from previous actions. That's the place where I'd like to be as often as possible – in the zone! To achieve that state in India, I knew that I needed to have good, restorative sleep. When I first arrived in Kolkata, I slept like a peaceful baby but by the end of January the sleep woes that I carried with me returned. I'd lie in bed at night feeling tired but not sleepy.

☾

My cold had knocked me off my feet, which was frustrating. When I went back to Kalighat, I knew I was only functioning at about 75 – 80%, but oh my – what a rough start and a rough day. It began when I left my

apartment to go to the Mother House. I was used to the sweet smell of to-
bacco fields in the North Carolina air after a spring rain. Well, Kolkata
had a strange, but undefinable smell some mornings that was smoke
mixed with who knows what. It made me slightly sick to my stomach, but
I pressed on.

When I arrived at Kalighat, the first thing I saw was the MC Ambulance. That was usually not a good sign. While I was standing there, several men came out the door with a corpse wrapped in a white cloth. The
cloth was held in place with ties and I could tell that the body inside was
quite small. My heart stopped, as I wondered which woman it was. Someone else asked if this was a male or a female. When the attendants said
the body was a male, I was relieved to know that it was not one of the
women I loved so much. I was proud of the Japanese volunteers who re-
spectfully stepped up to place the corpse in the ambulance. I was still outside when I saw two of our female residents, Sister A, and one of the
massies waiting for a cab. Shivani, who always wanted someone to sit and
talk with her, and the woman who loved to color, were being moved to a
different facility. Shivani was happy, and my lovely coloring woman was
sobbing because she didn't want to go. No matter who you are or where
you are, change can be difficult. Honestly, I thought this would be a great
move for both women. While they each needed some assistance to walk,
they were very alert. A more stimulating environment seemed like a perfect setting. Jayanti was moved to another home as well. I thought she
would likely thrive around other young people.

After lunch I was exhausted and decided to call an Uber for the two
mile walk home. I waited nearly forty minutes, despite the app indicating
that the driver was a mere two minutes away several times. Eventually he
cancelled because he couldn't find me. I was standing right in front of a
Kolkata landmark, so it shouldn't have been so complicated. The second
Uber driver took another fifteen minutes to reach me, although his location was listed as three minutes away. Ugh – I was done with Uber India
(at least for a day or two)!

☾

Morning comes again, even after the roughest of days. My cold was getting better, but sickness was rampant among the volunteers. Everyone said that the cause was the weather changing from "winter" to spring. Temperatures were climbing, so perhaps the change from air conditioning to the hot, hazy outdoors and back was part of the problem.

The mood at Kalighat was peaceful and lovely. Our volunteer army took over the 45B bus this week – there must have been fifteen of us. Some volunteers who were staying closer to Kalighat just met us there, instead of coming to the Mother House. A van load of our residents went off to the hospital in the morning. You might think that's a dreadful thing, but I didn't think the women minded at all. They had doctor visits and some treatments there, and doctors sent back follow-up instructions. One of the best things about going to the hospital was that the women got to dress up. I could see the joy on their faces when they got to put on a sari or a salwar, instead of a Kalighat "gown." The woman who sewed the gowns and the men's pajamas was a miracle worker – she made pieces of cloth fit all body types and she mended holes and other clothing issues daily, but I know the women loved dressing the way they did before they arrived here. I walked with a new resident to the van; she was headed to the doctor for a diagnosis. Sadly, I could see that every step was painful. The wounds on her legs and feet had already been dressed, but I didn't know her story yet.

Our social workers led mindfulness meditation in both the men's and women's sections for the first time. They played soft music and told the women that they could pray, meditate, or just sit quietly for about 10 minutes. Of course, it took at least that long to get the mobile women to slowly walk there and to wheel less mobile women to the meditation area (where the women sleep). It was nice and very peaceful. I hoped they would do it again soon.

A few days earlier several of us had met a new volunteer named Charlotte, from New Zealand. During our brief conversation at Blue Sky, she mentioned that her husband had died a few years ago. On her first day at Kalighat, I sat next to her during break. I asked her what her husband had died from – esophageal cancer, of course. I don't think that was just a coincidence; it was more like a God-wink moment. I looked forward to more conversations with her.

A miracle took place this week in Kolkata and it went largely unnoticed by the general populace – the sky turned blue. It was the first truly blue sky I'd seen since I'd arrived in early January. The sky was more often white and hazy with perhaps a tinge of blue. This brilliant sky was momentous and, unfortunately, a mixed blessing. As "winter" ended, the pollution and smog decreased, while temperatures rose. Highs in the 90's were predicted for the next few weeks and the "feels like" temperatures were usually 10-15 degrees higher. "Just wait until May and June," was the mantra of the local people.

☾

Valentina showed me a shortcut to Park Street from Sudder Street. Almost immediately, I recognized it as the way my students and I had walked to the Mother House from the YMCA eighteen years ago. I loved that as volunteers and fellow travelers we are always teaching and learning. I learned more every day – about the Missionaries of Charity, the volunteers, and the women in our collective care.

☾

The next morning, Sister A called out to me to notice that Aisha had asked for a second lunch, which was happily provided to her. Sister said to me, "Your love has helped her get better." I believe that the love at Nirmal Hriday comes from so many sources – the volunteers, the sisters, the massies, and the residents themselves. I was pleased to see the amazing

101

change in Aisha and to know that I had a small part in helping her to improve. Of course, many residents would never leave the care of the Missionaries of Charity, but they would certainly know love and kindness while they were here. And as for Aisha, I'd come to suspect that she knew more English than most of our women. We were beginning to have some actual conversations and we clearly understood each other.

I loved volunteer conversations because they were often wry and punchy. Steve, an Indian volunteer and worker, and one of the physical therapists were having toast for lunch. Knowing that Steve had been to England multiple times, I asked if he liked baked beans on toast for breakfast. Off we went. He LOVES this breakfast treat. I studied abroad in England during my sophomore year of college and could never handle what to me was a bizarre breakfast dish. Steve said that if he had died while in England, and an autopsy had been performed, they would have discovered that his insides were completely full of baked beans. That's an interesting picture! It sounds so silly in writing; perhaps you needed to be there to appreciate the humor.

At registration in the afternoon, I enjoyed some private, unspoken chuckles. Several groups of Indian students were trying to engage in local service by working in the MOC homes, to get credit for a college class they were taking. Just like some American students, they had waited until the last minute and were trying to figure out how to get in the needed hours. During the conversation they told Sister MM that they would like to work at one of the homes until 6:00 pm. She told them that afternoon volunteering is over at 5:00. This is a strict rule, to keep a schedule for the children. I felt like I was watching the students recalculate how they were going to complete their assignment on time.

☾

On Thursday, Kaitlyn, Valentina, Sara, and I had another adventure. Since it was our day off, I slept in, hung out at home, went to a coffee shop for breakfast, and met the three of them at the Park Street Metro. From there, following the directions we were given, we headed out to visit The Loyal Workshop. Shortly after Kaitlyn arrived in Kolkata, fellow Americans took her to a local café where she saw a gorgeous leather bag for sale. She remembered the name stitched onto the side — Loyal. Not long after, she picked up a pamphlet about The Loyal Workshop at the Baptist Missionary Society, where she was staying while in Kolkata. She showed it to me, and I told her I wanted to visit too. When we met and talked with Charlotte at Blue Sky, she mentioned that she was also in Kolkata to visit her son who worked at, you guessed it – LOYAL! Blue Sky is very small, and tables are close together, which encourages conversations like this one. The Loyal Workshop helps women who are fighting for freedom from the sex trade in Kolkata.

Let me share a little bit about the sex trade here. One area, Sonagachi (in North Kolkata), is reported to be South Asia's largest red-light district. The area contains several hundred multi-story brothels and upwards of 7,000 sex workers (some estimates are much higher — around 13,000). The second largest red-light area in the city is in the Bowbazar neighborhood with around 1,500 – 2,000 sex workers. Prostitution is legal, but related activities — such as soliciting in public, owning/running a brothel, prostitution in a hotel, child prostitution, pimping and pandering — are crimes. Prostitution is legal only if carried out in the private residence of a prostitute or others. That said, there are obviously many brothels operating illegally in the country. In Kolkata, it is widely known that the police turn a blind eye to such activities.

I wondered how this business happened. In the late 18th and 19th centuries, the British East India Company set up "comfort zones" for British troops. The troops helped establish brothels across India with a goal of making young Indian girls and women into sex tools to satisfy the men's needs. In the early 19th and 20th centuries, thousands of women and girls from Europe and Japan were trafficked into British India, where they worked as prostitutes. In 2007, the Ministry of Women and Child Development reported the presence of over 3 million female sex workers in India, with over 35% of them entering the trade before the age of eighteen. Most women enter the sex trade due to the lack of resources and jobs that would allow them to support their families; children of sex workers often follow their mothers into the trade.

The Loyal Workshop (TLW) was founded to provide an opportunity for freedom from the sex trade and works with women in the Bowbazar area. The founders believe that another world is possible: a world where sex slavery is relegated to the history books. As they note, "It is a brazen dream, but we are putting it into action in one city, in one red-light community, with one woman at a time." This was a dream a long time in the making. In 2002, the founders, Paul and Sarah Biesly from New Zealand, visited Kolkata for the first time and toured Freeset, a pioneering business helping women leave the sex trade. In 2010, they spent a year in Bangladesh, learning the local language – Bangla (also known as Bengali). A year later, when they moved to Kolkata to begin their market research, the Bieslys met another couple, Harry and Mandy Croucher. Harry became the designer of Loyal products. It took the Bieslys two additional years to form friendships in the red-light district and to recruit their first group of women, while also sourcing ethical leather locally and finding a workshop space. Three cohorts of women had been trained when we visited and were now working at TLW. The products they had learned how to make were beautiful.

TLW has a meet-up location that can be found on Google maps. We waited there for just a few minutes, until a staff member came to get us. He then led us through a maze of narrowing alleys until we reached the workshop space. We had a great tour and watched some of the women in the September 2016 cohort making their products. We saw their cool "passports" that mark their success in learning the various skills required to make each Loyal product. We were able to ask questions and to learn a bit more about what TLW opportunity had meant to each one. Standing on the roof, we pondered what it must be like to learn a new skill and to free yourself and your family.

Back in my apartment I reflected on the bravery of the women who were reaching for freedom and new beginnings. I also felt great admiration for the founders and employees. I loved this quote from their website:

> Beautiful things start small. We started with just five employees. The foundation of our business is people. These women are becoming loyal friends. They have complex lives full of abuse, poverty and oppression. To help them untangle themselves from oppressive situations takes time. And we're not in any hurry. This business exists for them. We ask you to stand with us, to show these women the loyal support they deserve. Buy a satchel. But even more than that, become an advocate for the woman who made your satchel. Her name is on the inside pocket and you can find out more about her on our meet the artisan page.

I choose to stand with these women!

☾

That night I had gone to bed early, prepared for the next day at Kalighat. When I woke up, it was clear that in the battle of "Mary versus the cold," the cold was now winning. My first hint that I wouldn't be going in was the realization that my eyes were caked with "goo." When I looked in the mirror, I could see that my eyes looked very small and my lids quite swollen. So, I went back to bed for more sleep. When I woke up and got dressed, I asked Visakha if she could recommend a doctor. She did, and I was ready to go right then — but his clinic hours were 5:30 pm – 7:30 pm. She told me how to get there, but in the haze of my cold, I wasn't too sure of the way. Thankfully, Brindaban agreed to accompany me. I was somewhat cheered up when he had to ask for directions five times. For 100 rupees ($1.50), I now had a clinic registration card. We got to Belle Vue Hospital and Clinic early, but the doctor did not show up until nearly 7:15. Thankfully, I liked Dr. Roy immediately. He said that my blood pressure was high and that concerned him a great deal. He prescribed eye drops (with steroids), medicine for my cold, and another blood pressure medication that could work in tandem with my Lisinopril. He then told me I needed to come back to the hospital for bloodwork and a chest x-ray. Although this didn't seem necessary, I was happy that the doctor may have gone overboard on the side of caution. I was very surprised that I had to pay him directly, but looking at the set-up, it appeared that the hospital charged doctors for the use of visitation rooms. The total for my doctor visit was $12.00. The pharmacy was located outside of the hospital and was open 24/7. The cost of three different drugs was less than three dollars.

I was incredibly hungry when we got home a little before 8:00 pm. I ordered in, using the Swiggy App. I had learned that I could have food delivered from dozens of local restaurants, although I usually ate my large meal at lunch and then had a very light dinner. I ordered Mediterranean mezze and was overwhelmed with fatoosh (real salad), falafel, hummus, chicken and veggies, and baba ghanoush. Served with teeny, tiny pita bread. That was a recipe for happiness!

☾

The next day it was hard to sit at home and wonder how the women of Kalighat were doing. Was Diya still sick and not eating? Was Aisha feeling stronger? Did Geetha finish her lunch (she did NOT like the Ensure-like product they fed her for strength)? Had any new women been admitted? On and on...

I headed back to the hospital for a blood draw and a chest x-ray. I was determined to get there early, as it was a fasting draw and I was already hungry. I only had to ask for directions once and was proud of myself. What makes finding addresses difficult in Kolkata is the way that numbers are laid out. Yes, they are sequential, but 4 and 6 may be next to each other or two blocks apart. The hospital is at 9 LOUDON Street, which seems like an easy find. Not so much — The name of LOUDON Street had been changed to Brahmachari, but most people didn't use the new name. Park Street is Mother Teresa Sarani (street). I got to 6 LOUDON street and walked 2 blocks until I hit 7. Then another block to 8. Of course, I also passed 8/1, 8/7, etc. Finally, I arrived at 9 — Belle Vue hospital! Who knew that directions could be this complicated? The clinic was very crowded, but I was able to walk in, pay $26 for the blood draw and chest x-ray, and get right in on both sides of the clinic. I was worried about needles being sterile, but the man who did the blood draw took the needle out of secure packaging. I have to say that it was the easiest blood draw I've ever had. I barely felt the needle go into my arm. I was immediately reminded of the difficulty the phlebotomist had when trying to even find one of Aisha's veins. The x-ray was also very efficient, and I was on my way back home in less than an hour.

I stopped off to get a bite to eat at one of the ubiquitous coffee shops in Kolkata. I had "the American," two grilled chicken sliders. I was to pick up test results in two days (hopefully after working). Medical records did not seem to be computerized here. I realized that I could have given the doctor my comparison test results from my physical in November through My Wake Health, but I hadn't thought about it at the time. But – good news – my eyes weren't gooey or halfway shut anymore (yea!!). My chest felt better. Now I was only waiting for the drainage to stop! I couldn't remember dealing with so much mucus in my nose and throat ever, and I wondered if I was allergic to something in India that was not found at home. I was ready to be back to 100% strength as soon as possible.

☾

As I've said before, begging occurs almost everywhere in India. On my way home from Peter Cat the day after my hospital visit, I had a conversation with a man on the street.

The man addressed me, "Hi!"
I followed his lead, "Hello."
"Where are you from?"
"US"
"You have a new President."
"Yes."
"God bless you."
"Thanks."
"I am 62, very old, and can't work. I am an artist, and these are some of my drawings."
"Ummm…" (What I'm thinking is that the pictures don't look hand drawn and colored.)
"Would you buy from me? They are 100 rupees each ($1.80)."
"I don't have any money." (which was true).
"Okay, all three for 180 rupees ($2.70)."
"I'm sorry but I don't have any money."
"Okay, all 3 for 100 rupees. I have no money and I'm very hungry."
"Please take this food (chicken korma, rice, and naan). It is delicious and there is a lot."
"No thank you!"
(I mental face-palmed…)

The beggars on Sudder Street had a different strategy. They would hassle you until you bought them some food (packaged) or baby formula, and after you left, they would sell it right back to the same merchant for cash. They knew that foreigners were often told not to give money on the street, so they changed their pitch accordingly! Such a tricky situation to be in. The Missionaries of Charity strongly discourage volunteers from giving to beggars. When we give, we help to perpetuate a system that is ultimately unsustainable.

Dealing with beggars has always been difficult for me. I never wanted to turn away from human beings in need, even though I would not give money. On A.J.C. Bose Road, on the way to the Mother House, there are many beggars. One older man sat in the same place every day; it was "home" to him. I looked at him each morning and we exchanged greetings. Despite the reality that I wasn't going to give him any money, I wanted to respect his worth and dignity. Honestly, sometimes my interactions with beggars just left me feeling sad and tired.

☾

After four long, boring days recovering in my apartment, I was finally well enough to return to Kalighat, and I did so with great joy. Oh, how I'd missed the women in our care. Aisha's cheeks were filling in, as she continued to eat with abandon. She was starting to look like a lovely young wife and mother, instead of a starving orphan. Tanvi was not happy and let us all know. She kept showing me the inside of her mouth, which looked normal to me. Anjali was getting stronger and could probably start walking with assistance if she trusted herself a little bit more. Geetha was out of it all day. She continued to cling unhappily to life. Often, when she refused to eat, she said that she just wanted to die. On this day, she wouldn't even accept her protein drink. Diya was feeling better than she was right before I got sick. She was back to her usual cycle of drinking lots of water and requesting lots of free rides to the bathroom. We moved women back and forth on plastic chairs, so I would often pretend that we were on a bus. There were express buses that could go very quickly, but there were also days with lots of traffic jams. Some women preferred to "crab walk," scoot, or crawl wherever they needed to go. When they were slow to move, they created difficult-to-maneuver-around traffic jams. Despite this, it was important for some of our residents to scoot or crawl, as it was the only true exercise they ever had. And, the floors were usually clean, as they were mopped frequently.

Meditation time had quickly become a part of our daily routine. My ability to sit and find a still point was sorely tested though, as several of the massies usually sat with us, talking loudly. On the other hand, the music was getting better. We now listened to an orchestral version of *Amazing Grace* and other songs.

When I returned home, I headed back to the clinic for my test results. My chest x-ray was completely normal, as were most of my other test results. I called the doctor to share these results, as requested. There did not seem to be any sharing of digital files. His first response was that my potassium was too low. He told me that starting immediately I should drink the juice of two coconuts every day. That was easy because they are sold outside of the Kali Temple. I also had to go back to see him at 6:30 the following evening.

When I got back home, Sunaina asked me what I paid for the doctor visit. She was aghast that it was 800 rupees, which she thought was quite expensive. At $12, I thought it was a bargain. I was just eager to feel better ASAP.

While walking home, I saw my friend on the street before she could call out, "Hey, North Carolina!" She told me I looked good, but she also said that the next time she sees me she expects me to have a hat on (not sure why). She asked me again how long I'm staying, then told me I need to buy a raincoat soon but NOT from New Market ("They'll rip you off."). She recommended Pantaloons or Trends, two popular clothing stores. I really did need a raincoat, sooner rather than later.

☾

The next day, our meditation time was even more challenging for me. I tried diligently for 15 minutes to find an inner, quiet place, but it was difficult when Aisha was screaming as her bed sore dressings were changed and Diya was shouting that she needed to go to the bathroom. I sent some baleful looks to the massies who were talking the day before, and at least they were a little more respectful. I was glad we were continuing with meditation, as some of the women seemed to be comforted by it. After meditation, I told Karima that from now on I would refer to her as Princess Karima. She kissed my hand and I think she liked this a lot. I had absolutely no idea how old she was — her age could have been anywhere from 25 to 60! Most of the women were considerably older.

I also spent a long time with Geetha during the morning shift. At this point, she could hardly whisper! I'd been at Kalighat for nearly two months, and frankly I was stunned that she was still with us. I loved talking softly with her, though. Each woman was becoming so precious to me. I fed Parul her snack mid-morning, but she grabbed the corner of my apron and decided to chew it instead. She didn't have many teeth, but she did have quite a grip. I had a tough time gently removing my apron from her mouth. I'd get it out and she'd grab it back, over and over.

In the evening, I went back to the doctor for my required check-up. I really liked him and thought he was very careful with his diagnosis. He commented that I looked extremely tired, and I was. I shared that my sinus drainage had not cleared up at all. He prescribed some antibiotics so that I could get rid of this yuck – fingers crossed. My blood pressure was now lower, but not enough to suit him. I was taking 20 mg of Lisinopril daily. Until a few months ago, I was taking 40mg daily but after several very low blood pressure readings my home doctor cut back on the dose. India has new stressors and heat, so Dr. Roy added the extra 20 mg back into my daily routine for now. Off I went to the pharmacy, where there was a long discussion about the prescription. Finally, one of the pharmacists said that the highest dosage pill of lisinopril in India is 10 mg, and with that they handed me the rest of my meds and sent me out — discussion OVER! I stepped into the next pharmacy and handed them my prescription. They gave me the same story, but I said that they should just give me two 10 mg pills per dose. There ensued a heated "behind the counter conversation" among the employees about whether they could fill my prescription. The salesclerk stayed out of it and gave me a little nod. He understood exactly what I was asking for, and I knew he would help to resolve the issue, which he did. Finally, I got a huge package of 5mg Lisinopril tablets with a reminder that I must take 4 per day, in addition to the pills I'd brought with me. Yea, logic prevailed!

CHAPTER XI

March

With the arrival of March came a new realization. I no longer felt like a "volunteer." It was shocking to me that I truly felt that Kolkata was my home. Despite the challenges of living in such a big, chaotic city, I was happy, really happy. I also realized that, while I knew the names of some of the women I interacted with the most, that wasn't fair to the others whose names I had not learned. My goal was to learn five new names a day – and I did. No one wants to be taken care of, in the long term, by others who can't even acknowledge them properly.

On March 1st, I was given the most beautiful gift. I was sitting on a plastic stool while massaging Deepika's feet. Like a few other women, she usually had swelling or edema of the feet and lower legs. We generally stroked her legs in the direction of her heart to help move excess fluid out of the affected area, as directed by one of the sisters. Afterward, we elevated her legs and wrapped them with compression bandages. I was talking softly with Deepika and Tanvi, who was sitting next to her. The women were eating their morning snack of mandarin oranges. I felt a tap on my leg, and when I turned slightly to face her, Tanvi popped a section of orange into my mouth. I nodded in gratitude (I hoped to have the lovely Indian nod/head waggle "down pat" by the time I left for America). Next, Deepika put a slice in my mouth. Overall, I probably had close to half of each orange. I do many things for the women and this felt like a precious thank you. Isn't it the case that the simplest gifts are sometimes the most meaningful? There was little else they could give me; they "owned" nothing. I cried at their sweet generosity.

A new woman was admitted later the same morning. She was confused, afraid, and in pain. It turned out that she too had big, deep bedsores. I now knew that bedsores demand medical attention before they cascade into a downward spiral of problems. I'd been in the room and heard the screams as bedsores were being cleaned and dressings changed. So far, I hadn't passed out (high school me would be so surprised)! Her arrival reminded me that Sister A is a miracle worker. She is completely committed to ensuring that anyone who needs care will have it. With the addition of this woman to Kalighat, I feared that we would be in for more screaming pain. By the time women arrive at Kalighat, their bedsores are often severe. Family members don't know how to treat them, and so they fester.

Before meditation time, our social workers added a new activity. All the women who were able to walk marched in a bit of a "conga line," about three laps around the sleeping area. I thought this was great because any movement helps to keep them limber. Several women who were not as steady on their feet did have to sit down early, which was fine. They TRIED! I loved seeing my fellow volunteers walking with the women and giving them subtle encouragement.

At lunchtime I fed Parul. For a woman who was skin and bones, she ate WAY more than I did. How was that possible? The key to feeding some of the women who can't feed themselves is to let them establish the pace. Today, when she wanted another mouthful, Parul pushed on my leg and it worked perfectly.

We had Indian visitors on a regular basis. I think they come for many reasons. One of them broke down crying today as she walked through the women's side of Kalighat. I don't know the catalyst, but one of the volunteers held her for a few minutes before she could compose herself again.

At lunch time, five of us headed back to Blue Sky. We came from the US (2), New Zealand, Russia, and Japan. The tables at Blue Sky are very close together, so it was common to start up conversations with others.

We invited a woman from France to join us. It was awkward for about 10 minutes, and then we began to feel like old friends. She looked about my age and was traveling around India on her own. She was blogging (in French), so we had something in common.

((

As much as I loved volunteering, I always looked forward to our day off and the adventures we shared. On this day, Charlotte, Debbie, Valentina and I went to the Victoria Memorial. We met in front of the Indian Museum on Park Street, crossed the road, and walked through the park that leads to the Memorial. The park is large, and very popular, especially on the weekends when families are outside picnicking and relaxing, and there are cricket games everywhere you turn. If only there weren't trash all over — it's actually a very beautiful area.

We stopped off for cold drinks before entering the Memorial grounds. The grounds were spotless, with beautiful flowers. This is what *Lonely Planet* says about the site: "Had it been built for a beautiful Indian princess rather than a dead colonial queen, the incredible Victoria Memorial would surely rate as one of India's greatest buildings. It's a vast, beautifully proportioned confection of white marble domes set in attractive, well-tended parkland. Think US Capitol meets Taj Mahal. Built to commemorate Queen Victoria's 1901 Diamond Jubilee, the structure was finally finished nearly 20 years after her death." It was very interesting, and we took some lovely outdoor photos, as pictures are not permitted inside. We sat and talked about all that colonialism hath wrought on the rest of the world after leaving the site. There was one display inside the museum that really caught our attention and led to our discussion. It was a panorama with life size (3-D) figures of Indian people during the colonial period that was set against a second panorama of a locked gate, with a winding road or driveway — clearly a house owned by someone British, as opposed to lower caste Indians of the time!

Charlotte wanted to take us to 8th Day Café, which she said was phe-
nomenal – and they served bagels and cream cheese. I'd never wanted a
bagel more than at that moment. At the gates of the museum, we checked
with several taxi drivers who told us they did not know the way to the
café. After a few tries, one guy said that YES, he knew the way for sure.
We got into the cab and it was clear that this guy had NO EARTHLY
IDEA how to get there. He stopped 5-7 times for (conflicting) directions.
We turned around several times. Somewhere on A.J.C. BOSE Road our
driver cut off another car. That driver got out of his car and walked toward our cab, which had the windows down. Next thing we knew, he had
grabbed our driver and punched him in the face. Then the two of them
started fist-fighting IN THE STREET. My friends asked what we should
do, and I quickly said we should get out of the car, which we did. We
didn't need to be around if the whole affair became CRAZIER THAN IT
WAS ALREADY!! Since we were close to my apartment, I led us to a different café I'd been to before and we had a nice lunch. On our way to the
café, our cab driver found us and demanded payment, which we gave
him (about 1/2 of what he wanted but absolutely the right rate for our
trip). When I got home, I checked my phone for directions to 8th Day
Café and discovered that it was only a 6-minute WALK from my apartment. I thought I might head over there soon, because I could not get the
possibility of eating a delicious bagel out of my head. I told my housekeepers about this experience via charades and the words we all knew.
They had commented on my story freely — Yes, this is also big city life.
They were glad that we were not hurt!

☾

Bhakti had not been well for the past few days. On Friday, while beds
were being changed, she slept on a mattress on the floor in a quiet place,
away from everyone else. I asked her if she wanted her snack (banana),
which I mashed in my hand. My stomach nearly staged a revolt, and I
tried to forget the slime I was creating, as I hate the taste, smell, and texture of bananas. She ate most of it, snoring between bites.

On Friday afternoon I found 8th Day Café, and it was worth the trip. I had a salad that I created myself with dressing on the side, and a bagel with cream cheese. Ah, the taste of comfort food! And it really was close to my apartment too. The cinnamon rolls in the glass case looked delicious, and I knew I'd return often for those and other delicious treats.

When I came home, Brindaban greeted me at the door looking baleful. My housekeepers were very interested in what I was writing so diligently, and they knew that I would be less than happy. For a few days, Brindaban greeted me at the door shaking his head "No," anticipating my first question. The first time that the cable company came, they couldn't find any problem whatsoever with our spotty Wi-Fi. This should have been predictable, as it seemed to happen no matter what needed fixed, completed, purchased, or changed. Everything in India took longer than anticipated!

☾

Over the weekend, for some reason, we had many volunteers working at Kalighat. Quite a few were there just for a day or two. I confess that this puzzles me. How do you go home and describe the one day that you spent at Kalighat to your family and friends? As I've mentioned previously, most volunteers spend their first day observing and trying to figure out what to do. It takes time and observation to learn the routine and the likes and dislikes of the women in our care.

And the big news of the weekend was that Aisha was up and walking. Wow, just wow. She had taught me so much about the necessity and healing power of HOPE. She was getting better for a special reason - to go home to her husband and children. When I talked to her about it in English, she answered with a brilliant smile. I'm not sure she understood everything I was saying, but she did understand quite a bit. We could now see the woman she was and would likely be again and not the deathbed patient we first met in January.

A new woman showed up on the steps of Kalighat and was admitted.

She also spoke some English and told me that her stomach was seizing. She asked for some calcium water and wanted it desperately. I took her to Sister A, who was in the dressings/procedures room. We got her the water, and she spied some biscuits. We gave her a few and she was very appreciative. In the process, we noticed that her feet were swollen with fluid. Sister drew a full syringe of fluid from one foot and drained the other manually since it had already been punctured. She then wrapped both feet in gauze bandages while I talked to the woman to distract her a bit from the procedure. I admired the combination of love, compassion, and medical skills that Sister, who is a nurse, used to help patients.

Because temperatures had climbed steadily over the last month, we were instructed not to give out blankets during rest time (shawls were distributed in the morning). It was really frustrating to know that some women really wanted them but weren't allowed to have them. I wished I could buy thin "summer" blankets for the women but didn't know if such a thing existed in India. And of course, I was NOT in charge (my mantra).

On Saturday, Charlotte, Debbie, Valentina, and I went to a vegetarian thali restaurant because it was Charlotte's last day in Kolkata. I said we were NOT celebrating that she was leaving, but rather that she was here. Our hands were washed in a beautiful basin, with hot water poured over them. Then many waiters came over to fill each small bowl on our plates. I am not a vegetarian because I don't know how to cook vegetables in interesting and tasty ways, but this was a true treat. We had a spinach dish that was divine (I asked for seconds), samosas, mixed veggies, sweet potato, several soups, bread with spicy gravy, condiments, five or six more delicious breads, and several desserts. There were a few things I didn't like, including the dish with tofu (see bananas). There was also a savory yogurt drink that was weird. Overall, we thought it was a great adventure that we could add to our book of experiences. At the beginning we had ZERO idea what to do, or what to eat first. The waiters were very helpful, and we could tell that they enjoyed watching us.

The first thing I noticed when I walked into Kalighat on Sunday was that Aisha was missing. Sister A told me right away that she felt Aisha was weak, and possibly anemic, so she sent her to the hospital for a blood transfusion. Aisha DID NOT want to go, but I was hopeful that she would be back soon and feeling better. She was not the only resident who resisted going to the hospital. Our women were well cared for and well-fed at Kalighat, and the hospital was an unknown. I doubt the food there was as tasty and nutritious as what we provided every day.

☾

Sunday was cloudy and breezy with a chance of rain. We were about to start the "fan fights" at Kalighat. One woman wanted the fan ON, but the woman next to her felt too cold as the air stirred. It was hard to know what to do. Sister said that we might need to move beds, depending on fan preferences! I thought the fans felt awesome, so I knew which side I'd prefer to be on.

At bedtime Farha, who never complained, was crying. I asked one of the Indian volunteers to help me talk with her. Farha had worked as both a maid and a nanny. One day, while cleaning, she had fallen down the steps, breaking her left arm and right leg, and causing a head injury as well. Both her arm and leg still hurt occasionally, and this morning she was in more pain than usual. Most of the time she still had a twinkle in her eyes that reminded me a little of Mary Poppins.

The woman who brought herself to the steps of on Kalighat kept telling me her story as well. What I understood was that she threw up for eight days straight and was very, very sick. She told the story quite dramatically, and both prayed and cried as she explained it all! I prayed silently with her, hoping that she would feel better soon. Bhakti was still sick too and hooked up to an IV line. She was very quiet, breathing softly all day. The massies really liked her and we were all concerned that her health was truly failing.

119

Sundays in Kolkata were quite different from the rest of the week. Before entering my apartment complex in the afternoon, I stood by the curb just listening to — NOTHING! No noise. If only Sunday came more than once a week!

☾

There was another new woman at Kalighat. On Monday, as lunch was being served, Sister A and I were discussing the feeding of one resident and we witnessed something stunning. The women were provided generous portions of food. In a day most of them ate much more than I do. After mixing her rice and dal together, our new woman shoveled — and I do mean shoveled — her food down in three huge bites. I had never seen anything like it. Sister A made sure she had more rice. On Tuesday, as I was peeling bananas for snack time, I could see the look in her eyes. Before I had finished peeling them, she was begging me for one. As soon as they were all peeled and ready to hand out, she grabbed one and pushed it down her throat in seconds. It pained me to know that there were so many hungry people in Kolkata. But I was also reminded of a harsh reality. Winston-Salem, North Carolina, where I have lived since 1985, is statistically one of the top metropolitan areas in the United States for food insufficiency for children. I was stunned when I first heard this statistic, thinking that it had to be wrong. It's certainly not something to be proud of. I felt a great deal of compassion for our new resident because it was clear that she had no idea when, or if, her next meal would come. She was very malnourished.

When I returned to my apartment, we STILL did not have Wi-Fi. The housekeepers and property manager were tiptoeing around me because they knew I was NOT happy. The repair guy came to look at it again. He literally LOOKED at it and never touched it. Then he said that to get it fixed we would need to register a complaint. Having done that for several days, we were all confused. Apparently, the former apartment manager, who was now in business school in another city, had to register the complaint. When contacted, she said she would, but she was busy with her studies and we were impatient. How NOT to run a business! To stay in touch with family and friends, I first went to a coffee house with my iPad, but their Wi-Fi was also spotty. Next, I went to a spa. My plan was to have a foot massage and blog at the same time. Unfortunately, the pedicure area was under renovation and closed. I opted instead for a foot, head, neck, and shoulder massage, and checked my email afterward. I was glad it worked out this way. Multi-tasking isn't effective most of the time!

((

Aisha was still at the hospital, but when I walked in on Tuesday morning, Sister A reported that she was walking everywhere and would be back at Kalighat soon. One of my first tasks of the day was to pick up Karima in the bathroom and take her back to the sitting area. She let me know that she had felt left out and wanted to be taken to mindfulness meditation. I promised that I would personally take her. Not long after that I passed by, and she reminded me that she wanted to go. I looked at the clock and said, "No, not yet." Karima pointed, and sure enough, the women were gathering. I hadn't realized that the clock on the wall was not working and that it had been 8:40 all morning!

Bhakti slept most of the day, but she did eat an entire banana that I mashed in my hand (only out of love). While I was feeding her, she talked and laughed several times. I'm not sure she was talking to me because her gaze was toward the wall. Perhaps she was moving between two worlds.

At tea break, the volunteer conversation turned to favorite foods and what we were most looking forward to eating when we returned home. For me, it would be beef, salad, veggies, and fruit! There was general agreement that fresh, uncooked fruits and vegetables were greatly missed in Kolkata. They were present everywhere but concerns about the water and travelers illnesses prevented most of us from eating them. Our conversations at break time ran the gamut from the ridiculous to the sublime, but getting to know each other and laugh together was an unexpected treat!

In a surprise move, the blankets returned for the afternoon rest period after being taken away a few days earlier due to the high heat. Most women wanted themselves covered for nap time and this was a good move in my opinion. Those who wanted one could use it and blankets were tucked underneath the pillows of the other women.

Debbie, Valentina, and I took a new volunteer to the Spanish café for lunch, and afterward we headed off to Big Bazaar, where other volunteers said they had gotten some great bargains on cool cotton clothing. We were all disappointed at the selection and quality of the clothes, but it did provide me with some déjà vu — to get to the store we passed the YMCA, where I stayed with students on our 1998-99 service trip. That area, sidewalks crowded with sellers of everything and nothing, gave me some serious claustrophobia.

On the way home, my back said, "Oh, hello — have you been forgetting about me?" The truth was that I hadn't thought about my back much at all, except for Friday mornings when we cleaned and re-made all the beds, a task that involved a lot of bending over and straightening back up again. We thought about taking a taxi back to A.J.C. Bose road, but I didn't need it. I loved walking everywhere. And on Tuesday afternoon, IT happened. Sometime after I got home at 3:30 and the end of my nap at 5:30, the internet repair person came and fixed our Wi-Fi. The housekeepers were delighted to share this development with me.

☾

I respected and admired Sister A and I told her this again on Wednesday. In my opinion, she gave MacGyver a run for his money. Like the TV character, she had a knack for finding unusual and interesting ways to solve problems. She was trying to figure out how to cover a wheelchair with a cushion that would be comfortable AND practical, as some of our women don't have much control of their bladders or bowels. I watched her take a rubber mat used as part of the bedding at Kalighat and figure out how to cut it just so to account for the various parts of the wheelchair. She cut in the appropriate places, then went upstairs to enlist the aid of Charita, the woman who did all the sewing at Kalighat. When the work was completed, the two of them showed me the cushion — perfectly cut and made with Velcro to hold it down in the right places! Genius… Sister A will take no credit for what she does. "All good things come from God," she says!

I was deeply humbled by the lack of waste displayed by the Missionaries of Charity. One day, I observed one of the massies cutting an empty toothpaste tube in half to squeeze out every last drop. She got enough toothpaste out for 3-4 more brushes. I admit that I would have thrown the same tube of toothpaste in the trash without a second thought. Charita was also at work against waste. Torn sheets were patched back together until they couldn't be fixed again. Then they were cut into smaller pieces to be used as rags, washcloths, or other useful items. When the ties came off a bib, new ones were sewn in their place. She hemmed daily. I loved the sound of the old treadle Singer she used; I remember watching and listening to my mom sewing on a similar machine. These actions made me much more conscious of what I waste and inspired me to do better. I was faithful about finishing off every water bottle I bought. I asked restaurants to give me "to go" boxes for anything I couldn't finish and, knowing that I don't always eat leftovers, I quietly dropped them off by the mats of people living on the streets. I knew I would continue to wrestle with my consumption and waste when I returned home.

Parul wasn't wasting one bite of her food! She was clearly unhappy that I was not feeding her fast enough. To encourage me to move more quickly, she grabbed my hair, pulling it out from under my headband and chomping down on it when she was ready for more. Eventually, I had to request assistance from another volunteer to free myself from her iron grip. And — she finished off every bite of lunch.

One of our women had been trying to make herself understood by someone (anyone). Some of the residents spoke Indian languages/dialects that the massies didn't understand either. I was sitting with the woman, listening but not truly understanding, when she suddenly smacked her forehead with her hand in a universal gesture of frustration. I couldn't help myself and burst out laughing. Then she started laughing too. If only she knew how many times I'd refrained from doing the exact same thing!

We were all thrilled when Aisha re-entered Kalighat near the end of our shift. She walked in — not slowly, not humped over — but tall and straight! It was hard to reconcile the pretty, young mom with the dying bag of skin and bones who had come to us weeks earlier.

The afternoon might have been a preview of the next few months. It poured BUCKETS just as our shift was over. We would have been completely soaked if we'd tried to walk to the metro stop, which was about a ten-minute walk from Kalighat. I called an Uber, and even though four of us probably walked no more than 50 feet, we were drenched. Our driver took us to Bar-B-Q where we shared Chinese rice and veggies, noodles and veggies, veggies and cashews, hot soup, and Chinese tea. It was actually (dare I say it?) COLD in the restaurant. Throughout the afternoon, the high was only in the low 70's, providing a brief respite from the unrelenting heat.

☾

The next day was our day off and we had planned to visit several temples. We knew that the forecast called for rain but decided to play it by ear. When I woke up to the sound of rain beating on my windows, I rolled over and went back to sleep. Instead of sightseeing, I cleaned up, then decided to head to 8th Day Bakery. When I walked outside I was stunned to see that my street (like many others) was flooded, and the water was coming up over the sidewalk. At 8th Day Café, red lentil soup and mushroom and gruyere quiche fit the bill just perfectly. I sat for several hours and finished my current novel. Then I decided I needed to swing into action and find myself a raincoat and rain boots. I set Google Maps for Quest Mall and headed out. I found the mall — it is HUGE! I don't love malls anyway, and this one was high end — Gucci, Rolex, Burberry, etc. In the big mall, I could not find one raincoat — not ONE! At every store they suggested I try at another place. I had no idea how I'd handle monsoon season without the proper clothing.

☾

When contemplating my trip, I knew that I would leave pieces of my heart in Kolkata, just as I knew I would bring home memories and love that would allow my heart to expand. On Friday, one of those pieces rocked me to my core. I'd been at work at Kalighat for an hour or so, and it was a VERY busy day, when I realized that I had not seen Deepika, the woman whose eyes looked just like Ben's. I quickly checked in the toilet area, then asked one of the massies what had happened to her. I was told that she was gone. We had heard several times that she had no home to go to despite her constant pleading to be taken there. Even a week earlier, one of the social workers told me that while they continued to tell her that they were still looking, they weren't hopeful that she had a place to go. Apparently, her neighbors came to Nirmal Hriday and agreed that they would take care of her. I took off for the volunteer area upstairs and had a little cry. She had declined and become increasingly confused since she'd arrived, perhaps in part because she had lost hope. I was SO happy for her because she got what she absolutely wanted and needed. I only wish I'd had a chance to say goodbye. I knew I would miss her so much. Although I was sad, I knew I had to get back to work. Most of the

125

morning shift was spent in deep cleaning and bed making activities. My back hurt less when I did these tasks than it did when I first arrived. I was reflecting as we cleaned about our well-oiled Kalighat team. We helped each other and worked together every day.

It was "one of those days" for Tanvi. Instead of taking her pills with the water handed to her, she held them in her mouth, then spit them on the floor, where a volunteer found them later. Everyone tried to persuade her to take them, but she was adamant! NO, NOT HAPPENING! The woman who came a week earlier and who ate every meal like it might be her last one, was not having afternoon bedtime. Several massies put her in bed and she started wailing. She said that she wanted to sleep on the floor. Sister A was working to make that happen when we left. Every day was a *different* challenge.

At lunch time, I gave in and ate street food on Sudder Street with some of the younger volunteers. This "restaurant" had been up and running for several years and was actually very good. My chicken wrap was delicious; however, the moment I stood up, I experienced ominous rumblings in my stomach and knew that I had to find a bathroom ASAP, or the afternoon would get a lot worse. Fortunately, a bathroom was found with seconds to spare before a very embarrassing situation. I pitied the person who unwittingly used that bathroom next.

☾

At home late that afternoon, I read more about Mother Teresa. In multiple places in the various homes run by the Missionaries of Charity are the words "I Thirst." I knew that those were words spoken by Jesus on the cross and assumed that they were a reminder to thirst for God. I like detective work, so I started looking to discover why these words were so important to Mother Teresa. In the 2016 *Time Magazine* special edition about Mother Teresa (*The Life and Times of a Modern Saint),* I found this:

In the particular phrase, "I thirst," which Jesus uttered in agony during his last hours on the cross, Mother Teresa discovered a mystical touchstone that she invested with multiple spiritual meanings. First, the fact that Jesus literally thirsted demonstrated that God had indeed become human, out of compassion for humankind. Second, Jesus's command in the Gospels imposes a duty to alleviate the thirst (and hunger and illness) of his beloved poor. Third, Teresa understood Christ as 'thirsting' for the love of humans and their souls [This included those of non-Christians, but she was adamant that they were to be won over by good example, not by some kind of food-for-salvation trade-off]. And finally, as she explained to church authorities, since Mother herself thirsted for Jesus in her life, she must give herself over entirely to what he had called her to do.

Young Agnes joined the Sisters of Loreto and took her new name in honor of Saint Thérèse of Lisieux when she was eighteen. For over two decades she lived out her call, teaching children at the Loreto School in Calcutta. After an experience in which she explained that "Christ spoke to her," Teresa told church officials that He told her to leave the convent and establish a radically new religious order. She explained that nuns in her order would live among, dress like, and serve the "poorest of the poor." "From his command to care for 'the least of these' in the Gospel of Matthew, 'I was hungry, and you gave me something to eat, I was thirsty...' — *she derived a simple mandate to help. He has told us that he is the hungry one. He is the naked one. He is the thirsty one. Each is Jesus in his distressing disguise.*

I was glad I found this explanation, as the words would now have a deeper meaning for me.

☾

127

March 12th and 13th were the Indian holiday, Holi — also known as the Festival of Colors and the Festival of Love. The festival represents the triumph of good over evil, the arrival of spring and end of winter, a shedding of past errors, a time to mend conflicts, and a day to forgive and forget. It is a celebration for families and friends to get together, play like children, forgive and repair broken relationships, and eat special foods. It is also celebrated as thanksgiving for a good harvest. Holi is celebrated at the approach of the spring equinox on the full moon. Indeed, the moon was beautiful, big, and bright orange!

Volunteers had some interesting conversations on the first day of Holi: "I don't want to be holied, do you?" "Wow, did you see him get holied?" I'm fairly certain that "holied" is not a real word, but it was definitely part of our vocabulary. Many of us rubbed coconut oil on our arms and legs when we left Kalighat. Colors, which can be liquid or powder, can be hard to get off the skin and the oil prevents "sticking." So, basically, we just "Pammed" ourselves. The children took great delight in covering everyone. The last time I was in India on Holi was in 2001. That year I was covered in colors and I remember that the powder burned a little bit when it touched my skin. Two of the more popular ways to color others now are via SQUIRT GUN or WATER BALLOONS. So much fun! My daughter loves to run half-marathons, and she has participated in several "color runs," which have become popular over the last few years. Surely these runs, where participants are doused in colored powder at various check points, have their genesis in Holi.

I had a great ending to the day. I took an Uber to Salt Lake to get together with Ananda Mitra, my friend and colleague from Wake Forest, who grew up in Kolkata. Joining us was our mutual friend Avijit Basu, who had helped Ananda coordinate his summer India programs with students, and who had been helpful to me since I'd arrived in January. Talking about home felt good and I loved our time together! I was amazed that, when we talked about places in Kolkata, I knew where things were and could participate in the conversation easily.

☾

After Holi, things got back to normal quickly. On Tuesday we got on the 45B, but there are multiple buses on the same route, with the same number. The bus driver assistant (ticket taker, etc.) was new. When he took my money, he asked where I was going. I replied, "Kalighat." "What?" "Kalighat." The Indian man sitting across from me tugged on the assistant's pants to get his attention. "She said she is going to **Call (long pause) EEE (long pause) Got...** Bus driver assistant: "Oh, okay!" Wait, what? The two versions of Kalighat sounded exactly the same to me.

Meanwhile, our bus driver for the day was surely working on his carnival ride operator's license. Up and down, up and down. We really had to hang on tight. I thought that at some point I would likely go flying down the aisle or end up in the bus driver's lap since I was sitting up front. To top it off, the bus driver assistant announced that we were at the Kalighat stop and we needed to get off. We did, then looked around. Of the ten of us, no one knew where we were. As the bus sped off, the assistant waved his arm in a direction that made no sense. Thank goodness for Google maps! We finally got there.

☾

Suddenly, Kalighat seemed more like a hospital ward than a residence. Over several days, a few very sick women had arrived, while some of our residents were still under the weather. There were women in bed with IV's attached at various spots around the sleeping area. One new woman had terminal cancer. At lunch time, I tried to sit her up to feed her, but she was too weak and unsteady. Instead, I hugged her to me and fed her very slowly. I prayed for her throughout the time I was feeding her, as it was clear that she would be transitioning soon.

At break time, I started talking with a new volunteer. He had volunteered for a day or two, and then got sick for a few days (Welcome to

Kolkata) and was now feeling better. I learned that he was from Italy. Not ten minutes later a group walked in for a brief tour of Kalighat. The leader of the group said to me, "We are from Italy. Are there any Italian volunteers who can speak with us?" I don't believe in "coincidences," so this was powerful.

☾

I had no plans for Thursday, and that was perfect. I'd asked various people where I could find the raincoat that I was sure would be vital during the upcoming monsoon season. I had been told that Duckback was the very best. I checked out Google Maps and found that it was only a 5-minute walk from my apartment. I'd already been burned several times by Google Maps though, so I was a little leery of the distance and walking time given. Nevertheless, I found Duckback House easily; however, although Google Maps indicated that the company showroom was here, it was not. The Duckback building had many businesses inside, but none of them involved raincoats of any kind. I decided that I'd just order one from Amazon India.

One the way home, I passed a sign once again that had made me chuckle many times. It was interesting to see the ways in which Mother Teresa's name and legacy were used to encourage Indian citizens to "do better." This particular sign said, "God cannot be found amid noise – Avoid unnecessary use of horn." In my opinion, not even a saint could persuade drivers here to stop the beeping. Noise pollution at its finest. And during Kalighat meditation time I was slowly learning how to breathe and find inner solitude through the din. Perhaps the challenge was an opportunity.

Visakha, who looked after my apartment and the one upstairs (Airbnb), along with her work for one of the owners, had been very helpful since I arrived. Her office was just outside of the apartment door. A few weeks after I arrived, she was joined by her friend Sunaina. Friday was going to be Sunaina's last day, as she was leaving to work at her family's clothing store. While I knew I would see her again, it wouldn't be every day, so I suggested that we order in lunch and spend time together. We had Chinese/Tibetan food and it was delicious. We talked through the afternoon, until we were hungry again. We went for dessert next, ordering in lemon curd tart, devil's food cake, and chocolate truffle pastry. Delicious!! We took some selfies to remember a perfect afternoon.

☾

Back at Nirmal Hriday the next morning, I was reminded that while it is a home for the dying destitute, it is also a place of great joy. I loved the days when there was laughter throughout the building!! During the year that Ben was sick, we learned just how important gallows humor was when dealing with pain and sorrow. The same thing was true at Kalighat — humor was so valuable.

When I walked into the women's ward, one of the massies handed me a toothbrush and said, "See if you can get Tanvi to brush her teeth, because she won't do it for us." I took her the toothbrush with a smile and asked her to use it. She opened her mouth wide and showed me that she has exactly 3 teeth on the left side and three teeth on the right side. So, why should she have to brush them? Her logic made me laugh, and then it made her laugh too!

After lunch, Anjali told me that no one fed her and that she was hungry. I sat with her and told her that for lunch she had rice, potatoes, spinach, and curried egg. "I did?" "You did!" And we laughed…

A priest from Ireland who was volunteering at Kalighat had made a quick trip to Delhi and Agra. He told us the story of his travel woes and we groaned, and then we laughed! It was St. Patrick's Day and I played *Ireland's Call* by Celtic Thunder at tea break in his honor.

When I wasn't working with our women, I was peeling hard boiled eggs and cutting green beans for dinner. On the bus to Kalighat, we had been talking about how the simplest of jobs can be the most sacred, so I laughed when one of the sisters asked me to do these basic kitchen chores just a few hours later.

☾

Compassion fatigue was something that we talked about on a regular basis. No matter how much we loved our work, those of us who were long term volunteers needed time to rest and recharge, or we might find ourselves unable to serve with great love. I'd been needing a break, just to get away from it all for a few days. My friend Kaitlyn had invited me to go to Varanasi not long after she arrived, but while I wanted to travel with her, I could never work up much interest in going there for more than a day or two. My friend Valentina, from Moscow, invited me to go to Sundarbans National Park with her, and that sounded like something we would both enjoy. Sundarbans is a natural region in the Bay of Bengal (river delta) and a UNESCO World Heritage site that includes a tiger preserve, a biosphere reserve, and a national park. The Sundarbans spans from the Hooghly River in West Bengal, India, to the Baleswar River in Bangladesh. Although we knew that tiger sightings can be rare, we still thought this would be a fun place to visit. We purchased tickets and were told to meet at 8:00 am by the travel agency on Sutter Street and were joined shortly after by our tour guide and fellow travelers. Overall, there were 13 of us in a small van. We were given cream cheese and veggie sandwiches, which were delicious, and gulab jamun, which is basically dessert for breakfast. After breakfast I slept for a while, until we stopped for chai. It was the strangest chai I've ever tasted — more like coffee with sugar and milk than chai. Our bus driver and tour guide were enjoying tea and talking with local people so much that finally all of us were saying, "Chalo, chalo (let's go)!" After tea break, we began talking with each other. Our fellow travelers included three middle-aged couples from

Kolkata who were good friends, and a young man with his wife and mother. We chatted a bit before we arrived at the Tiger Reserve and got on our boat.

After we got onboard, we enjoyed taking photos and selfies. As we got underway, Valentina and I sat up front enjoying the sunshine and fresh air. I have sat at the front of many boats all over the world and was reflecting on the similarities of river life. And then the torrential rain came with no warning. When the lightning and thunder started, I felt like we might be on the Titanic. Not only that, but it started **hailing.** As our tour guide said, "It's raining ice cubes." The light kept changing, which made for interesting photos. Later, all we could see was a gray blob of land. We did get to know each other a lot better when we were huddled together, soaking wet from head to toe, in the middle of the boat! It felt a bit surreal, and we all shook our heads at the strange turn of events.

The rain stopped just as we reached our hotel. There were no face-plants, but several of our fellow travelers slipped and slid in the mud as we disembarked. For the record, I learned that some Indians use English swear words when they are frustrated and angry. There was a hotel in front of us and I thought, "This place doesn't look bad at all," but we kept walking around the side of the building until we arrived at an "eco" hotel, which looked more primitive than "green." Our room was perfectly adequate though, and I quickly got out of my rain-laden clothes before I settled down for a short power nap. We were awakened several hours later by a knock on our door and the word that it was time to leave for our sunset cruise. The weather was now beautiful, with a slight breeze, which made the cruise delightful. We again took lots of photos and enjoyed more chai and delicious pakoras. We got back to the "resort" about 9:00 pm and were ready for dinner. While we waited, we were treated to music and dancing by local people. We waited, waited, and waited some more. We finally ate at 10:00 pm. I didn't eat much, as I have occasional heartburn when I go to bed soon after eating.

☾

I woke up early the next morning when one of the cooks knocked on our door with chai (it's a wonderful way to wake up). We got on the boat to head to the first of three watchtowers. We were reminded again that Sundarbans is the largest mangrove forest/jungle in the world. Every four years, there is a census of tigers. In 2013, there were 103 tigers reported on the Indian side and over 300 on the Bangladesh side. We also learned that tigers are great long jumpers and can swim very fast. They are not great high jumpers though, so there are mesh "fences" around the perimeter of the preserve. Because of the fences and the dense jungle beyond, visitors face little danger. On the other hand, the jungle can be a dangerous place for the local people, who hunt, fish, and keep bees (to sell honey). On average, 35-40 men are killed by tigers (who usually attack from behind) every year. There is a local village where the "tiger attack" widows make and sell handicrafts in order to survive. Yikes.

At one of the watchtower areas, there was a monkey sitting at the entrance. As his head acknowledged every visitor I thought he was counting us!! I also saw the biggest lizard I have EVER seen. Never, ever want to see one that big again. It was maybe 3 feet long and totally creeped me out!

There are "roads" cut into the jungle area, and sometimes the tigers cross them, but alas, we saw no tigers. Our guide told me that they only spot tigers 3-4 days a month. We did see a wild boar family and a deer family, along with a white crocodile (so hard to see from the boat, as it blended into the surroundings perfectly). We learned about Banbibi, who is a guardian spirit of the forests, worshipped by both Hindu and Muslim residents of Sundarbans.

We had a very late breakfast of hard-boiled eggs, luchi (bread), and potatoes on the boat. We were a little bit grumpy before breakfast and felt better afterward. After more touring we had a nice lunch with prawns, chicken, rice, veggies, salad, tomato chutney, and papad.

Late in the afternoon we returned to our hotel to drop people off who were staying for a second night and to get into several jeeps for a "5 minute" drive to another boat (to get back to our starting point and return to Kolkata). Our travel agent told us that staying the extra night really wasn't necessary and that the third day wouldn't be much different from the second. Valentina and I ended up in a small jeep with three big guys and the driver. But you can do anything for 5 minutes, right? Fifteen minutes later I said to the guys, "Didn't they say **5 minutes?**" We all heard it but when the guys asked our driver how much longer, he said, "**10 minutes more.**" New math, India style. Since I was sitting by the window, I did get to take lots of village photos. Again, I marveled at how villages around the world are alike in so many ways... We finally made it to the water taxi, which was crowded with evening commuters. On the way home, the three Indian couples began complaining to our guide about the fact that they would not be let out at their homes, as stated in the travel brochure. Instead, they were dumped out at a street corner a few blocks from their houses, still yelling at the driver and travel agent.

☾

After a 2-day break, it felt great to walk into Kalighat on Monday morning. It warmed my heart to see our women sitting in their usual spaces and places. I went around and greeted all of them and then got right to work. After lunch, I put Bhakti in bed, helping one of the massies. For some reason, she did not land well, and I knew that she was feeling some pain. I looked her in the eyes to tell her I was very sorry, and she pulled my hair out from under my headband. It hurt and I was momentarily shocked, so I got up quickly to gather myself as the tears came. After a few minutes I went and sat quietly by her bed and told her again, softly, that I was sorry. She told me that she was sorry too and gave me a kiss.

Earlier in the morning, I'd had a similarly jarring experience. I was sitting and talking with one of the women, when I saw Anjali slide forward on her chair just enough to be able to pee on the floor. As soon as I could, I went to the bathroom and brought some water, so that she could wash off. I slipped and accidentally spilled water on her and she was off on a rant. I stepped away until she calmed herself, then went to apologize. She looked at me and said: "God sees everything. He is almighty and powerful." I was stunned! She spoke to me in perfect, clear English. Another volunteer was there also, so later I quizzed her to see if she heard the same thing, and she did. She also shared that Anjali was resisting her exercises because she is "ready to die." I reminded Anjali that we loved her very much. My love for these women was unconditional, and I felt horrible when any of my actions caused them pain. What a shock – two women spoke to me in English. I realized that by withholding this information, they could maintain a bit of control over their circumstances.

In the afternoon, after a much-needed nap, I met Valentina at the movie theatre to see LION. The theatre was the most beautiful I've ever seen — recliners for some seats with tables for food and beverage, huge screen, great audio and video quality, and 300 – 400 seats. The concession stand had multiple restaurants and types of gourmet food. The Kolkata scenes in the movie made my heart beat quickly (the city was captured very well). What a poignant story of a young man trying to find his mother and home without hurting his adopted parents in the process! I love Dev Patel and thought this was his most mature and nuanced role yet.

When I returned home from the movie, my housekeepers let me know that I needed to improve my Bengali more quickly, so they gave a list of new words to learn as soon as possible. My first full sentence was, "I want a big (cup of) chai" to Sukumar, and he brought it to me. Brindaban laughed because he had taught me the phrase a few hours earlier, while Sukumar was at the market, and had already given me my first chai. Two big cups of chai in one evening!

☾

It took me two days to realize that I'd been coughing since I returned to the city. Welcome back! With every cough, I felt like I was spewing little pieces of Kolkata everywhere. I was taking vitamin C and walking a few miles every day. Despite the cough, I felt stronger than ever. It was the first day of spring, and while temperatures at my North Carolina home were in the 60's and 70's, we'd settled into the mid-90's in Kolkata. Every breeze felt like a breath of fresh air. We were grateful for overhead fans at outdoor restaurants that kept us comfortable. I loved the days when the Kalighat crew would eat lunch together. On the 22nd, our lunch group included volunteers from France, Belgium, Ireland, and the US, and covered a large span of ages from 19 (pre-college "gap year") to those of us in our 60's!

☾

Kalighat was cleaned often and only rarely smelled bad. I couldn't say the same for many US nursing homes I have visited. This week there seemed to be another caca storm, though. I sat down twice to check the bottom of my shoes to make sure that I hadn't stepped into it and spread it around the women's ward. I'm happy to report that the bottoms of my shoes were clean!

With fewer volunteers at Kalighat this time of year, we were busy every moment answering calls of "Auntie, auntie." As I wrote that last line, I thought of Shivani, who left for another home a month ago. Her "Oh, auntie" as she patted a spot next to her on the bed meant sit down and talk a while. We helped women brush their teeth this morning and provided water and a basin they could spit into. We also gave out medicine at the direction of the sisters. We were watching carefully because some of the women just didn't want to take their pills, including several who believed they were being poisoned. On the other hand, ordinary days at Kalighat often included both little miracles and great love. Anjali told me today that "God is good, and God is great!" Indeed He is, Anjali!

☾

I had special plans for my Thursday off. In the morning I headed off to Café Coffee Day for tea and a pastry. I had an appointment for a cut and color at one of the spas near my house. I wasn't paying attention when I left the café, and about a half block later I stepped in some sewage sludge and almost lost my breakfast. Unlike the day before, I did not have to check the bottom of my shoes. I was a walking stink bomb and it was a gift that kept on giving. If there had been a trash can, the lack of which I've discussed before, I would have dumped my Rainbows in it immediately and without a second thought. My North Carolina beach and hanging out sandals have been perfectly molded to my feet for at least the last 10 years. Still… I started walking in my bare feet despite the hot roads and sidewalks beneath. The horrible smell came right along, and every now and then I got a nice whiff of unpleasantness! I knew I couldn't walk into the salon like this, so I stopped at Tea Junction for large bottled waters and did my best to clean my feet and shoes. I managed to snag as many napkins as possible but there weren't nearly enough. I also asked for a fresh lime soda, sweet. I took a big sip and literally did a projectile spit, as the tea wallah had merely added sugar to a very salty drink. It was disgusting and just added to my ire. My clean-up efforts were not entirely successful, but at least I was finally presentable. I told my story at the salon and they sent me to the washroom so that I could clean up a little more AND gave me some slippers to put on while I was sitting in the stylist's chair.

Before I came to India, I'd asked my home stylist if she would be able to "fix" any hair mistakes that might happen here. She said yes and that made me feel better. When I went to make the appointment for my overdue cut and color, the stylist and I reviewed his color chart. I told him that I wanted it to be as close to my hair color as possible. I was worried when he showed me the burgundy as a possibility — That was a big NO from me. We agreed on copper and auburn, mixed. I admit to being totally surprised when he was done. I loved it!! I asked him why he chose his profession and he told me that he had played around with his own hair color from the time he was a child. He said that it felt great to him to see clients looking happy and feeling self-confident as a result of his work.

Following my haircut, I checked out a new three-story Fashion Big Bazaar (known as FBB) that had opened at the end of my block while Valentina and I were visiting Sundarbans. It was interesting to see the different choices for Western wear versus ethnic wear. Few clothes on the planet are more comfortable than Indian ethnic wear, I must say. During my previous shopping experiences, I had been surprised at how closely salespeople followed customers in Indian stores. It felt uncomfortable to me. I think that, for the most part, they wanted to be instantly available if I needed help. I had to bite my lip though to keep from telling them that if I needed their help, I'd ask for it. I asked Visakha about it and she said it happens in most stores and annoys her too. It's also interesting that in many shops, there are male salespeople in the women's department. While I shopped, I enjoyed surreptitiously watching them try to "learn" my shopping style and preferences and find me clothes that they thought I'd like. They needed to keep trying....I asked one of the salesmen, "What is the difference between churidars and leggings?" He told me that "churidars are full length and leggings are ankle length." Got the difference? I didn't really understand, because both stop at the ankle; however, churidars are bunched around the ankle and look like they were designed for *really* tall women.

☾

Another Friday at Kalighat meant another round of deep cleaning and bed making. The weeks were going by so, so fast, and I wished that time would slow down. As the days went on, I kept learning more about the need for touch at Kalighat. I had learned NOT to touch Banhi. She sat on her chair every day with her knees pulled up to her chest and the back of her gown over her head. She resembled a turtle, encased in a shell of her own making. She was blind OR had very limited sight. I imagined that she had lived on the street where being touched might indicate possible danger. I knelt or bent down in front of her to talk. I saw her listening very carefully. I'd asked if I could touch her in the past, but I'd gotten no response. She was more comfortable not being touched and I tried to honor that.

None of the volunteers spent much time with Vanya. She looked at the world with a scowl on her face and never encouraged interaction. Other women got more attention because they liked it and wanted to interact with us. One foot and part of her leg had been amputated, and she was not particularly mobile. When she was frustrated or angry, she lashed out and hit those around her. So, on this morning I was giving head massages and rubbing oil into the women's hair. Some loved the rubbing and gentle scratching. I had often washed Ben's hair for this very reason. Some of the women held out their hands for me to give them a little oil and preferred to rub it into their own hair. I had finished massaging the woman next to Vanya and decided to see if she would allow me to finally massage her head. I started and there was no resistance. After a while I felt her pulling me down and thought she wanted me to stop. She was crying and gave me a blessing, then pulled me into a big hug. Now both of us were crying. There had been a lot of crying at Kalighat recently — and then there were the residents (Yes, the tender-hearted volunteers cried a lot)! Vanya taught me a needed lesson; those who may be the hardest to love are exactly those who need it the most. I struggled with my own shame as I realized that I'd judged her unfairly. I reminded myself that unconditional love is not always easy, but I vowed to do better.

The woman who had arrived a few weeks earlier and eaten her big lunch in three enormous bites was becoming more comfortable at Kalighat. I was massaging her legs and asked her if she was ready for lunch. She said, "Yes, but I don't like soup." Soup is not actually served at

Kalighat, so I think she was talking about the (somewhat) soupy dal over rice that is part of most meals. When I asked her what she did like to eat, she said, "Chicken, fish, and rice!" We were both silent for a while and then she asked me (in English), "What are you thinking?" In fact, I was deep in thought, and what I was thinking was that I wanted her to get well so that she could leave Kalighat. I wanted her to be healthy and reminded her of how sick Aisha was when she arrived. I wanted her to get better too. I didn't know how old she was, but I guessed somewhere in her late 20's or early 30's. During a conversation later, she told me that she was 54. She was quiet after I shared my thoughts and nodded in assent.

Once again, there was a group of departures of residents and volunteers. The volunteer I knew that I would miss most of all was Father Damian from Ireland. It had taken us a few weeks to start sharing deeply, and I had come to respect and admire him and his work. Two of our residents went home on Thursday – Zoya and Kashvi. Zoya always had a smile for each volunteer. I loved her welded silver ankle bracelets. They had been given to her by her late husband and she refused to have them removed. We had some fun conversations and I would miss her greatly. Kashvi was quieter and kept to herself. I knew she how very much wanted to go home, so I was happy for her.

Another resident had surprised me with her English. Sister was inserting an NG Tube for a new resident who refused to eat or take her medicine. She was feisty and had also tried to pull out her IV lines. The woman whose bed was next to hers whispered to me in perfect English, "If she won't even take her medicine, how can she get better?" My response was that it would be unlikely that she'd get better if she wouldn't accept help. I worked at composure when residents revealed their English comprehension to me because I believed that it was a sign of trust. I couldn't help but wonder how many other women had been hiding their ability to speak and understand my language!

☾

Once again Kalighat felt more like a hospital than a residence. Geetha who had been at death's door for months continued to hang on, barely eating. She told us frequently that she was ready to die. Parul, on the other hand, ate like a champion, rarely leaving a bite of food on her plate. Ekta, who was conscious, but still seemed out of it, ate a little, albeit very slowly, otherwise her food would simply dribble out of her mouth. Maya had to be watched, because she tried to pull out her IV lines every time we turned our backs. Sister did chest compressions on a woman who was riddled with cancer, bringing her back from the brink of death. I handed her the supplies as she set up an IV line to give her fluids. Finding viable veins was just so difficult.

I was in the medical room to talk with and distract one of our newer residents while she was having her dressings changed. I liked the opportunity to help in this way, and I learned that I was not nearly as squeamish as I was in high school when I ruled out a career in medicine because I didn't think I could handle the blood. This woman was brought in with large open wounds on her head, with maggots crawling in and out. She had not taken a bath for four years. And she wanted to tell all of us her tale of woe — over, and over, and over! Even Sister A's patience had about run out!

I had to confess that I was losing my patience with several of the massies. There was always some ongoing tension between massies and volunteers. Volunteers came to Kolkata to do small acts with great love, while massies felt that they needed to maintain order and routine. If no volunteers came, the massies would be doing much of the "heavy lifting" in the homes. Some of them had been there for many years and knew the long-term residents quite well. Still, I didn't like it when they handled our women roughly or refused to honor their simple requests. This was a common sentiment among volunteers, and I had heard some speak out, begging the massies to be kinder. I was irked because one of our women wanted a new gown. Hers was not particularly wet, but she was unhappy. She was not a complainer, so when she asked for something, I liked to accommodate her needs. Our least favorite massie came over and started yelling and angrily took the new gown off, putting the old one back on, while our resident cried softly. I had to remind myself over and over that this was their workplace and we were the guest. "Keep calm and keep on loving the residents — and the massies too." Breathe in, breathe out!

Having settled into my Kolkata life, I might have found it easy to regard each day as ordinary, but I refused to do that. I believe that each day is a precious gift that is not to be wasted away. Victor Frankl wrote in *Man's Search for Meaning* that,

> We who lived in concentration camps can remember the men who walked through the huts comforting others, giving away their last piece of bread. They may have been few in number, but they offer sufficient proof that everything can be taken from a man but one thing: the last of human freedoms — to choose one's attitude in any given set of circumstances, to choose one's own way.

This was true, and I had both taught and learned it many times. The ultimate choice and greatest freedom is to choose our attitude in any situation. For me that means living and leading with love. I could grumble and say that I don't like to get up early, which many of you know is true! I could view our days at Kalighat as boring or ordinary, but I simply could not. What I could say was that each day gave me an extraordinary opportunity to learn and to love. Each day had a rhythm and pace of its own.

The simple joys of Kalighat included:

Seeing the women for the first time each morning as I descended the staircase.

Doing "ordinary" tasks like getting pane (water) for women.

Sitting with Anjali at bedtime when she told me that I was "good and kind."

Talking with new women for the first time.

Praying with another woman who was pouring out her heart to God.

Exercising with the women who were mobile.

Drying Upasna's tears and holding her close.

Sitting with different women during meditation time.

With joys, there were also challenges. I'd been spending more time with Ruchika, the relatively new arrival who ate ravenously. She had parasites, which explained why she was always hungry. At lunchtime she refused to eat because there were carrots on her plate. I think she may have thrown her plate at one point (I was busy doing something else). I was working hard to forge a relationship with her that was loving but no-nonsense. Yes, ordinary days can be truly extraordinary when we are willing to embrace the beautiful messiness of life.

☾

Kalighat continued to look and feel more like a hospital ward. Three women were on IV's — Maya who still refused to eat; the woman who was riddled with cancer, and a recent arrival who had seemed relatively healthy when she arrived. Ekta was eating better and was starting to talk a little. I asked her if she was willing to fight to get well and she nodded that she was – A good sign! Women left as well, including some who had come to us very sick. Good food, proper medications and vitamins, and loving care went a long way!

Meditation had become a regular part of our daily routine. I usually kept my eyes closed to set a good example. Some days, when I surreptitiously opened them; however, I had to work hard to refrain from laughing. One this day, a whole row of women had ditched meditation, laid back, and taken mid-meditation naps. After meditation, we now had exercise time and I had become the leader. I looked back from the head of the "conga" line and felt like the mama duck in *Make Way for Ducklings*. Some of the women loved to wave their arms while we danced/walked our way around, and that made it fun too. More very sick women AND our active/mobile ladies kept Kalighat hopping.

It always took a long time to feed Ekta, and when I did, I missed putting other women to bed. When she was done, I walked around making sure that all was well and that everyone was settled in. I sat and talked for a while with the woman who had arrived with maggots. While I sat with her, she told me her story three or four different times in Bengali. While I didn't understand the words, I knew the story, which allowed me to nod in all the right places.

When our shift was over, Kathy (one of my American friends) and I went with some of the younger female volunteers to Bar-B-Q, our favorite restaurant. We ordered a variety of dishes and passed our plates around. Their Chinese and Indian menus were both extensive, and we loved trying out new dishes along with our favorites: dal makheni, chicken tikka masala, and Chinese veggies. It wasn't a meal unless we had lots of naan as well. We stopped by the Oxford Bookstore, so that several women could pick up copies of *Shantaram* (which several of us were reading on our Kindles), by Gregory Roberts. And just like that, we had an Indian book club.

☾

Ben was a master at remembering people's names. I would sometimes laugh, though, when he would greet a newcomer effusively, like a long-lost best friend. "Who is that?" I would ask. He would then sheepishly confess, "I have no idea!" I've never been able to remember names like that. At the same time, I knew that it was important to me to know the names of the women at Kalighat. I also knew that this wouldn't be easy, especially since some of the Indian names were completely new to me. I'd made it a game and now I knew most of their names. It remained challenging though, since new women arrived constantly.

I'd heard speakers talk about creating images in your head to remember names, and I was tickled that it was working for me. It became a fun game, and it really helped the women to know that I cared enough about them to remember their names. I love the Christian worship song "*You Are Mine*" by David Haas. "*Do not be afraid, I am with you.* **I have called you each by name.** *Come and follow me — I will bring you home. I love you and you are mine.*" All of us have names and we want to be known. When I went to bed at night, instead of counting sheep, I visualized the women of Kalighat and recited their names — bed by bed. This was complicated a little bit by the bed shuffling that had started happening to accommodate ceiling fan preferences.

We'd begun having farewell parties for the Kalighat volunteers who were saying, "So long for now." Blue and Beyond was our rooftop bar and restaurant of choice. It was on the 9th floor of the Lindsay Hotel, and no matter how hot and humid it was on the street, there always seemed to be a nice breeze on the rooftop. It was now time for Sofie (France) to depart. She is a nurse and I really admired her loving spirit as she tended to the Kalighat women. There were volunteers from the US, Chile, Spain, France, Russia, and New Zealand represented at the party. As Valentina and I walked home, I mused that Kolkata has a vibrant night life that we didn't get to enjoy very often, given our early wake-up time each morning.

☾

Another Thursday arrived and another day off was just what I needed. I had breakfast at home and continued reading *Arranged Marriages,* a collection of short stories by Chitra Banerjee Divakaruni. The highlight of my day was heading out to Quest Mall with a group of friends to see *Beauty and the Beast.* It was a bonus that the theater was showing the movie in 3-D. Most of the time I find 3-D annoying, but in this case I truly felt transported into the beautiful story and scenery. Emma Watson did not disappoint, and the Beast was easier to love than I might have expected.

We now knew the pre-movie routine. A public service announcement encouraging citizens to dispose of trash properly (as if that would work), a gruesome PSA to remind everyone to avoid hitting innocent people crossing the street (worse than the driver's ed films in high school), and the singing of the national anthem. At some point near the middle of the film, there was usually an intermission, which was most likely designed to encourage patrons to eat more food. The intermissions sometimes seemed oddly placed, even in the middle of a tense or important scene. Following the break, movies were started up again with no fanfare whatsoever. You needed to get your food and get back in your seat ASAP or risk missing key plot points.

My Uber drivers were great on the way to and from the movie, which was always a plus. One of them asked me if I knew that Park Circus is called 7 Points by most Bengalis. He asked me if I knew why, but then answered before I could get a word out that it is because seven streets meet in one big intersection there. He also said that Park Circus is actually home to several circus companies during the winter months. I really do learn something new every day. I figured that the name Park Circus came from the rowdy, out-of-control driving that happened in that vicinity.

While heading home from the mall in my Uber, I could see crowds of people, eating out, shopping, and having a wonderful time. Some malls and markets in Kolkata were open until 10:00, 11:00, or even later, which helped to explain the relatively fluid opening times for some businesses in the morning (often after 10:00 am). Temperatures were much cooler at night, which made it delightful to be outside.

☾

My very favorite time at Kalighat was the last 45 minutes of the morning when we put the women down for their afternoon rest. Part of it was routine - washing hands, taking women to the toilet and/or providing bed pans, pulling women to bed on plastic chairs, and taking care of personal needs (replacing wet gowns, getting last drinks of water, etc.). I liked it when everyone was in bed and I could check-in with individual women. When I stopped by Kavya's bed to give her a hug because she had had several dressings changed AND an injection, which had clearly hurt, I could tell that this was not her best day. Kathy was holding her hand, which made it better! It had been a rough morning. I blew her a kiss and she did the same to me.

Next, I sat with Rushika, who slept on a mat on the floor next to Kavya. She still didn't like sleeping in a bed, so this was a workable solution for her. She liked to sleep sitting up with her head on the bed of the woman next to her on the other side. I sat and put my head on the other woman's bed too and she laughed. I asked if her lunch was okay and she said yes. Then she apologized to me because her English isn't very strong. She understood most English and could speak quite a bit too. I told her that I was very tired after a long morning. She said, "Isn't your duty done soon? You can go home and have a rest!"

When I sat with Anjali, she asked me if I had "taken lunch" yet. I said no and she reminded me that I need to eat. This was followed by a big kiss. Diya called out to me, and I saw that her water bottle was missing. When I found a new one for her, I was rewarded with an awesome smile.

A new woman arrived at Kalighat who was so strikingly beautiful that I could not stop staring at her. She clearly had Chinese AND Indian features, like some of the people I'd met years earlier in Mizoram. I wondered if we would ever know her backstory, as she was mute. But when she smiled, she was luminous.

The Kalighat volunteers went our separate ways after getting off the Metro at Park Street. I headed to the bookstore for chai, a chicken mustard sandwich, and a small apple tart. It was delicious.

CHAPTER XII

April

With the arrival of April, I was halfway through my Kolkata experience. I was amazed at how quickly the time had gone. On the 1st, many of our women were scheduled for haircuts, including some who were going to rock a new bald look. Seriously, lice can be a difficult problem in groups, and several of our women already had the bad little mamas and babies. On more than one occasion my children were sent home from elementary school with a notice to check their hair carefully, as other children in the class had lice. I also must confess that my children were the cause of one of those letters. So much cleaning of everything in the house and all the combing of their thick hair! Karima was sad after her head was shaved because she "looked like a boy," but I told her (truthfully) that she still and always looked like a beautiful princess. And the bald look made her gorgeous eyebrows even more prominent!

Parul was not at ALL happy with me as I struggled to shave her head with an old razor while wishing I had one of mine, along with some shaving cream. It would have made the job so much easier! She also wanted to snatch the razor from my hand and tried to grab it, but I was faster. To distract her, I gave her a small candy that she really enjoyed. Geetha was half-shaved when one of the massies came to get her so that she could have her dressings changed. We'd completed the front of her head but not the back; I reminded them to let us finish the job afterward. There was so much going on, that we never did finish her cut. I told Sister when we put Geetha to bed that she looked so uncomfortable — she had bed sores and needed to be turned a certain way for the most comfortable sleep. She also had arthritis though, and she couldn't move her arms very well. When Sister went to move her to a better position, she realized that her head was not fully shaved so she got the supplies and shaved her in bed, with my assistance. I could see the adult lice (louses, right?) jumping and running away. Thank goodness for the head coverings that I wore daily. While engrossed in head shaving, Maria (Spain) and I had joked that we should open a hair salon in the future. Fortunately, it didn't take us too long to realize that that would be a terrible idea.

Ekta would not eat breakfast or lunch. I was able to get a few liquids into her throat, but she spit up everything a few minutes later. I was concerned that she would soon stop eating altogether. Maya wasn't eating either, and sister had sent her to the hospital. I couldn't imagine that she'd ever leave there alive. She was very, very sick! And the new woman who looked so Chinese had a name – Adra! When I greeted her by name, she gave me a huge smile.

☾

When I woke up on Thursday morning, I immediately realized that my back was at war with the rest of my body. I'd been working hard to listen to my body and not push as hard as I often wanted to do. So, I rested for a while and did a little bit of housekeeping – paying bills, cleaning my room, doing laundry, and reading for a while.

Later that afternoon I took a short walk over to Café Coffee Day. Although it was convenient, only a block from my apartment, my experiences there had been less than stellar. They never had half of what was on the menu, which was already limited. I ended up with a decent chicken wrap and a drink. My cold, non-water drink of choice in India was fresh lime soda (sweet). It was a refreshing mix of soda water, fresh lime (muddled), and sugar. Or, you could get it with salt. Some of my friends now asked for it plain, with no salt OR sugar. Coffee Day didn't have fresh lime soda, so I asked for something "not too sweet." I was told that classic lemonade was my best bet. Guess what — it came about as salty as a drink could possibly get! Yuck. And for the record I don't like Gatorade either.

I came home sweaty and quite hot, as the "feels like" temperature was 108°F! I planned to go to bed early as I was always eager to get back to Kalighat after my day off.

☾

I loved the moment each morning when I walked down the stairs at Kalighat. It only took a few minutes to figure out who was feeling good and who was feeling not so good each day. After I greeted the women, I started looking after individual needs. One woman, Lasya, rarely asked for anything herself, but made sure her neighbors were taken care of every day. On most days she wanted a cup of water, so I just went ahead and brought her one today. She didn't seem particularly happy about it though. Next, she patted the empty seat beside her. I thought she was inquiring about the woman who usually sat there, so I went off to see if she was in the bathroom (she wasn't). When I came back to the sitting area, Lasya was still patting the place next to her, so I sat down. She snuggled right up to me and after a while she put her head on my shoulder. It was interesting to be still and watch the other volunteers work. I had to fight my American urge to get up and get busy. On the other hand, our spot felt like a little oasis of calm amidst the busyness. I'm not sure how long we sat together, but it was perhaps 15 blissful minutes that meant the world to me.

As I was leaving at the end of the morning, I stopped by the beds of many women to say, "see you tomorrow." One of those women was our Adra, who was brought to Kalighat after she was found wandering and looking confused at one of the Kolkata train stations. I was cautioned to tread lightly, as she had hit several women during the morning, but she gave me a wan smile as I stopped by her bed. I realized that just like grief itself, there were stages that women went through after they arrived at Kalighat. When they first arrived, most women looked and acted confused. Often, they were very ill and had received little to no care. There had usually been a triggering event that led them to our door — family members brought them, someone found them on the streets, and/or another facility had refused to take them in. They were generally very quiet.

After they'd been at Nirmal Hriday for a while, their new reality sank in and some got angry — not at Kalighat, but at the circumstances that led them there. In some cases, they provided a phone number or an address for family/relatives, and the social workers did the follow-up. Unfortunately, the information some women gave was inaccurate and their families were not found or finding them took a considerable amount of time. If you've seen *Lion,* you know how easily this can happen. Some women simply do not remember that they were living on the streets.

After a while, there was acceptance. Women at Nirmal Hriday were fed well, slept in comfortable beds, and had their medical needs met at the home or the hospital. Most importantly, they were loved!! Yet, despite this acceptance, many women longed for "home." Really though, don't we all long for home, wherever or whatever that might be? Some women rejoiced when it was time to go and others were incredibly sad.

☾

There was a big surprise waiting for us at Kalighat – two new massies had been hired. They both seemed very nice and I appreciated the way they talked to and interacted with the residents. The volunteers noticed that this was quite a sea-change and we heartily approved.

As I walked through the ward, I looked around and saw Upasna huddled on the floor. I plopped down next to her for a while and talked with her softly, my arm around her. She was fragile in every way and was so tiny that she reminded me of a wood sprite.

It wasn't long before I heard that one of the newer women had died before we arrived for our shift. She had become critically ill only a day earlier, so this was a surprise. I realized in retrospect that she must have been much sicker than she looked.

There were five new volunteers, some of them American nursing students, who would be graduating in a few weeks. I had lunch with them at the Spanish Café on Sudder Street and sat with them as they shopped at Sunshine.

☾

My deep aversion to begging in Kolkata continued unabated. I didn't want to ignore other humans, particularly those with very little to no privilege whatsoever. It felt paradoxical to love the women of Kalighat so very much and turn a blind eye to beggars. In the morning I usually passed several beggars and I spoke to them every day. When they saw me coming, they smiled — just the way that I did whenever I saw them. I didn't give them money, but I did try to recognize and acknowledge their humanity! Some of our women had begged on the streets at one time, and it had taken a toll on their bodies, not to mention their souls. I'd recently had several frustrating experiences with beggars. A woman had approached me on Sudder Street while I was waiting for an Uber that couldn't come fast enough to suit me. At first, she'd asked me politely for money for her family. I'd told her no, that I didn't give money on the streets. It didn't take her long to start yelling at me and telling me that I was NOT obeying the will of God. I think she was a bit surprised that I held fast. She left me in a huff and my Uber arrived shortly afterward.

There was a young man on Park Street who had first approached me shortly after I'd arrived in the city. He started by asking me where I was from and I told him. Then he asked if I was a Christian and I told him I was. He told me that he was a Christian too and that he loved God. *At this point, I already knew he would ask for money.* He told me that he was going to pray for me, and I said that was fine. Then came the sad story of his family's recent woes. His poor father couldn't even eat. Could I give him a little money to buy some food? In mid-March, he had approached again – "Remember me?" He tried the same story this week. I suggested that he talk with someone at his church, but he didn't like my answer at all. Worst of all were the adorable begging children. Those with excellent English often gave themselves away as "trained professionals." During my first trip to Vietnam in 2002, I'd encountered many beautiful, smart, English-speaking, beggar children. In the years since then, there have been fewer and fewer beggars on the streets, as police rounded them up frequently in order to ameliorate the problem. In addition, Vietnam is a more communal society, and families generally take care of their own members. I wished that India took the problem more seriously. I wondered where and how they would even start to create the necessary change.

☾

Any other Thursday I would have been relaxing or sightseeing, but this Thursday was different. Sister N, who supervised Nirmal Hriday, had asked for two male and three female volunteers so that the massies, staff, and sisters could spend time meeting, praying, and having a special mass. I'd volunteered to come in since I didn't have any firm plans, but afterward I'd begun wondering if the three of us would be okay alone with our nearly 50 women. That was a lot of needs to tend to when short-staffed. I was relieved to see that three novices would join us in caring for the women.

I arrived just after 9:30 and some of the women were astonished to see ANY volunteers present. Surprisingly, it was a delightful morning, although there was little time to spend with individuals. A few of the women were a bit "under the weather," but most were in good spirits. Hugs, kisses, and blessings came from unusual places! The woman whose bed was next to the place where new, very sick patients are placed (with extra space for IVs) winked at me when cries of "Auntie, auntie" came from all over the room. She was the woman who had revealed to me just a few weeks earlier that she spoke English well. Prisha, who had been a resident at Kalighat for many years, helped where she could. We didn't call her the "big boss" without good reason. Aisha proved that she could be the "little boss," as she helped women to the bathroom and back and provided general assistance!

My favorite moment of the morning was when Adra gave me a big hug and motioned to one of the social workers. She had been watching this exchange and told me that Adra would be leaving Kalighat sometime soon. As I'd mentioned previously, Adra could not speak, and I wondered how the social worker had found her home. Recognizing that Adra's facial features were similar to those of various Indian and Chinese tribal people, she brought in a picture book with tribal dress styles illustrated. Adra's eyes lit up as she pointed to one type of clothing. Now the social worker was preparing to contact that tribe to find a place for Adra. At the very least she would be "at home," and hopefully someday she would be reunited with her family.

When all the women were resting, and our shift was done, we were ready to leave and get some food, but Sister A insisted that we sit down and eat with the massies and sisters. I was a little leery, but I was so glad we did. Lunch was chicken and rice and it was delicious. It made me feel good to realize that it was the same food we'd served our women earlier. And I was still messy when eating with my right hand. My friends and I ended our afternoon with dim sum at Bar-B-Q!

☾

Another Friday meant another round of bedmaking! The day passed with lightning speed, which was surprising. Beds were stripped, cleaned, and stacked so that the floor could be deep cleaned, and soon after all beds and mattresses were put back in place and new bottom sheets, rubber liners, and draw (top) sheets were added, along with new pillows and pillowcases. This was all done in less than an hour and a half. Male volunteers were allowed to help us with this, and I appreciated them so much. If they hadn't been available, we would have done all of the heavy lifting, which could be rough.

Several women (including staff) had throbbing headaches and I think this was largely due to the weather. Rain was in the weekend forecast, and the barometric pressure was changing. I still needed a raincoat!

Have you ever had a meal that was so perfect, whether simple or fancy, that it made you cry? My hand is up, as that was my Friday lunch. Everyone seemed to have different things to do when we got off the metro and, knowing I would need to be at orientation by 2:50, I decided to head to Flurys. My club sandwich was amazing, so delicious that I could have wept. And the mango ice cream there was like the nectar of the gods. Only four new volunteers showed up at registration, the lowest number since I'd been helping. I was grateful to get home in time for a power nap.

☾

Because Thursday was our day off, I was never actually sure which day it was. I often confused Friday with Sunday or Monday. Since I'd worked on Thursday, I took my day off on Saturday — an actual "weekend." During the morning I slept, read, and cleaned, then decided to head to the mall for some retail therapy and good food. I woke up thinking about pasta, so I went searching for good Italian food that was NOT pizza. The only pizza I'd had since arriving in India was from Domino's – and it tasted awful!

At the end of the day, I realized that you knew you lived in Kolkata when:

> *In the 5 minutes it took for your Uber to arrive, you were*
> *soaking wet from sweating profusely. The "feels like" temp*

this afternoon was 106 and it felt at least that hot! I was so grateful for air conditioning AND fans…

You could watch cars from all directions drive straight toward you yet remain moderately disinterested. Traffic was crazy but always seemed to sort itself out.

You appreciated mall security that ran all handbags through x-ray screening. Quest is a big, beautiful mall and in today's crazy world, I appreciated the screening of people and bags. I did have to laugh at the cinema screenings at Quest, as they took any food in your bag away from you, including gum. You could pick it up after the movie (or not.) Last time I went to the movies there, I didn't think that going back for the three small pieces I had left was worth the walk.

You are a "foodie" and you had SO MANY different types of food to choose from. At the moment, I needed to feed my Italian food cravings! I checked out Seraphina, which was recommended to me by Indian friends. I lingered over my lunch of tomato/basil soup, homemade bread, farfalle with shrimp and lemon cream sauce, and prosecco. This was followed by a delicious caffe latte. The only thing that could have made the meal more perfect would have been a canoli!

Your Uber driver grew up in the city, didn't like Google Maps, and couldn't figure out where you live SO you showed him how to get around like a boss! Wink, smile… I never know how to get to anywhere without the assistance of a GPS, but THIS city is easy to traverse.

You were standing on the street talking to someone when an

*ill wind blew, and something putrid, fetid assaulted your
nose. Oh, Calcutta!*

☾

I was looking forward to working at Kalighat and attending mass there
on Palm Sunday. On Saturday night I went to bed earlier than usual but
couldn't sleep. For the first time since I'd arrived in India, noise kept me
awake for much of the night. It sounded like some of the teenage boys in
my apartment complex had started a rock band. I was happy to learn that
there was a puja on Saturday and that the loud music wasn't about to become a permanent part of my Kolkata life! Since the noise had kept me
up hours beyond my usual bedtime, I was sleepy when I woke up, and
quickly re-set my alarm for two hours later. When I woke up for the second time, I dressed quickly and then hopped into an Uber with a driver
who was surely related to auto racing driver Helio Castroneves. The
streets of Kolkata were his arena as we went weaving in and out of traffic.
He was one of the few Uber drivers who dropped me off AT Kalighat —
most dropped me off 5-8 minutes away because the streets were crowded,
and traffic was slow.

Palm Sunday mass took 90 minutes! My favorite part of the service
was walking through Kalighat with our palms in hand. The service was
lovely, but I missed taking communion since I'm not Catholic. Our
women were in good spirits, which was always a delight!

☾

On Sunday evening, sleep eluded me once again, so I Ubered back to
Kalighat on Monday morning. The extra two hours of sleep were completely worth it! Another piece of my heart was shattered when I had to
say goodbye to Adra, who was being moved to a shelter in the region
where she lived. She was so happy to be going to someplace more familiar, and I understood completely.

☾

On Tuesday it was clear that Geetha was declining quickly although when I arrived in January, I never imagined that she would cling to life until April. She ate less and less every day, despite the care that was taken to provide her with a special, nutritious diet. No matter how gently we moved her (and we tried very hard to move her with the utmost of care), we could often see her wince in pain.

Over the course of any given morning, Ruchika could go through many different moods. She was in good spirits as we arrived. I was busy immediately, running here and there to take care of multiple needs including taking women to the toilet, peeling oranges for snack time, massaging achy arms and legs, and sitting with our sickest residents. At 9:20 we had meditation time, followed by walking. Walking time had become fun for our women and we kept it as lively as possible by singing, clapping, dancing, or whatever else worked to motivate our mobile women to move more.

Shortly after we finished walking, I checked on Ruchika and saw ominous storm clouds on her face. I leaned in to ask her what was wrong. "I saw you," she said. "I WANT TO WALK AGAIN TOO!" I asked her if she was willing to fight for it, and she said "YES." She had a similar conversation with Kathy, another American volunteer. Then she worked with the physical therapists for a while, slowly pulling herself up to a stand. She was serious and had Aisha's determination. I was looking forward to celebrating with her as she regained strength and perhaps even walked again.

The most disconcerting part of the day was seeing Prisha sick. Because she had been at Kalighat for many years, she was affectionately known as "the big boss." She fearlessly called out other residents when they whined or demanded attention, and she regularly told volunteers where to go and what to do. Every morning, Prisha put on her glasses and read the paper

161

from cover to cover. I really appreciated her guidance each day. She'd been a little "off" for a few days, but we didn't think much of it. Now though, she had a fever and was delirious. I was hopeful that she would feel better soon. As we were leaving at the end of our shift, we commented that seeing Prisha sick was disturbing to all of us, as she was usually so healthy!

I went out with friends in the evening. From our tuk-tuk (auto rickshaw) — with four people in the front and three in the back — I watched as shop owners began closing for the evening. The "street food" culture went on, however, long past midnight! Most restaurants didn't open for dinner before 7:00 or 7:30. We were out for a bittersweet reason. Valentina, my Russian/Armenian friend from Moscow, was leaving Kolkata at the end of the week to head to Darjeeling. With numerous Holy Week activities throughout the week, we decided to celebrate with her a little early. I was heading to Darjeeling the following week and would meet up with her there. Although we'd have to say goodbye after that, at least this party was not our final farewell. Both of us were happy that the high temperatures in Darjeeling were in the 60's, instead of the high 90's. This would be a lovely change of pace. My housekeepers laughed at me when I came back. I went out at about 7:00 pm, nicely dressed and freshly showered in beautiful Indian clothing and came back all wet and sweaty. "It's HOT," they said, "but wait until May." It felt like some odd hazing ritual that every Kolkata resident laughed when they mentioned May weather to the uninitiated.

☾

After a late night with friends, I figured the next day would be hard, but it wasn't. The long-term volunteers had a nice rhythm with each other and our women. Teamwork was our mantra. New short-term volunteers arriving every week, which meant that there were multiple opportunities to teach, learn, and share. When I worked at Kalighat eighteen years ago, there were few volunteers and no one to tell us what to do, which I remembered as very frustrating. I'd felt useless when I was unable to respond quickly to even simple requests.

Ruchika was proving to us that she was serious about walking because she began to work harder on her exercises. Prisha was feeling a bit better, but was not her usual, feisty self. She did "bless out" a few women throughout the morning, so I thought she was indeed on the road to recovery. We had another good walking session this morning after our meditation time. I was the leader on most mornings, and I felt a little bit like a mother duck with all my ducklings trailing behind.

☾

Not all days were great, though. The next day, our day off, was just weird and it was a perfect reality check. I felt like India was trying to "spit me out." Those were words that a friend of mine used several years ago when she had an accident in Uganda. Her experience was an incredible ordeal though, and mine was just a day in which I let my India frustrations fly.... And speaking of flies — some days you are the windshield and some days you are the bug! I intended to read, watch a movie, and do some personal work. I got up, had breakfast, and cleaned. The cable went out again, for no known reason, and the Wi-Fi was slow. The temperatures were climbing daily, so I decided to stay in and order food from Swiggy, a great phone app that allowed the user to order food from over 1,000 local restaurants. I ordered a chicken burrito bowl that looked and sounded delicious. Each menu item was shown complete with picture. I ordered, then waited — it often took an hour, but the delivery charges were minimal. Finally, the delivery guy called and said that the restaurant was out of this item. What? I waited an hour for this? Discouraged and "hangry," I started looking for something else. I found something that looked good from a trustworthy restaurant and started to place my order, then saw that the restaurant would not accept COD payments. No problem, I could use my debit card — except that I couldn't. While my credit card worked fine in retail establishments, I always had trouble in India when I tried to use it online for Uber and now Swiggy. Between this and demonetization/remonetization, financial transactions could be challenging to say the least. I re-entered my credit card multiple times to no avail. Visakha ended up ordering something for me (because she could see that my mood was not good, which was quite unusual), but the entrée was too spicy, and the dessert was too sweet. I was in desperate need of a steak, baked potatoes, and one of my friend's delicious salads!!

No place is perfect and romanticizing a place has always been a dangerous practice. I knew that tomorrow would likely be better. I'd deal with the heat, have some good chai and a fresh lime soda with no salt, and love on the women of Kalighat. I would sadly say "so long" to my friend Valentina but would rejoice that I'd see her next week in Darjeeling.... As Easter Sunday approached, my thoughts were truly on things that were at the core of who I am and whose I am. I gave thanks for good days and great days here and at home, as well as those not so good days.

☾

I was determined to get back on track on Good Friday. My early bedtime was derailed when I woke up with stomach cramps not long after I fell asleep. Fortunately, I was able to get back to sleep and woke up feeling good. There was no breakfast at the Mother House, because the sisters were in prayer. That meant two more hours of blessed sleep once again before I Ubered to Kalighat.

When I arrived, I checked to see if all our women were present and accounted for. I saw that several volunteers were sitting with Geetha and my heart sank. I walked over and saw that she was actively dying, although the process could take several days. We sang to her, prayed for her, and gave her some water from a soaked cloth, as Sister requested. The last gave me chills when I thought about Jesus on the cross, also thirsty, and drinking from a sponge. During the morning other volunteers stopped by her bed, and some of the sisters from the men's side came to check on her as well. She tried to speak several times, but we could not hear her.

During my first week at Kalighat in January, I did not think Geetha would live through my entire stay. I WAS surprised that she had rallied many times over the course of the last few months. At times she ate well, and I always appreciated the opportunity to feed her. It had been clear for the past few weeks though that her body was shutting down and we had only been able to entice her to eat very small portions of liquified food. She told us many times that she was ready to go. Even though none of the volunteers had had the opportunity to know her when she was healthier, we loved her dearly. I didn't know if she would be there the next day, but I knew how much I would miss her when she was gone.

Although it was difficult, we tried to keep things "normal" for our other women. We had a good meditation session and many women walked beforehand. We hoped that this would become part of the day schedule even after we left Kolkata for home.

☾

With all our Easter preparations, I was surprised to learn that Saturday was New Year's Day in West Bengal! There were throngs of people at the Kali Temple and I had to wind my way through the already narrow streets, past the fruit and vegetable stands, to get to Kalighat. On Bengali New Year's Day, gifts are given, and new clothes are worn. I saw many families all decked out and heading to various temples as I roamed around the city. Many people were carrying large woven baskets with gifts inside. There were stacks and stacks of notebooks for sale and I saw many buyers. Along Kali Temple road there were other small gifts for sale as well.

Inside of Kalighat it was a bit more peaceful. Imagine my surprise when one of the first things I saw was Geetha sitting up. She smiled several times as if to say, "Not yet." She also ate some food, which had not been a given recently.

Diya was missing Valentina and when I greeted her, she pinched my arm. I was taken aback but another volunteer took me aside and said that one of the massies had been rough with her and that's what she was showing me.

The rest of the morning was very busy with everything from giving out snacks to washing hands to sitting with the meditation group to prepping the women for lunch. We couldn't walk because one of the massies was washing the floor when it was time to start and we did not want our women to slip and fall.

The "oh no you didn't" moment of the day went to one of our women who will remain nameless. Shortly before lunch, she woke up from a rest. I don't know how she ended up in bed, as we worked hard to keep our women sitting up in the morning. Too much "bed-time" could lead to bedsores and, whenever possible, we wanted our women to be engaged. Anyway, during her "rest" she had pooped all over her bed. When she woke up, she started flinging it on the floor — after all, who wants poop in their bed! When I sat with her for a few minutes before I left at noon, she didn't remember what had happened at all. Sometimes the lack of recall is a good thing, I suppose. I was feeding another woman and she didn't like her food; therefore, she was quite mad at me. Another volunteer asked me to help her move a resident and I did. When I returned, the woman I was feeding gave me a BIG smile, as if all had been fine between us....

☾

A few days before he died, Ben said to us very clearly and with a sense of wonder, "It's so pretty!!" "What's so pretty?" we asked. "Heaven — it's a multiplicity of colors!!" We were very surprised by how absolutely certain he was about this brief parting of the veil. A multiplicity of colors is exactly the way that Kalighat felt when we walked in to celebrate Easter morning with our women. The beds had new sheets with bright, beautiful flowers and our women were dressed in new gowns that also had flowers on them. Kathy brought cake with her, so we served it to the residents at snack time. I was lucky to be feeding Parul because Farha, who sat next to her, always shared her snacks with me. The cake was delicious. I felt like I was on a sugar high all day, as we had sweet buns for breakfast along with coffee with lots of sugar. At our break time we had sweet buns again but with chai this time. I had two fresh lime sodas at lunch, and on it went. Perhaps this was the adult version of eating too much candy out of your childhood Easter basket at one time!

After snack time we spruced our women up with new bangles and earrings. They loved it and we could see that they felt pretty wearing their Easter finery! I appreciated the mass and the message, but I really missed singing familiar Easter hymns. The music at Kalighat was like nothing I'd ever heard before and I didn't like it much at all. After mass, our women had a special lunch. Surprisingly, Geetha ate well and even had some chocolate cake and juice. A poignant reminder that things happen in God's timing, not ours. The sisters invited us to eat at Kalighat, and most volunteers stayed. We had lunch — round #2 — at Fairlawn on Sudder because we all wanted our fresh lime sodas, which really tasted great in the heat!!

Have you ever used a familiar expression and then had to explain it to someone from another culture? That happened to me when I returned home, and I realized that what I was trying to say was totally lost in translation. I was trying to explain to my housekeepers that when I leave the house in the morning I look (and feel) fresh, but by the time I get home in the afternoon I look bedraggled, like something "the cat dragged in." As I tried to explain, it was clear that it made no sense to them! I'm not a mime, but I could usually make myself understood — just not this time. Perhaps there is an Indian expression like "bless her heart," but I'm not aware of it yet. If there is, I'm sure that people were blessing my bedraggled appearance behind my back as I walked along Park Street on my way home.

☾

Time at Kalighat felt like it was going by so quickly. I looked around and saw volunteers sitting with different residents the morning after Easter, and I felt so much love radiating throughout the room. We worked well as a team too! I fed Geetha and she ate well, although she remained in bed except when her dressings were changed. The heat was bothering some of the residents in the same ways it bothered us. Thank goodness for the ceiling fans, although there were occasional "words" between the women who wanted them on and the women who wanted them off!

We all went our separate ways at lunch. I headed off to the café at the Oxford Bookstore, which was quite nice. I stopped to buy a book downstairs so that I could read and eat at the same time (I always have a book with me). Because of demonetization and remonetization issues in India, shopping could be difficult. I handed the salesclerk a 2000-rupee note (about $30) for my 199-rupee purchase, and he just shook his head, not happening. It was frustrating that ATMs ONLY spit out 2000-rupee notes AND that unless you were making a large purchase, no one would cash them. So, after purchasing the book with my card, I went upstairs to a delightful lunch of fresh lime soda (how every restaurant was judged), a chicken sandwich, French fries, and apple crumble — and a fresh lime soda "to go." This came to about 680 rupees $10), so I was hopeful that it would be enough to "tip the scale" and get the manager to accept my 2000 rupee note but NO, still not enough. I ended up using my card again, but I did talk with my server about how frustrating this situation can be. He asked me for my 2000 note a few minutes later and came back with smaller notes in hand. I thanked him profusely (albeit quietly). I had to laugh at myself later. This was NOT a serious problem, but rather an inconvenience…

I was excited that I would be heading to Darjeeling for a vacation in two days. I knew before I arrived in India that I would travel several times, but when I fell in love with the women of Nirmal Hriday, it was harder to imagine getting away. That said, I didn't want to become locked in compassion fatigue, and so I began planning a trip. After careful review, I chose Darjeeling for several reasons. First, I am a tea drinker and Darjeeling has always been one of my favorites. I'd never been to a tea plantation, and I was looking forward to it. Second, I was hoping to at least SEE the Himalayas, but knew that would depend on the weather (fingers crossed). Third, the high temperature for the next few days was 68° F, which sounded delightful! Fourth, it would be good to get away before I settled back in for May and June. And finally, Valentina was there, and we would get to spend some more time together.

☾

After I arrived in Kolkata, I learned that Mother Teresa had a life-changing experience while traveling to Darjeeling on the train. The quote below is from *Time* magazine's special edition, *Mother Teresa at 100: The Life and Works of a Modern Saint.*

> In the summer of 1946, Calcutta was shaken by religious rioting. Normally the nuns would remain cloistered behind their walls, but Teresa, by then headmistress (of the Loreto School), ventured into the city to gather food for her charges. The brutality she witnessed shook her deeply. Seeing that she was nearing exhaustion, her religious superiors sent her in September to a retreat in Darjeeling. The train trip from the Bengali lowlands to the city in the Himalayan foothills is a dramatic one, filled with hairpin turns and sudden vistas as the clouds part to reveal the splendor of the mountains. The people who later became Teresa's followers always knew that something happened on that trip to change her path forever, but it was only after her death that the publication of her

letters revealed to the world that, beginning on that train, she heard the voice of Jesus, and shortly afterward had several visions of Christ on the cross. She described her experience as an "impassioned dramatic dialogue." Every year on September 10 the Missionaries of Charity have commemorated her experience on that train as Inspiration Day. When (Mother Teresa) returned from Darjeeling, she began petitioning the Calcutta archdiocese for permission to form her own order.

Before I left for Darjeeling, I'd had to say goodbye to Father Etienne from France, whose last day of volunteering would be while I was gone. Because I knew I would miss his party, I invited him to lunch at Peter Cat. There were seven of us at the table and we all had a great time. I was the only one who had been to the restaurant previously! They all loved it and I was reminded of the many, many times that Ben and I shared dining recommendations with our friends. I realized that I was doing the same thing in India. Father Etienne was witty, kind, and compassionate, and I would miss him a lot!!

☾

I like to be organized and EARLY on travel days and would rather sit at an airport gate reading, writing, or people watching, than make a last-minute dash. Do you see where this is headed? I was up, packed, and sitting in the living room waiting for my driver to arrive fifteen minutes ahead of schedule. When he was fifteen minutes late, I called, and he said he was "making his way." I had no idea if he had left already OR if he was just starting out (in which case he would be an hour late). I texted my friend (his employer) to ask if the driver had left, and he called me back and said the driver was just arriving at my house. To me this meant that he was pulling into the driveway, so Sukumar and I stood outside waiting. It was ten more minutes before the driver arrived. When he got out of the car, he kept telling us there was a traffic jam. Yes, but there is

ALWAYS a traffic jam in Kolkata! I sat down and settled myself and off we went. It only took a few minutes before I realized that the AC wasn't working, and it was boiling hot. So, we opened the windows, which made it even hotter, but the breeze felt really good. Drivers in Kolkata often turned their engines off when traffic was stalled, as my driver did after about fifteen minutes…

Guess what happened next? When he tried to start the car, NOTHING happened. We were stranded in the middle of the road. He ran over to the side of the street and grabbed two guys to push the car while he tried to restart it. It worked but I was pretty sure the same thing would happen again if we were stuck in traffic and it didn't take long for that to happen. I asked him to try to get a taxi, but no one wanted to go to the airport. I said I would request an UBER, and he said okay. The UBER driver was two minutes away when I had to cancel because the driver persuaded two other guys to help him move the car to a side street about 1/4 mile away. Fortunately, I was able to get a second UBER quickly and was finally on my way again. Apparently, all the coolant had drained out of the car. It smelled so bad and I was worried because my granddaughter had had something similar happen a few weeks earlier in my old (old, old) car on an Oklahoma highway. Thankfully she was okay, but the car was now at the junkyard.

I did make my flight, but it was close. The jet was beautiful and new, although I'd never heard of the airline — IndiGo — previously. I have to say (ahem, United Airlines) that even though I bought my food on the plane, it was not expensive and actually delicious! The pilot said there would be turbulence as we neared Bagdogra, but fortunately it was a smooth ride.

It was a three-hour ride from Bagdogra to Darjeeling. I had requested that the hotel send me a car, and the driver was there to meet me. We got in the car and took off, passing many tea gardens. After about an hour we stopped for tea and toilet. I needed to go, but it was dicey. If I stumbled and fell off the narrow ramp, there was a steep drop-off down the hill. I slept for the next hour and a half for self-preservation — I knew that this part of the drive would be steep curves, switchbacks, and hairpin corners and, as someone prone to motion sickness, I did not want to succumb to my nemesis, so being able to sleep was a blessing.

I woke up in Kurseong, a hill station in the Darjeeling district. The houses were built into the sides of the mountain, reminding me of Mizoram, where I'd worked with a consulting team sixteen years earlier, which is also in Northern India. We arrived in Darjeeling mid-afternoon and I was already enjoying the heat, or lack thereof.

I was staying at Windamere, an old colonial hotel built during the British Raj. I knew it would be charming and I was right. I had a large room with a queen size bed, a beautiful sitting area, and a bathroom with a bathtub. After a short rest, I headed down the hall to tea – finger sandwiches, jam cake, scones, and biscotti, all in a red parlor with a fireplace. I sat and chatted with two American couples — one living in Mumbai and the other living in Bhutan.

I went back to my room to read, and there was a knock on the door — The prepared staff member entered and started the fire in my fireplace! Yes, my fireplace!!! Later there was another knock on the door, and another gentleman came in to put a hot water bottle under my sheets so that the bed would be warm when I settled in for the night.

I was stunned when I walked to the dining room for dinner. The hotel had recreated an evening in 1939, complete with scratchy recorded music from the period. I felt like I had walked into a J. Peterman catalogue. And at that moment, I felt lonely. Where was the dashing gentleman who would give me the shivers when our eyes met? Dinner was a five-course meal: watercress soup with crouton toast; Italian leg of lamb with roasted potatoes and green beans; thyme-flavored carrots; butter chicken, rice, paneer, dal, okra, and Indian breads; lemon pudding cake with custard (one of the best desserts I'd ever had); and locally grown tea. It was so much better than I'd anticipated. I'd been dealing with showers nearly four months, so after dinner I enjoyed a steaming hot bath as I listened to the rain tapping on my windows.

☾

I was greeted with a mystical view when I walked out of my room for breakfast. The mountains and the mist created a dreamy quality that reminded me of Shangri-la. So beautiful.... And if you haven't read it, I encourage you to find a copy of *Lost Horizon* by James Hilton. It's my favorite novel and it never grows old. Oops, I just innocently shared a major plot point, but it is SO worth the read.

My tour guide picked me up right on time, and we started the morning touring a small Buddhist Monastery near Darjeeling. It was a beautiful place, although it was one of the smaller and poorer monasteries in the area, with only 15-20 monks residing there. One of the various sects of Buddhism, this monastery is part of the "yellow hat" group whose spiritual leader is the Dali Lama. The lights were out but the candlelight was beautiful. The monk we met and spoke with let me spin the very large prayer wheel.

We then headed to Batasia Loop and the War Memorial. The Batasia Loop is a spiral railway created to lower the gradient of ascent of the Darjeeling Himalayan Railway. At this point, the train spirals around over itself through a tunnel and over a hilltop. This is the Toy Train I mentioned previously which is not, in fact, a toy, but rather a passenger train that runs on a toy-like track. The War Memorial commemorates those killed defending the Motherland. It was built in 1995, and I was surprised to see that the last name added died in January 2017. My guide said that the soldier was likely killed in a skirmish with Pakistan. The flowers at the Memorial were beautiful.

We stopped for a cup of tea at a little restaurant. Interestingly, people do not drink chai here. They REALLY love their Darjeeling. I was told that Assam tea is used for chai because it doesn't taste good unless milk and sugar are added. A little tea rivalry perhaps?

Next on the agenda was a stop at another, much larger monastery that is home to 400-500 monks (including young boys). Although the main worship space was closed to visitors, we chatted with women who spend part of their days turning giant pray wheels "for exercise." This sounds like an excellent mind-body activity! We also listened to the children chanting above us as a part of their education.

I was really interested to learn more about tea gardens and tea growing. Confession: Although I drink tea every day, I had no idea what actual tea leaves and tea gardens look like.

The next stop was the rock garden. It was a beautiful area with trees, flowers, waterfalls, a stream, and yes, rocks. The azaleas were beautiful; I'd been thinking about mine at home, wondering if they were blooming. We sat and watched a native dance performance and a local man doing native bird calls. I also ate the delicious lunch that had been packed by the hotel to look like a present. Another feast - 2-cheese sandwiches, an apple, hard boiled eggs, cookies, a chocolate bar, juice, and water!

Our first stop of the afternoon was at a local Japanese peace pagoda. My guide showed me that these were being built around the world, including one in Massachusetts. I started taking pictures and didn't realize for a minute that my friend Valentina was sitting right there. I went upstairs to do some drumming and sat next to my friend Sara. I'd forgotten that she too was headed to Darjeeling, perhaps because she had taken a more circuitous route. The pagoda was beautiful, and the message was critical to our survival as a planet. We finished the afternoon with a tea tasting. I loved the fact that they had so many kinds of teas and teas from different estates. When the tasting was done, I purchased 2nd flush (picking), Oolong, and White tea to take home. I asked the owner about his favorite tea and he told me it is almost always 2nd flush or picking of the season, which takes place in May.

Dinner was another feast: potato and onion soup; home style fish with cheesy potato mash (incredible), butternut squash, and lady fingers (Am I the only one who didn't know that is another name for okra?); a different Indian chicken dish, black dal, cooked tomatoes, paneer, and breads; a nice, light dessert — good but not as amazing as dessert on the first night, and tea or coffee.

☾

I started Friday morning with another five-course breakfast. If I'd stayed at Windamere much longer, I would have had to be rolled back to Kolkata! Then I had a very nice massage at the wellness center. I'd only had one massage since arriving in Kolkata, as the spas were generally overpriced. Following my massage, I came back to my room and lost myself in *Shantaram* by Gregory David Roberts. The writing was exquisite, and the story was quite a wild ride. Of course, reading it in India also added to my enjoyment, since it reflected so much of the culture.

I had a five-course lunch, and one of the items was mixed grill. They served BEEF, which was very good. I took several other "meats," but realized almost immediately that they were liver — gag, spit, etc. After lunch I headed to the "Mall," the outdoor area in the center of town, to meet Valentina. I had a drink while she had lunch and we talked. After lunch we window shopped and bought tea from local estates.

I came back to my room and rested, but there was no way that I could manage tea AND dinner. At dinner time I had the soup starter and the crepes entree but passed on the Indian food and dessert (I know, right?). I realized that if I ate even one more bite, I would be a totally unhappy camper all night long.

☾

On Saturday morning I got up late, skipped breakfast except for tea, and kept reading. I also spent time thinking about my life after returning to the United States and what I wanted it to look like. I felt like a new person and wanted to make sure that I incorporated what I had learned in India into my new routines at home. I went to lunch — I ate everything but in small portions — and I walked to the Mall. There was great excitement because a big film shoot was happening! Darjeeling reminded me very much of a ski resort — majestic mountains, cool temps, interesting shops, and fascinating people. I wandered through curio shops and tea houses and had a delightful time. I got back just in time for tea (more food), a little rest, and reading time by my fireplace.

☾

My travel back to Kolkata was much smoother than my trip to Darjeeling. The hotel staff lined up to say farewell to me, and I was completely charmed. The vacation respite was EXACTLY what I needed before returning to Kolkata for the next few months. When I left Darjeeling, it was quite chilly, and I could feel the temperature rise as we slowly drove down the mountain. I reached the Bagdogra airport in plenty of time for my flight and I relaxed with a fresh lime soda and my book!

One more interesting fact to share about Darjeeling… The name is commonly said to be a corruption of Dorje-ling, "the place of the thunderbolt," the name of a monastery that once stood on a well-known eminence in the modern town, now known as Observatory Hill, where Windamere is located. Of course, there are some who disagree.

On reflection, I was concerned about Darjeeling because it reminded me of Siem Reap, Cambodia (Temples of Angkor) and Machu Picchu. These are amazing places that were not designed for the massive influx of tourists they receive now. The infrastructures are fragile, and I wondered what viable solutions might look like. At Machu Picchu, there is talk of severely restricting access by capping the number of visitors per day and/or limiting areas that are open to visitors. In Siem Reap, the sidewalks buckle, power outages occur intermittently, and sometimes businesses can't accept credit cards because there aren't enough open phone lines. In Darjeeling the narrow roads are about the width of 1.5 cars (and many of the cars are SUVs or jeeps hauling visitors.) If you are driving through town, you must stop multiple times to let cars in the opposite lane pass, and sometimes you must back up to let another car go by. Cars pass within a hair's width of each other. At least drivers are incredibly patient!

I also acknowledged my mixed emotions about staying at a colonial hotel. I asked my guide and several others what they believed was the result of colonialism. They all said that colonialism was both good and bad. When the British left, the tea estates remained, and today they are owned by Indians and governed by the Tea Board of India. Darjeeling is a thriving tourist destination, and this too began during the British Raj. It's complicated and I would continue to process my experience there when I returned to the city.

☾

After a great vacation, I wanted to have a gentle re-entry. Too often, when we rush back to work and commitments, we feel that relaxed vacation vibe ebb away faster than we'd like. So, I stayed home, washed (more black water in the bucket), did some non-blog writing, watched a movie (*Pacifier*), ordered in for lunch, and read. Believe it not, the key lime pie I got for dessert was the best I've ever eaten!

☾

I knew there would be changes at Kalighat during the week I was away, but they came hard and fast. Most significantly, Geetha died peacefully on Friday. I would have been MORE surprised had I walked in and found her still clinging to life — but I'd said that before. I knew I would miss her very much and would always remember her fortitude and self-determination. When she did not want to eat, or had had enough, she would close her lips with a vice-like grip. You were loved, sweet Geetha!

Ruchika, Nidhi, and another woman were transferred to Shanti Dan, a home for women and girls that is also run by the Missionaries of Charity. This new environment would be good for them as they would have more stimulation throughout the day. I would miss them all, especially Ruchika. This move would be a new start for her, and I was hopeful that her eating issues would be resolved. Since the day she told me with great longing that she wanted to walk again, I'd been determined to help her achieve this goal, so that she could eventually go home to her family.

The biggest surprise of all was that Aisha had gone home to her husband and children. What a journey we'd been on from her dire illness the night she came to Kalighat to her recovery, which felt like a joyous, unfolding miracle!

The only sad part was how deeply I would miss her. I'd told her that I loved her many, many, times and before I left for Darjeeling, I gave her a huge hug! I hoped I'd be able to keep an eye on her progress through the social workers.

We had several new residents. I spent time in the dressings room with one of them. She had a deep, nasty wound on her leg that one of the sisters was cleaning and re-dressing. I was holding her hands because she was squirming and kicking to get away from the sister's reach. We had to call in a massie to help hold her legs as well. At one point she was able to wrest one arm out of my grip, and as I went to re-grasp it, I realized that she is a biter. I saw her wide-open mouth coming straight toward me. She was quick, but I was quicker. I began talking to her quietly and telling her everything that the sister was doing and, more importantly, WHY she was doing it. She calmed down, and I had several chances to check in with her later. We also had a new resident who fell off a train; her face was badly damaged, among other things. Indian trains are NOT for the faint of heart! A new young woman with cirrhosis of the liver had breathing issues and needed oxygen. With her distended abdomen, a result of the disease, she looked like she was nine months pregnant!

The heat felt brutal, especially after such respite in Darjeeling. I had to admit that it got to me. As we were putting women down to rest after lunch, I began to feel light-headed and could tell that the pressure in my ears kept changing in the same way it does when I'm on a descending plane. I told several other volunteers to watch out for me, and they totally had my back!

☾

It has been said that the eyes are a window to the soul, and I agree. So many inner thoughts, feelings, and struggles can be reflected there. When Maya arrived at Kalighat, she refused to eat. When she did eat, she felt even worse. She was given IV fluids and went to the hospital for additional treatment. She was back at Kalighat now and looked and felt like a new woman. I sat with her for a while. We didn't say much but we communicated so many things with our eyes: how good it was to feel better, to see each other, and to recognize the spark of the divine radiating through the space we occupied. On the other hand, when I looked at Shalini's eyes, I saw gathering storm clouds. It felt like a monsoon was coming from her direction. She had been so sad recently and not herself. Occasionally we still saw her beautiful smile, but those instances were few and far between.

Diya's eyes looked cloudy and confused. She had cataracts in one eye, and in the other eye I saw — something that looked like confusion. She was one of the Hindi speakers at Kalighat, so was not easy for her or her caretakers to understand each other.

In Anjali's eyes I saw exhaustion. She told us that she was tired, but she had good days too. Her back had started hurting and she wanted frequent massages, which we lovingly provided.

I had an Uber experience in the afternoon that was a throwback to my messy airport run the week before. When I requested the ride from Shishu Bhavan to my apartment, the app said that my driver was three minutes away. Twenty minutes later, the app claimed that the driver was one minute away. I finally cancelled that car and requested another. Same driver (I'd never had that happen before). It still took five more minutes until I saw the guy waving to me from across the street. Instead of stopping in front of Shishu Bhavan, like all the other drivers did, he wanted me to cross crazy busy A.J.C. Bose Road during rush hour. I was not too happy as I gingerly crossed the street. When I got in the car, he asked me how to get to my house. I explained that it was straight down the road and then two right turns (and I named the roads where the turns took place). He asked me about every one-hundred feet if he should turn yet. No, No, and No! But finally, we turned onto Shakespeare Sarani (street), and he got pulled over by the police. He turned off the cool car, which began to heat up rapidly. When he came back to get some papers and to tell me his radiator was leaking, I gave him the fee and walked home. Mercy!

☾

Relationships are like onions. As we get to know someone, we peel back layer after layer, revealing the soul of the person inhabiting the body. Darpana started talking with me about the problem with one of her eyes. I was leaning in to listen to her when she said, "Why don't you sit down so that we can talk more easily?" ZING — I realized as soon as she asked that my posture didn't look like that of someone who was willing to sit down and have a conversation. Chagrined, I sat down. With approximately 50 women in our care at any given time, we were pulled in many directions at once. While sometimes it was necessary, I was not a fan of multitasking. Although requests for my assistance came from all corners, I realized that Darpana was inviting me in, and I was not going to decline. The two of us spent 20 minutes chatting, and I was completely blown away by the conversation, which took place entirely in English. She told me about her father and growing up in Pune. She talked about earning her MBA, and she told me that she loved to read. Unfortunately, her eye condition had kept her from reading for a while. She then shared a funny story about one of her friends. This woman used to invite her over to eat, but she was a terrible cook! What to do? Darpani proclaimed that she had been a good cook herself and that she shouldn't have accepted her friend's invitations. She also revealed that the doctor had told her that her eye issues could be resolved with surgery and medications. She hoped this was the case and wanted to go home soon. I prayed that she did have a place to go home to, as so many women did not.

Later in the morning, I heard an interesting conversation between Sister A and a volunteer who had been in Kolkata for ten days and was leaving the next day. The volunteer was very unhappy that one of our residents, who vociferously demanded to be taken to her bed by mid-morning, had not been allowed to do so. Sister patiently explained why that was NOT a good idea (and I completely agreed with her)! To me, the volunteer's frustration was a little bit like coming into a movie theater about half-way through a film. You didn't know what had happened prior to your arrival and you had to figure things out with incomplete knowledge and information. Short-term volunteers often had no back-story or history regarding those we served, which made it difficult for them to understand patient-care decisions.

My back hurt more than usual, and I knew I'd go to bed early. Bed-making day involved a lot of bending over which could be difficult, AND we had a few new residents who were heavy and difficult to move around. We couldn't always wait for another volunteer if everyone was busy. I had asked my prayer partners to pray for my strength and stamina, and today was one of the days I needed those prayers the most.

There was a surprise that made the day incredibly special – Aisha and her cute children came to visit! Volunteers and staff lined up to give them BIG hugs! The sisters had been concerned about the family — they had very few resources — and I learned that her husband had been offered a job at Kalighat that would begin soon. In addition, the Missionaries of Charity provided basic food rations to the family. Aisha pitched right in, getting water for some women, and helping in other ways as needed. Her little girl handed out bowls of watermelon at break time, and she was very proud of herself. Aisha's little boy (2 1/2) was shy and wanted to stay close to mom. She had been at Kalighat for quite a while and had been sorely missed by her family. It must have been hard for her little ones to have mom gone. Before leaving, Aisha laid down with her kids in her old bed and took a nap.

It was also a sad day, as Kathy was leaving after two months of volunteering. She was kind and compassionate, and she would be dearly missed. A group of nearly twenty volunteers celebrated with her at BBQ. We were seated in an alcove above other diners, which was probably a good thing since we were a bit rowdy. We shared Indian and Chinese food and drank fresh lime sodas. The waiters were called upon to take many group photos. Either someone decided that we would celebrate Kathy's (un) birthday, or one of the waiters simply wanted in on the fun and brought balloons to the table. Of course, we sang the volunteers' goodbye song (three verses), and there were hugs all around.

A day earlier, the heat had gotten to me as we were leaving the metro station after volunteering, leaving me a little wobbly. Juanita was very concerned and would have stayed with me if I'd asked. I told her I'd sit for a while, until I felt better, then walk home. I gave her my number and she called twice to check on me. In the heat, we needed to be good to ourselves and move slowly. Today, it was my turn to help her. Like me, she was okay but just had a "heat moment." The "feels like" temp was 115 again! I wondered how high it would climb....

☾

On April 30th, we had our monthly volunteer program from mid-afternoon into the evening. We met at the Bishop's residence, just a few blocks from my apartment. There were about 40 of us, and we began our time together singing and watching simple skits, illustrating timeless truths in parable form. After the skits we had sharing circles in English, French, Spanish, and Japanese. The sister who facilitated the English-speaking circle related each of the skits to interesting stories about Mother Teresa. She said that many, many times Mother would take small, simple actions, encouraging others to do the same. She also said that Mother love exuded from every pore in her body. This sharing was my favorite part of the program because it felt like such a privilege to learn more about the Saint of Kolkata. After the sharing program we had an hour of prayer, followed by a simple dinner.

CHAPTER XIII

May

When May arrived, I was reminded that my time in India was moving very quickly. I vowed to make the most of my remaining two months in the country and at Kalighat. May 1st was International Workers' Day (like our September Labor Day). In India, the first May Day was celebrated in 1923 in Chennai (Madras). Now, organizations and trade unions arranged pageants; children entered contests, so they could understand better the importance of fairness for workers; and political leaders made speeches. Some of us were asked if we would work from 8:00-5:00 on the first, as the massies and staff would be involved in various activities. It looked and sounded like they were having fun, and I was grateful for the team building that was now taking place at Kalighat! We all needed each other. My fellow volunteers and I knew how much we wanted and needed happy massies after working without them all day long.

It appeared that another of our women was close to death. She was no longer responsive and could barely swallow a little water given to her from a gauze pad. I stayed by her side for much of the morning, holding her hand and talking softly to her. Upasna was also sick, and that made me very sad. Later, during the afternoon, she did sit up briefly and ask for water, which was good. The morning passed so quickly that I almost missed teatime. I ran up the stairs and gulped down two small cups as fast as possible, then ran downstairs to start putting bibs on the women who needed them before serving lunch.

After everyone was in bed and accounted for, those of us staying all day ate together and then settled down for brief "naps." The quote marks are indicators that I found it hard to take an actual nap on a hard bench. I was immediately reminded of my privilege. I couldn't really imagine what it would be like to sleep on the hard ground or on a bench for years and years. Around 2:00-2:30, our women began waking up. Instead of their usual chai and biscuits for afternoon snack, the women had ice cream — messy but delicious. I knew that because someone always wanted to give me their food; today, it was Maya who shared. At 4:00, Sister A told those of us who had been there since 8:00 that we could leave. She sent us off with mango juice boxes. I went out into the hot streets with my constant accessory, my small absorbent face towel that let me blot my face before my ever-present sweat rolled into my eyes.

I had been afforded many interesting opportunities in Kolkata because my landlord was an amazing human, involved in many different aspects of cultural and religious life in the city. Among other things, he was the president of FACES, a non-profit NGO founded in 2006. FACES is an association of long-established alumni of multi-disciplinary schools and colleges of Kolkata. The group sponsored, along with The Creative Arts and in collaboration with the Indian Council for Cultural Relations, BEYOND BORDERS, an all-women's production celebrating the spirit of inclusiveness. Although much of the play was in Hindi, I understood the major themes but wished I'd had a better understanding of the nuances surrounding each scene. From the director's notes,

> *Like everyone else, my thoughts and actions are affected by*
> *what is happening around us. I am constantly looking for an-*
> *swers to the questions that crop up in my mind; searching for*
> *the various 'whys' whose 'because' I can rarely find...My art,*
> *like any other artist's, is a journey to continuously delve*
> *deeper within myself and the circumstances around, to dig for*
> *the deepest layer that could be the root cause for something.*
> *Our all-women production of 'Beyond Borders' explores*

*boundaries of nationality, caste, color, ethnicity, gender, body,
and mind... Geographical borders created by man can be
seen, religious borders can be debated... but maximum devas-
tation happens by the boundaries that humans create within
their minds. Each boundary that we create — is it a figment of
our imagination, is it our insecurity, our envy, our greed, our
hunger for power, our pent-up anger, or simply our inability
to understand a point of view that is different from ours?*

The play was derived from personal accounts, stories, and poems. One
of American poet Neal Hall's compelling poems was a significant back-
ground piece for the production. Even better, he was there and read a bit
of his poetry before the production. SO. VERY. POWERFUL.

(

The next day, I was just undone. It was hot, hot, hot from the moment
I stepped outside in the early morning. Leaving Kalighat at lunch time
was the worst. By the time I got to the metro station I was wet all over.
The metro station is air conditioned, with fans as well, but I didn't have
any time to bask in the delightful coolness, as my train came just as I ran
down the steps. At the second stop, Rabindra Sadan, the doors opened
and closed over and over. Then the train sat there for 10-15 minutes. I
was in claustrophobic hell as the packed train didn't move and instead
grew hotter and hotter. There were some announcements made (in Bengali only) that there was some kind of problem or delay. By the time we
got to Park Street I was in complete pity party mode. WHY DID IT
HAVE TO BE SO INSANELY HOT? WHY DID EVERYONE HAVE TO
PUSH AND SHOVE? And on and on.

I was walking down the first set of stairs leaving the Metro station
(down, around, up, out, left, up to the street) when the Muslim woman
next to me wearing a burka wobbled in my direction. I thought she had
tripped, but I quickly realized that she was passing out. I caught her and

sat her down next to me. A security guard came running from behind us and her husband, who was in front of us, turned around, saw what was happening, and came running back. Her gave her some water and after a few minutes she felt better. I left feeling ashamed of my pity party just prior to our encounter. I can't even imagine how HOT she must have felt. Message received!

☾

Our very sick woman died during that night. I was not surprised, as her breathing had been so labored the past few days. I was asked to pull all the linens off the bed and to take the mattress to the roof to dry in the sun. That task made the loss much more real. And there were several women who could leave us soon. Chaaya, who had stomach cancer, took a terrible turn for the worse while we were working, and I didn't think she would survive much longer.

After meditation time, we had our usual walk around the sleeping area when I heard one of the volunteers say that Maya was bleeding. During her first stay with us, Sister A had no choice but to put her arms in restraints, as she would pull out her IV line every chance she got. After her arms were restrained, she was able to pull out her IV line with one of her feet, which resulted in restraints at her ankles as well. During that first stay, she was very ill and refused to eat even one bite of food. We thought then that death was very near. She returned to Kalighat a few weeks ago after a short hospital stay. We were so pleased because she was eating well and walking. Earlier, she had eaten about a quarter of her lunch — and when she was done, she just started spitting rice at us. The cause of the bleeding? She had indeed pulled out her IV line, resulting in a bloody mess. We had to restrain her arms again, AND she tried her old trick, kicking the IV line out with her foot. I spent much of the morning comforting her but, as you can imagine, she was not a very happy camper. Spitting out her rice at us was a way to share her frustration.

I headed to the Oxford Bookstore Café for lunch. Afterward, I walked about halfway down the block and ran into my friend, Bernie, the woman who had talked with me about the American election. She gave me the business because I was not aware of the situation in Kashmir, where kids were throwing stones at the Police. Apparently, this had been going on for a while. Bernie was very well informed and was so knowledgeable about American politics. I knew I needed to read the Indian newspapers more carefully so that next time we ran into each other I could respond in the affirmative and share my opinions on events in India as well as the US.

☾

My day off was absolute bliss. I was happy to do absolutely nothing. I had a great breakfast — luchi (light, slightly sweet puffed bread) and aloo (potatoes). For my big meal I ordered in momos (dumplings) and chicken and sweet corn soup (my favorite). I watched several movies, read a little, and just relaxed.

☾

When I arrived at Kalighat the next morning, I learned that Chaaya had died during the night. She had taken a major turn for the worse on Wednesday, so I was not surprised. She was in a lot of pain and I was relieved that she didn't have to suffer any more. I was also worried about the volunteer crew. Two female volunteers left early because they did not feel well, and others of us just felt a little "off." We kept reminding each other to drink as much water as possible, at least three medium-size bottles every day, along with chai and juice, and to rest when we were weary. During our shift, Anjali, who now wanted to be called Rathi, started showing everyone an underarm growth that looked like an epidermoid cyst. Sylvie took her into the dressings and wound care area, where one of the sisters worked hard to lance it. Sister A worked on it as well. Rathi did not like the treatment one little bit and yelled at all of us for a while. When she calmed down and the beds were all made, we let her relax. "I am very old and very tired. I need to rest in my bed," she reiterated! It was a plea we knew all too well. I knew I would remember it and the way it was delivered all my life. Just before lunch she said to me, "I do not want to be alone. Stay with me." I did stay for a while, then told her I needed to help serve lunch. "How many minutes until you come back?" "Five," I said. I did return and she ate well, although I asked her how she enjoyed her lunch when I was leaving, and she told me that no one gave her any food…

I loved the sitcom *Will and Grace* when it was on TV. I learned in Kolkata that it would return in the fall, and I looked forward to enjoying it again. In one of the funniest episodes, Grace was in a foul mood and commented, "Today I'm giving out lollipops and ass-whoopings, and I'm all out of lollipops." I felt a little bit like that today! In early April, I received an email from my NC bank that my Visa debit card was one of thousands (millions?) involved in a security breach and that a new card had been issued to me. I called and explained that I was living in India, so they Fedexed a new card to my India address, despite the concern I expressed about getting mail delivered promptly. I expected it to arrive while I was in Darjeeling, so I was shocked that it wasn't at my apartment when I came back to Kolkata. Instead, it was being held hostage by FEDEX INDIA over customs clearance. I'd sent them every document they wanted, including several that were sent twice. FEDEX in the US had contacted them as well. I kept telling them that I was an individual and that I was not importing or exporting anything nor was I doing business here. After volunteering, I walked to the American Consulate to see if they could help. They promised to call FEDEX early the next week. I just hoped I'd have my new card by May 19th, when my current card would no longer work.

☾

There are things that, once seen, cannot be unseen. Animal sacrifices happen daily at the Kali Temple, which is next to Kalighat. I knew this was happening, but I didn't have to see it. That is, until this afternoon when I saw a teenager carrying a black baby goat. It took me a minute to process the reality. One boy was carrying the head of the animal, and his friend was carrying the (separated) body.

We said goodbye to a YWAM (Youth with a Mission) group this week. They were off to trek for a month in Nepal. None of the houses had a full complement of volunteers and might not until July and August, which are popular times for volunteers to travel to Kolkata. Volunteers had finally started arriving who would be here after I left. I appreciated the continuity of care that they would provide.

On my way home, I stopped into one of my favorite shops, just for tea. I loved tea times here and hoped to preserve the space for quiet reflection and beverage when I return home. Surprisingly, I didn't have to use my sweat rag to mop my face today. I didn't know whether I was getting used to the heat or if today was actually cooler and less humid. In any case, I was grateful.

☾

One day another long term volunteer casually asked, "Hey, Mary — Have you had scabies yet?"

"nooooooo……" I replied cautiously.

"Ugh! I've had scabies (mites) three times. My blood is very sweet."

I shuddered. "I have psychological scabies. Every time I hear people talk about them; I itch EVERYWHERE!"

(Just writing this made me feel extremely itchy.)

☾

191

Most of the women of Kalighat were feeling good this morning. It was surprising then to see Darpana sleeping at the table. When it was time for lunch, we realized that she was ill, rather than just tired. It was always disconcerting when one our "well" women was suddenly among the sick. I hoped that she would feel better the next day.

I had brunch at Flurys on my way home and it was amazing! I had delicious eggs Benedict, my favorite brunch treat, along with cereal and fruit. I walked home slowly, just savoring the day!

☾

I loved the laughter at Kalighat. It brought me the greatest joy in the midst of busy days. I have always understood the importance of humor, even in the most difficult situations. Today's biggest laughs came at bedtime. I was leaving the bathroom with a resident I had cleaned up and was putting to bed. As I turned the corner, I heard lots of shouting in my direction — "Careful, look out, stop! She's making...." And what was she making? Well, aside from a giant mess, she was making caca from halfway through the sleeping area to the bathroom. The woman who was "making" had quite a blissful look on her face; she was likely the ONLY one who was happy with the situation. The rest of us were laughing so hard. As I moved on to put several other women in bed, I heard more commotion in the area where the incident had taken place. I went over and there was lots of excited chatter. Sister explained to me that in the process of cleaning up the floor, someone had grabbed a mop to use. Sister didn't like the fact that there was so much "dust" on the mop, and she pulled it off with a twisting motion only to discover that it was ALIVE. I heard all kinds of possibilities — a lizard, a scorpion (definitely NOT), and (most likely) a caterpillar of some kind. It became like a fish story; the critter grew exponentially as the story went on.

For our morning shift, there were about ten sisters present whom we'd never seen before. We learned that they were in Kolkata for formation study and work. It was nice to talk and get to know them a bit. They would serve with us all week.

Anjali continued asking us to call her Rathi. Apparently, when she arrived at Kalighat her name was given as Anjali but now she answered to both. Quite a mystery. Perhaps she remembered more of her life, or it was possible that she had taken on the name of someone else she knew. At least half of my conversations with her were in English, which was such a delightful surprise.

I realized that I had exactly a month and a half left in Kolkata. If this experience was a bell curve, I'd have been on the downhill side. The first six weeks were all about getting used to the country and city and, of course, to volunteering at Kalighat. The middle twelve weeks were all about moving from inexperience to "flow," and coming to love the women more and more deeply. I could see that I was now starting to step back slowly from my Kolkata life and experience to think once again about my life back in North Carolina. I'd been spending time each day thinking about what I'd learned.

☾

I was talking with my mom and she asked me how many female residents we had at Kalighat, since I didn't share stories about all of them. Typically, there were about 48, but there had been times when we'd added mattresses on the floor and other times when not all beds were full. Changing numbers had to do with who came or was brought in, who had been sent to a more appropriate residence, who had been discharged, and the women who had died. Speaking about women moving to new residential homes, I learned from a social worker that Diya, Bhavna, and two newer women, would be leaving later in the week for a care facility in another state. Diya was the first woman who caught my attention at Kalighat. She was the one who reminded me about "security blankets" in different forms. Hers were a bed pan and a water bottle. She couldn't use the bed pan and sometimes couldn't open the water on her own, but she needed them beside her bed to go to sleep and I totally got it. I would be so sad not to see her again, but the move would be good for her. Only rarely were there consistent caretakers who spoke Hindi, so often it wasn't totally clear what Diya wanted and needed. I loved putting her to bed. She would often grab my chin and give me a big kiss that kept me going all afternoon.

Bhavna was one of the women I was planning to talk about, in response to my mom's question. She had big cognitive and physical challenges. She spent most of her time with her knees tucked into her chest, bobbing her head up and down. But she quieted down when you talked to her or stroked her hair. Although it was often difficult to discern how aware she was of what was happening around her, she was excited each time I put on her bib for mealtime.

Anushka was another interesting woman. She sat with her legs under her, and with her round belly she looked like a happy Buddha. Her eyes were generally closed, and I assumed she was completely blind. She could make a scene like nobody's business, usually when she didn't get her own way. Today her bib was put on, but lunch didn't come fast enough to suit her, so she started banging on the table. I'd seen her throw her food on the floor when she didn't like it, which is why she was often fed by others. The funniest thing about Anushka was that she could get naked in the blink of an eye. She did NOT like a wet gown (who would) OR any gown with a hole in the wrong place or side slits. I changed her wet gown last week and turned my back on her for a minute to help someone else. When I turned back around, she was naked again, because she had found a tiny hole in her gown that she did not like. I had to get and inspect a new gown before putting it on her.

Indira loved to be on the floor and she often hung out there for most of the morning. When you said, "good morning" to her, she responded with "good morning, good morning, good morning!" She had broken her leg, but I don't know how that happened. I thought her plaster cast would slow her down, but it hadn't so far. When I passed by, she always held her hand out, and whenever I could, I stopped and sat with her. She often recited "abim, abim, abim" over and over. As far as anyone knew, it didn't mean anything. Sometimes I sat and recited it with her, and she liked that very much.

I was VERY tired all morning, and every time one of the women yawned it set off my yawning as well, which cracked them up. I was talking with Anjali/Rathi at bedtime and asked her if she missed her children, thinking of those she taught. She responded that she didn't have any children of her own but that her husband was a Christian "preacher." What are the odds? I was totally stunned.

While getting ready that morning, I had accidentally hit my eye with my mascara wand, but all seemed fine. My eyes gave me no problems until late afternoon when they became red and itchy. By the time I got home, I felt very uncomfortable. I took a nap, hoping my eyes would feel better when I awakened, but there was no change.

☾

When I woke the next morning, up my eyelid was swollen over my eye and the light sensitivity was atrocious. Apparently, I had conjunctivitis (per the doctor at Mercy Hospital across the street), so no volunteering for a few days, as it was highly contagious! I was disappointed but decided to use my time off to begin making lists of things I needed to do when I returned home. I was happy to have something productive to do, as I missed being at Kalighat so much!

☾

A day later I felt infinitely better. When I woke up, my eyes were still red BUT the goo was gone, my eyes were fully OPEN, and there was no pain! I couldn't help but reflect on my emergency room visit. The hospital was about five minutes from my apartment, and I went with a staff member I'd met. It was so quick and easy! I received prescriptions for three medicines that cost less than five dollars total. I couldn't help but worry about family and friends at home who might lose their access to healthcare if the Affordable Care Act was eliminated. The Missionaries of Charity had multiple dispensaries throughout Kolkata where the poor could visit a doctor and receive critical medicine. I hoped that we could find a way to insure all Americans.

I gave away a few more pieces of my heart when I returned to Kalighat. Diya had been told that she was leaving, and when I said that I was going to miss her, she started to sob. Then we were both crying. It was so wonderful to know her, and I was grateful for all that she had taught me.

I learned that morning that Ganika was also leaving. I went and sat on her bed and she knew I was saying something important. She pointed to her ear to remind me that she is deaf — which, of course, I knew very well. I realized not long after she arrived at Kalighat that she couldn't hear me, although we had wonderfully animated discussions. So, I pantomimed — me, my heart, you. You, waving goodbye. Me, crying. She understood! I also said goodbye to Tanvi, who was quite stoic. If she understood that she was leaving Kalighat, she didn't show it. This was a prelude to the next few weeks, as the goodbyes would come quickly. How do you leave a place that is so important to you? I wasn't totally sure, but I was taking it one day at a time....

☾

On Mother's Day, I was surprised to learn that the holiday is celebrated not only in the United States, but in 45 other countries as well, including India. Several times, as I wandered around after volunteering, I witnessed mothers and children together celebrating. I really missed my son and daughter, as well as my mom, and was looking forward to seeing them as soon as I returned home.

I was also reflecting on the life of St. Teresa. It was still a bit hard for me to write it that way, because I believed that MOTHER was the designation that fit most perfectly. Here is an excerpt from *Mother Teresa's Road to Sainthood*, written by Fr. Angelo Scolozzi.

> *Since my first contact with Mother Teresa, I have had no other desire than to follow her footsteps as she followed Jesus. From my infancy, I had been longing to have an idea of the love one would feel in the presence of Mary, the Mother of Jesus. I felt this flow of loving goodness when I first glimpsed Mother Teresa in 1976 at her motherhouse in Calcutta. I was waiting in a small courtyard and saw her approaching between the gray buildings, with her bare feet and white sari with the blue border. She passed through a beam of light, and suddenly I understood; my longing was fulfilled.*

A champion of the poor, Mother Teresa loved children. When she founded the Missionaries of Charity, she conducted classes for children, teaching them hygiene and faith lessons. The children loved Sister Teresa, often bringing others to hear her lessons. Soon, she was paying personal visits to the families of the children; in the slums and huts she saw extreme destitution. She was unable to ignore what she saw. The truth is, we are all like children — needing unconditional love to thrive. Volunteering with the Missionaries of Charity had been illuminating for me. As I learned more and more about St. Teresa, I desired to love others as she loved. Stories and anecdotes that had been shared with me revealed that her love never waned or wavered, even as she experienced her own dark nights of the soul.

☾

I felt better, and since my eyes weren't even red, I believed it was safe to return to Kalighat. Three days of rest and the right medicine had made such a difference! I imagined a world where everyone had affordable access to basic health care! It felt so good to be back at Kalighat. At the same time, I was shocked to learn that Vanya had died. For a few days last week, she wasn't hungry, leaving food on her plate at lunch. Given the increasing heat, I didn't think too much of it though. Apparently, she had declined very rapidly. Vanya had been a great mirror and teacher for me. I never paid much attention to her because of her menacing scowl. Some women weren't as interested in attention and comfort from volunteers as others. On the day I was giving scalp massages with hair oil for the women sitting in her row, and decided to give her one, she had cried and held me in her arms. I'd felt ashamed, as I realized that I had judged her unfairly and had assumed that she was not interested in human contact. After that experience, I'd worked hard to go deeper with the women of Kalighat.

As May marched on relentlessly, every day at Kalighat became increasingly precious to me. One day, in the not too distant future, I was going to have to say "so long for now" to my beautiful women. What I would remember most of all from Kalighat was the laughter. There had been so much of it during my stay. For example, one day Bhakti decided to open her mouth really wide to show me her teeth, so I did the same to her and we laughed and laughed together. Farha (coloring) gave me sweet little smiles when I talked with her and we giggled together at nap time. Karima laughed when she was happy, and she liked to be teased just a little. Upasna had a little laugh that I'd recognize anywhere. I loved to hear it, but she had been tired for a few weeks and hadn't wanted to do much. Several mornings I'd found her on the floor with her breakfast plate. Some women liked to be on the floor, so I never insisted they get up. I plopped myself down next to her to talk.

Maya was very out of sorts. She didn't really want to be up and kept falling asleep on different beds. During meditation, when she was supposed to sit up, she lay down. She didn't want to walk during exercise time, but I asked another volunteer to walk with her and she did about half of the "laps" around the room. She didn't like her lunch and got angry with the sisters and massies. She tried to take other women's food and we couldn't allow her to do that. I put her in bed and asked her if she would take a nap. She said she would, so I sat for a while and stroked her hair. After a few minutes I left to help with another resident. When I turned around, Maya was gone. I heard commotion near the sitting room and saw Prisha gesturing to a wandering Maya and telling her to get back in bed. This happened three more times before the bell rang telling volunteers that our shift was over! As I was leaving, Sister A was laughing — "She sleeps when it is time to be up and gets up when it is time to sleep." Oh, Maya!!

Rathi had been asking on a regular basis if she could pray for me. I always said yes, and she put her hand on my head and started praying in rapid Hindi, always ending with a big AMEN. I received two long prayers this morning; I must have needed some extra help! She informed us that she was not hungry at lunchtime and that she would let someone know if she wanted to eat. What she always DID want was chai, which the women had most afternoons.

☾

Maybe it was the weather, but some of the women of Kalighat were really cranky — and then there were the residents. I spent quite a while chasing after Meera, as she was clearly hot and not having it. She had only been with us for a few days. She was a wanderer and I had chased her all over Kalighat, to keep her from getting lost. She left Kalighat this afternoon for another home but provided much laughter while she was with us. She was very, very tiny and could take off her gown in one second flat, without even having to unbutton it. She liked to be free and naked, and I put her gown on her over and over today. Finally, she fell asleep naked in someone else's bed. Sister said to put a sheet over her and let her be, so I did.

Other women felt exhausted and didn't want to do much and I completely understood. Rathi was in quite a mood for part of the day. She would bless us, pray for us, then bless us out. I have to say this delicately. She was incredibly upset that we would not give her scissors, because she wanted to cut her hair. Not anyplace that you could see her hair, but in a more private area — ahem! It was not a question of misunderstanding; it was perfectly clear. I hoped she would forget about this request in the coming days, but she did not.

It was Sister R's feast day, which is celebrated like a birthday. The massies brought her a bouquet of flowers and made a flower garland for her to wear, we sang to her, had special treats, and even danced a little. I really enjoyed the way her face lit up.

☾

Sadly, Aisha had returned as a resident. For the time being, her children were being cared for at Shishu Bhavan, as her husband was working at Kalighat and couldn't be with them at home. She still helped us out and looked good, but she needed to get stronger. At the very end of the day, I was putting several women in bed, when I heard a major commotion at the other end of the room. I was shocked when I ran in that direction and realized that it was Aisha who was screaming and thrashing around with about five sisters holding her down. She had a meltdown, because she wanted to go home with her husband. It was very unsettling, yet at the same time, her fire and passion to be home with her family gave her the fighting spirit she needed in order to get well again. I talked with her about it on Sunday and told her how much she scared me. She knew it too!

☾

Empathy remained alive and well at Kalighat. The physical therapists were hard at work despite the heat. They had several women busy practicing standing up from a sitting position, using the ladder rungs that were on the wall for that purpose. It was all too much for Barkha. She heard Karima complaining and then Pallavi whimpering. She let everyone know that this was an awful thing, yelling at the therapists, massies, sisters, and anyone else who would listen. She just wanted it to stop.

Aama had an unhappy morning, and she too was on the receiving end of great empathy. She had a paralyzed arm (which she held up on her chest) and leg. The therapist put a brace on her leg and a different contraption on her arm, to help give her greater range of motion (gradually). I wasn't sure that this therapy would help her, but as Ben had often gently reminded me, I'm not that kind of doctor. Still, Aama clearly hurt, as she spent half of the morning crying. Thankfully, the braces were removed after lunch so that she could sleep more comfortably.

All of us had great empathy for Ishita, who had arrived recently. She had breast cancer with multiple external tumors that looked incredibly painful; I'd never seen anything that looked quite like those. Of all the things I'd seen at Kalighat, her tumors affected me the most. I could scarcely look at her without crying. She could barely lift her head, and I didn't think she would be with us for very long.

When Aisha had her meltdown, I was comforting Farha, who was crying and covering her ears, along with Shalini and Aama, who were also crying. The women KNOW what suffering looks and sounds like, and they hate it.

Kavya, with her sweet smile, had "show and tell" with me every day. She had two leg wounds that were frequently "dressed." I got to see her new bandages, blow air kisses, and remark on how much smaller her dressings were — a very good sign. Today she noticed my rash and started counting each red spot. She carefully inspected both arms and legs. She got up to a fairly high number. We were all sharing possible remedies to reduce the itchiness. At first, I didn't know if this was scabies, prickly heat, or something else. What I did know is that on several different nights I'd scratched spot after spot. It was a never-ending story. When I began noticing multiple red, itchy spots between my fingers, and Googled rashes, I was more certain that I was indeed dealing with scabies. The constant itchiness made sleep even more difficult.

☾

When the "feels like" temperature hit 117° F, with nearly 100 % humidity, I thought I'd reached my limit. When I left Kalighat at noon and headed for the metro stop, I had to walk very, very slowly, stopping at various shops along the way. Most of the shopowners were sympathetic, offering me stools to sit on until I was ready to start moving again.

We were all feeling the heat, including the residents of Kalighat. Some women, particularly those who were the most mobile, rested in their beds. Ishita's breathing was even more labored than it had been. Volunteers took turns sitting with her and providing what little comfort they could. After I helped her swallow her morning medicines, I let her rest the back of her head on me. Soon after, I left her to bring other women to meditation time and then to head upstairs for teatime. As I was leaving teatime, after two cups of tea, and two cups of water (got to keep hydrated), another long-term volunteer whispered to me that Ishita had just died. I went downstairs and helped to wrap her body in a white sheet and tie it up. Then several sisters and volunteers moved it to wait for a driver. Of course, any death affected the residents, putting everyone in a solemn mood. One of the younger volunteers confided to me that she had never seen a dead body before, and I reminded her that Ishita was now free of pain and in a better place.

In the afternoon, I went to St. Mary's church to witness the final vows of twenty new sisters. Sister MM had been telling us for weeks that the service would be beautiful and encouraging us to attend. The mass was lovely, but the unairconditioned church was hot, with fans only. My favorite part of the service was listening to the sisters, postulants, and novices sing. Many were in a loft that circled the church, and they sounded like a heavenly choir. The women said parts of their vows together and parts individually. Sister Prema, the current Superior General of the Missionaries of Charity, took written statements of their vows as each sister signed them. The service went on and on and after a while, I felt dizzy every time we had to stand or kneel.

When the two-hour service was finally over, we walked outside and after standing for a few minutes, I felt the need to sit. I called an Uber, and when I went to stand up again, I was very dizzy and passed out. Fortunately, my volunteering friends were there and completely took charge. They got me to my Uber, along with a cold drink and a snack. I was disappointed that I had had so many problems with the heat for much of May. I got home, took a shower, dusted off my rash, and fell into a deep sleep. I knew I just needed to move more slowly.

☾

On my day off, Visakha, Sunaina, and I had planned to go out to Mamagoto's. Brindaban and Sukumar asked us if they could make lunch for us instead. It was a feast with dal, rice, chicken, fried something, chutney, mishti doi (a sweet yogurt dessert), and mango. I was stuffed, but in a glorious way. We were celebrating Visakha's last day of work before she headed to Hyderabad to work on her master's degree in women's studies. I was so proud of her! She had hoped to study at Harvard, but she hadn't yet been able to secure a student visa. I encouraged her to continue trying to get her visa so that she could eventually get her PhD in the United States. I loved my Indian "family."

☾

Fortunately, Friday was relatively cooler, which made bed-cleaning and re-making chores a little easier. I spent most of the morning in the medical/dressing room, holding patients during procedures. My fellow volunteer, who often had this task, was out today, so I stepped in.

Farha had an area on her foot that needed a new dressing. She was crying out in pain, so I gave her a lemon drop (she loves candy). I took her back to the table where she sat, and she said she needed to use the toilet. I then put her back in her plastic chair and turned around to head in a different direction. The legs of our plastic chairs can be very flimsy, and as we moved, one leg totally collapsed. In an instant, both of us were on the floor. I was scraped up but only worried about her. She was crying, but otherwise okay. I kept loving on her and telling her that I was so sorry until she stopped crying a few minutes later. I figured that she wouldn't want me to take her anywhere else, but she insisted that I put her to bed and gave me multiple kisses before I left. I am just grateful she was not hurt. I remember falling on ice with Jordan and on cobblestones with Jenna, and I learned that our instinct is to protect the other. I knew that I would love on Farha even more the next day. Something similar had happened to Sister A the week before. She was in the bathroom helping one of our women when the chair collapsed. She called for help, but no one heard her. Finally, I heard her and ran to the bathroom to help her out. I was concerned that someday one of our women would be hurt unintentionally by a fall from a collapsing chair.

☾

What a delightful day at Kalighat! Most of our women were in great spirits, although there was always someone who was unhappy. Time seemed to fly as we got teeth brushed, served thick (yummy) mango juice as a snack, cut nails, and gave massages. Sister A was concerned because the arrival of hot, hot weather meant that residents didn't want to do much, if anything. So, while this stifling weather continued, all of us were asked to take a more active role in helping with exercise and physical therapy. Kavya and I worked with pulleys; I was the resistance. Banhi was less willing to play, but Sister A cajoled her a bit and she exercised in spurts. Rathi had many memory lapses, but it allowed her to greet me for the day over and over. She did a lot of praying today, but she was frustrated with me after lunch because I was sweaty. Before she prayed for me, she insisted that I dry myself off, as she did not want to touch my wet arms and face. She really likes to be DRY. There was enough time during the morning for several of us to sit and chat with residents. We were often too busy to do this, so I really enjoyed this opportunity. Some days there just wasn't time to rest, even for a few minutes.

At lunchtime, my young friend Celina introduced me to a new restaurant — A Step Up. The food was delicious, and the conversation rich!! The depth of her compassion really resonated with me. I wasn't nearly as mature in my early twenties....

The toughest part of my day was saying goodbye to Sister MM, the volunteer coordinator. She was headed to the United States to visit family and secure her Indian visa renewal. She was not scheduled to return to India until several weeks after I left for home. I worked at registration for her every Monday, Wednesday, and Friday. I greatly admired her and felt blessed to have had the opportunity to make her work a little bit easier...

☾

On my day off, my thoughts turned to the practical realities of life. I began making long lists of things I needed to do when I got home. I now found myself living more in both worlds instead of being thoroughly absorbed in my Indian life. I ordered my lunch from Edesia, a restaurant I liked very much. Cream of chicken soup is very popular in India, and theirs was excellent. I also ordered chicken-mango salad, and it was delicious, but quite unexpectedly spicy. And, as always, fresh lime soda. I'll have to perfect the recipe when I get home.

It rained all afternoon and into the night. I could hear the thunder rolling as I drifted off to sleep. Rain was forecast for the rest of the week and the high temperatures were predicted to be 10-12 degrees cooler than they had been. I was incredibly energetic all day and I realized that we do indeed have limits. I'm not at my best when the "feels like" temperatures top 110°F.

$$\mathbb{C}$$

I spent most of the morning with a new resident, Vaani. She'd arrived a week earlier and appeared to be very sick. Her eyes were bulging out of her face and her skin was very yellow. When I walked into the women's ward, I saw that she had been hooked up to an IV for fluids. She'd told one of the younger volunteers that she had liver issues. I didn't need a medical degree to see that now. She seemed to be in a lot of pain and clearly dehydrated. She asked for water over and over. I didn't know if she would rally or not. I was happy to see some younger volunteers sitting with her, as I knew some of them had been really shaken by Ishita's death last week.

When I came back downstairs after teatime, I immediately went to Vaani's bed to check in. Her breathing was less labored, and her fever was down a bit. I would have remained with her, but the women were having a "no-pep" walking time. With no music or energy, they were walking slowly around the sleeping area. I jumped in and started clapping — clap, clap, clap clap clap, clap clap clap clap — Let's go. The next time around, I changed the cheer to "Chalo" — which coincidentally means "let's go" in Bengali. The women joined me in clapping and one of our newer residents started singing. I'd really enjoyed the small part I'd had in changing something so rote and boring into a fun activity for all!

On the way home, I tried a new restaurant - Hakuna Matata on Park Street. I started with the best pumpkin soup I've ever had, followed by — get this — a barbecued corn burger, and it was actually satisfying. It came with onion rings and French fries. I still had lots of restaurants I wanted to try and so little time to do so.

☾

The next day at Kalighat was a peaceful one and most of our women were very content. I helped in the dressings room for a while. Right now, these were easy dressing changes — just "ouchies" instead of screaming pain. Even Sita, who still watched me warily because of the times I'd had to hold her hands over her head to keep her from biting, barely showed any emotion as her large leg wound was cleaned and re-dressed.

Rathi blew hot and cold all morning. At one point she was angry with everyone and blasted us all with a tirade in Hindi. The problem? She wanted to change her perfectly clean and dry gown. Later she wanted to wash AND dry herself — but refused to go to the bathroom to do so. After she calmed down, which she can do in an instant, she quietly folded her hands and sat still. She asked once if I was Sylvie, another long-term volunteer from France. I told her that Sylvie was not there but would be back in a few days. "Where did she go?" I wasn't sure, but I told Rathi that she was in Agra. Her eyes got really big — "Oh, the Taj Mahal."

In the afternoon, I stopped on Sudder Street to see my old friends at Sunshine, which is a cool shop with mountains of merchandise in a very small space. They invited me to have lunch with them, which I did. I also picked up an orange/pink wall hanging for the woman who loves that color combination more than any other, my daughter Jenna.

I ended the day watching America's Funniest Home Videos with the housekeepers. They always cracked up when watching, which made me laugh extra hard!!

CHAPTER XIV

June

The beginning of June brought simply beautiful, ordinary days. On Wednesday we had two very sick women. Vaani's fever was down but still too high. A new woman was on oxygen, with severe breathing issues. Again, it was great to see our younger volunteers sitting with them. Presence is so important! Everyone else was doing well.

Kavita, one of our physical therapists, asked me to make sure the women walked for a while. Staff members have break at 10:00, and massies take turns going on their breaks. Meditation had been moved to 10:30, during our volunteer break time, so the plan was walking, followed by meditation. It felt a lot like summer camp! Can you believe that the most introverted person in the place had become the leader of exercise time? Anyway — I laughed and joked and clapped and sang and cajoled — and our women kept moving. When they stopped and sat down, other volunteers got them up and moving once again. One of our women loved to sing, and we put her near me, so that I could play off of what she was doing!

☾

On Thursday, I slept in a bit, which was always nice. I took Visakha to Mamagoto for a farewell lunch. We had shrimp tempura, chicken dumplings, a lamb noodle bowl for two, and a side order of beef. There was no way we could finish it all (she got the leftovers). We did need dessert though — of course! Toffee cake with ice cream and caramel topping was a perfect ending! I did a bit of shopping in the afternoon, then, completely exhausted, I went home to rest. The weather had heated up again, making all of us a bit more tired.

☾

On Friday, the heat was back full force and I was soaking wet by midmorning. The only times I enjoy being wet are in the bathtub, jacuzzi, and at the beach, so these days were hard. I planned to donate the clothes I brought with me, as I never wanted to see them again. It felt like no amount of washing could ever get them clean. Bedmaking was the likely reason I felt so overheated (only two more bedmaking Fridays for me). We cleaned in record time! The two women who were sick on Wednesday were still in bad shape. They had to sit up while we were cleaning, but as soon as we were done, one of the sisters asked me to put them back in bed. This was a day full of tasks, rather than resident care, but both were important.

☾

The next morning, I just had to laugh. Many of our women were exercising and involved in physical therapy. Most of them did not like it one bit! There were grunts, groans, and a few screams. Eventually, it was snack time. Because I'd been at Kalighat for so long, I was often tasked with snack preparation. This morning's snacks were mango and watermelon, which we put into bowls and distributed to all our women. Then we received a gift from the upstairs kitchen — a bowl of ice pops — the kind in the long plastic sleeve that you cut the top off of and suck on. They were in various stages of melting from completely frozen to totally liquid. It was easy to see that this was going to be a very sticky mess — and it was! I mean, would you give a large group of pre-school children this same snack? The women seemed to love them, with a few angling for seconds or thirds. Sylvie, who had been a great volunteer partner, was leaving the next day. It was another poignant reminder that my time in India was coming to an end.

☾

Weariness was a general theme among volunteers in early June. I skipped a day of volunteering and was told by the volunteers who had worked that the heat was brutal. The next morning, we learned at breakfast that two sisters had died the day before. One death followed a long cancer battle, and the other was completely unexpected (heart attack). A third sister died this morning. Many of the Kalighat sisters were at the funeral and didn't return until 11:00 am.

Siya died on Saturday evening and I was not surprised. I'd never seen or heard anyone breathe like her before. I'm not even sure I could describe it. It wasn't the death rattle, which had made me shudder when Ben was actively dying. Vaani, on the other hand, was still hanging on. She cracked us up because she told us she was CRAVING chocolate. I told her that I always craved chocolate too and got a big smile. I searched and found a small chocolate candy and gave it to her. She chewed on it for quite a while, then spit it out. For the record, I didn't care much for these mocha-flavored chocolates either. On a more serious note, she kept asking to see her daughter. We weren't sure, but we'd heard that her daughter was living at Prem Dan, another home run by the Missionaries of Charity. I talked about this with Sister A and it sounded to me like a face-to-face reunion might be in the works. I hoped so because I knew it would mean everything to Vaani.

I asked Maya to walk with me, so we went around and around the sleeping area. If she had her way, I would never let go of her hand or get up from my spot next to her on the bed. While I was saying goodbye and giving out nap time hugs and kisses at noon, Maya called me over and I saw that she was tied to her bed again. She had been found wandering around in the men's ward, which was a definite no-no. I told her I could not untie her but that I'd sit and talk for a few minutes. When I asked her if she had been over to the men's ward, she nodded yes and frowned at the same time. Oh, Maya! She would always have a piece of my heart!

☾

I spent the first half-hour of the next morning remaking beds. There had been many "accidents" overnight. I enjoyed making beds, and I sang to myself while I worked. Sometimes they played the strangest music at Kalighat. At one point during the morning it was "My Heart Will Go On" (I was singing bad karaoke to that), hymn medleys, and Bollywood themes.

I'd been trying to spend more time with Shalini. She was teased quite a bit and had a very tender heart. At the end of the morning, however, she was not too happy with me. One of the new volunteers put her in the wrong bed for nap time (one over from her regular bed). She was on Karima's bed and I knew Karima would have a fit when she was wheeled back from the bathroom. I quietly and calmly showed Shalini the beds on her side of the room about ten different times, naming the woman who slept in each one. She yelled every time I reviewed this with her. At one point she used an Austin Powers (Well, Dr. Evil) "zip it" on me, and I broke out laughing. I did it back to her and I saw a tiny smile, but then it was back to the battle of wills. When I left, she was still clinging to Karima's bed.

☾

There were many quiet, lovely days at Kalighat in June. A full census for women at Kalighat is 48, and during my stay we'd had more women than that, with some sleeping on mattresses on the floor. In early June we had only 38 women staying with us. There was no particular reason that the number was down, just a natural ebb and flow. It made our days a little less busy, which gave us more time to spend with individual women.

212

Upasna hadn't been feeling well for the past few days. Overnight, she was put on IV fluids. Sometime during the night, she had to go to the bathroom, so she pulled her IV out of her arm. Once in the bathroom, she tripped and fell, and was now sporting a big bump and bandage on her head, as well as a funky new hairdo, as shaving was required to clean the wound properly. She seemed confused and lost today. Farha had a fever and remained in bed all morning. Her request several times today was for help turning on her side in bed.

☾

The next morning, Vaani was still in bed, although we sat her in a chair for a while to ease pressure on the areas where we could see that bed sores were developing. Today she reminded me of a chipmunk or squirrel. Sister A told her she needed to eat lunch, so several of us sat her up and fed her slowly. She appeared to be chewing and swallowing. Her food looked like rice pudding — rice, milk, and a little mashed banana. When she finally indicated she'd had enough, we stayed to make sure we could make her comfortable in bed. She looked like she wanted to spit out the last bite she'd had, but by the time she was done, I think she'd spit out everything we'd fed her. It was not regurgitated — it was stored somewhere in her mouth or cheeks. Wow....

Maya's wandering continued. Someone was always bringing her back from somewhere. She received an injection at lunch time that knocked her out before I left. I worried about her and I sadly understood that I'd probably never know what happened to the women of Kalighat after I left.

It was Aruna's day to be unhappy with the physical therapists. She too had a hand that remained clenched shut. Today she'd had the contraption on her arm that held her hand in an open position, and she was having none of it. She cried on my shoulder for a long time. She was one of our quieter women and a real sweetheart. Banhi was also in physical therapy, and it was easy to see that she had greater range of motion and that she was allowing some touch, which was a first for her.

I enjoyed "Wake Forest Tuesdays" at Kalighat. Our school colors are black and gold although yellow often substitutes for gold in Wake Forest "gear." And on Tuesdays, the women wore black gowns with big yellow/gold flowers. I smiled every time I descended the stairs to see this beautiful sight! Go Deacs!

I had lunch at Flurys. I loved their mango ice cream and wondered if I would be able to find it anywhere at home. Later in the afternoon I had my hair cut and colored at a salon near my apartment. I used the same stylist who did my hair in March. He was quite an artiste, and he loved making women look and feel beautiful. He was proud of his work and I thought it looked absolutely perfect.

☾

Some days felt like they unfolded in slow motion, like this one. No rushing around, just gentle care. I'd been trying to get more sleep so that I was "all in" for my last two weeks at Kalighat. This morning I helped with medicine distribution, as some of the younger sisters didn't know the names of our residents. I also prepped the morning snack — curd (yogurt) with Rice Krispies mixed in. It was the first day in the last month or so that the morning snack had not been mango or mango juice. We DID have mango for volunteer teatime, which made me a very happy camper! The mangoes available in the US taste NOTHING like the delicious nectar of the gods that I first tasted in Vietnam. I'm sure that I had more than my fair share, since there were a few volunteers who didn't like the fruit. Whaaaaaat?

I was worried about tiny Upasna. Since she'd ripped out her IV a few nights earlier, it had been hard to keep her hydrated. One of the sisters and I tried to feed her lunch today and she ate a tiny amount. I didn't think she weighed more than 60-70 pounds, as I could easily pick her up and put her in bed.

Vaani was about the same. She wasn't comfortable, although we'd tried to help her with whatever she needed. We could see the beginning of bed sores, so Sister was adamant that we move her several times each morning.

As the "walking club" leader at Kalighat, I tried to encourage the women with my silly clapping, commentary, high fives, and dancing. Soon another volunteer would need to step up and do this. Lathika, who loved music, was not quite in the mood to sing as we walked around the sleeping area, but I got her to hum a little. I really LOVED it when residents grabbed the hands of other women and encouraged them to walk too!

I ate at Marco Polo for lunch and had excellent penne pasta with chicken and red sauce. I kept trying to eat at as many restaurants as possible before I left for home.

We finally had a heavy rain during the afternoon, while I was volunteering at registration. We were in an enclosed area and I did not get wet, or should I say wetter than I already was from massive sweating.

☾

While I was in India our world felt a little crazy. Violence could pop up anywhere, even where you'd least expect it. I had been reading Indian newspapers with great interest around the violent protests in Darjeeling during early June. The Chief Minister of West Bengal, Mamata Banerjee, had visited Darjeeling a week earlier, and the Gorkha Janmukti Morcha (GJM) rallied in protest. Harsh words had been thrown back and forth over the last month around compulsory language learning. The GJM was protesting Mamata's recent declaration that Bengali will become compulsory for students up to class 10 in government schools across the state. In Kolkata, some are angry at the very idea of students being required to learn three languages — Bengali, Hindi, and English. The GJM was lobbying for a separate state, to be called Gorkhaland. They were demanding Nepali be taught, possibly with Hindi and English (if necessary). Most people in Darjeeling and other hill towns don't speak Bengali and did not want the language imposed on their children. As the protests became louder and more violent, police tried to contain the protesters. When they could not do so, the army was called in. Tourists reported hearing bombs go off in and around the mall, as countless people ran for cover. Vehicles were burned, some police were injured (one report said up to 52), tear gas was fired, and stones were thrown by thousands of GJM supporters. There had been a mad scramble to get tourists out of the area quickly and safely. More protests and shutdowns were expected to begin soon. Wow — this did not sound like the idyllic spot I'd visited less than two months earlier.

☾

Vaani and Upasna were both still very sick, and it seemed unlikely that either would live much longer. Upasna had a lung infection, and Vaani's condition continued to worsen. I asked other volunteers how much they thought Upasna weighed. They laughed at my estimate of 60-70 pounds and said they thought she weighed 50 pounds or less. They were probably right, because she felt like a feather in my arms.

☾

I woke up on my last Thursday off in Kolkata — to the delightful sound of rain! It lulled me right back to sleep. When I woke up again and looked out my window, I was surprised to see a beautiful blue sky. I asked if it had rained earlier and was told no. Hum…I guess my AC had been making some interesting noises.

I stopped into a "small" store at the end of my street for some "close to last-minute" shopping. Small is in quotes because the store that you could see from the sidewalk was quite tiny. The "action" took place upstairs. I went up, sat down, and told the owner what I was looking for. Soon several assistants started bringing me outfits to look at and approve of or discard. When I was finished with round one of try-ons, I came out of the dressing room, sat back down, ate the biscuits and tea provided, and watched while another woman tried a few things on. Several husbands were in the store and were brought sandwiches and salad. Such a pleasant way to spend part of an afternoon. I'd miss shopping in Kolkata!

☾

Every day remaining at Kalighat was precious to me. Surprisingly, Vaani was doing much better. Not long after I arrived on Friday morning, I was sitting by her bed, and she raised one hand up. I wondered if she was pointing to heaven, but when she started rotating her hand, I laughingly realized that she wanted the fan on. We joked about it now, because one fan was not enough for her. She wanted at least the five or six fans closest to her bed going at once. Earlier in the week there were men cleaning and repairing fans. Vaani was not happy with this because I said she would need to wait a while for cooling relief. I didn't want to set the wrong fan to spinning, as they were not well marked.

Rathi had suddenly taken a turn for the worse. She had appeared fine several weeks ago, but now she lay in bed and would rarely talk. I sat on her bed and recited her life story, which she had shared with me many times, hoping to get some sort of recognition and response from her. "You are a beautiful Hindi lady. You have three brothers: Benjamin, Yousef, and Rubin. Your husband was a pastor and you were a teacher. The first words you ever spoke to me in English were 'God sees everything — He is almighty and powerful.' You are eighty-three years old. You don't like to kiss my forehead when I am sweaty. Do you remember?" She said, without opening her eyes, "I am a teacher." Those were the last words I ever heard her speak.

Tiny Upasna was starting to cough and cough. I hoped that this meant the infection and congestion in her lungs were starting to clear up. Her tiny whimpering cries hurt my heart.

☾

My last two days of volunteering were deeply emotional. I arrived on Monday morning to learn that Rathi had died hours earlier. I loved her so much and knew I would miss her terribly. On Tuesday morning, I got up and walked to the Mother House for breakfast for the last time. The volunteers sing to those who are leaving, and Sister M noted that I'd been there for a long time. After lots of farewell hugs, I headed off to Kalighat. I expected that there would be lots of ugly crying all morning long, but I held it together until I said goodbye. I brought sweets for the residents, and they enjoyed this special treat. I was jolted when I learned that Upasna had died the night before. These losses really made me feel that I had come full circle with the women of Kalighat and that it was time to say goodbye. I saw Vanni, who was being sent to the hospital, as I was arriving in the morning. She looked better than I had seen her for some time (she died in the hospital a few days later). I was so emotional as I ended my volunteering. More pieces of my heart were shattered!

The minute I left Kalighat, I started sobbing. I was going to miss my volunteering friends — I was so proud of all of them. Saying so long was hard, but I hoped we would meet again. I had more friends all over the world now. Time to start the homestay tour! The next day, I would finish packing, run a few errands, read, and write, before leaving for the airport and home on Thursday.

After

CHAPTER XV

Braver, Stronger, Smarter

You are braver than you believe, stronger than you seem, and smarter than you think.

- Christopher Robin to Winnie the Pooh, A.A. Milne

When I shared my plan to live in India for six months and volunteer with the Missionaries of Charity, my family, friends, and colleagues had a variety of responses. Some of them listened, then commented that I most certainly was braver than they would ever be. I smiled and thanked them while thinking to myself that I didn't feel very brave at all. In fact, I was probably more terrified than anything else. Yet I felt called to respond to the voice of God that would not let me rest. Throughout my India life, I was tested and challenged. There were moments so frustrating that I wanted to tear my hair out and times when I would have hopped on the first plane back to the US for the comfort and security of the familiar and beloved. Yet, something always stopped me: the recognition that I was supposed to do this, my love for the women of Kalighat, my desire to serve, and my wish to challenge myself. Instead of looking forward too far, I developed the ability to remain present and focused each day. The longer I lived in India, the more unburdened I felt from that which no longer mattered. I learned that I'm stronger than I imagined. The heat was completely enervating; my bed was hard; my body had bumps, bruises, and bites everywhere, and I itched constantly. When I went shopping and looked at myself in the dressing room mirror, it looked like I had the pox (I did not). Apparently, this is common during May, the hottest month of the year. Despite all of this, I thrived! And I'd come to understand something else. Yes, I may have been brave enough to live on the other side of the world from home, but we are all brave in some ways, whether we believe it or not. A note to all of you:

I have watched you raise kind, creative, intelligent, and loving children despite external circumstances that might suggest that this would be difficult.

I have seen you tend lovingly to friends and family who are ill or in need without resentment.

I have observed your resolute courage as you navigate health and other life challenges without apparent negativity or self-doubt (And honestly, even WITH some self-doubt).

I have admired your ability to leave your place or position to start anew.

I have watched you learn a new language (after a certain age), take up running, painting, or you name it, not concerned about how "good" you will be at first, but always soaking up new knowledge and experiences.

Being brave, for me, means getting up in the morning (whether I feel like it or not), putting one foot in front of the other, and walking. I hope you know that you are brave too — and likely in ways that I am not! Here's to bravery!!

CHAPTER XVI

Everyone has a Story

Everyone has a story to tell. Everyone is a writer. Some stories are written in books and some are confined to hearts...Remember, there is a cost for every story in your life. A cost for making your story better. And it is you who will have to pay for it. So, decide carefully what you want. Which story you want to tell.

—Savi Sharma, author of *Everyone Has A Story and This Is Not Your Story*

I have always loved stories. One of my earliest childhood memories was going to the public library every few weeks or so with my dad to pick out new books to read. There were so many interesting stories that it was hard to choose. During college, I worked each summer at the Free Library of Philadelphia (Haddington Branch). While there, I loved to read to children during story hours. I also earned a teaching certificate in educational media, and during my student teaching, I read *James and the Giant Peach* by Roald Dahl to several classes each week. At various times in my adult life, I have thought about becoming a professional storyteller.

In Kolkata I had the opportunity to listen to countless stories. A favorite volunteer question at teatime was "How did you get here?" — not an airline itinerary, but rather a question of the soul and the answering of a particular call. We learned about the stories of our Kalighat residents more slowly and in a variety of ways — through the sisters and massies, through the efforts of the social workers, through the unfolding of events at Nirmal Hriday, and through the women themselves.

Not so very long ago, before I arrived in India, someone tried to change my story, and I almost let them get away with it because I was in a very thorny place. I eventually woke up and realized that my story is my autobiography; I AM THE AUTHOR! No one can change my story unless I allow them to do so. Kolkata has become a dear part of my life and my continuing story. Everything that happened there has been written on these pages and on my heart. Earlier, I wrote about *Man's Search for Meaning* by Victor Frankl, who was an Austrian neurologist and psychiatrist. Frankl, who was Jewish, was sent to a death camp during WWII. "Even in the degradation and abject misery of a concentration camp, Frankl was able to exercise the most important freedom of all — the freedom to determine one's own attitude and spiritual wellbeing. No sadistic Nazi SS guard was able to take that away from him or control the inner life of Frankl's soul. One of the ways he found the strength to fight to stay alive was to think of his wife. Frankl clearly saw that it was those who had nothing to live for who died quickest in the concentration camp. As Nietzsche said, 'He who has a why for life can put up with any how.'"

Frankl's words have been very important for me throughout my life. Although I have experienced deep sorrow and grief, I choose to make my story one about love, joy, and above all, hope! My attitude is a hymn of praise and gratitude. I'd felt Ben's presence on this journey, and I knew he was proud of me. And for the first time in a while, I was proud of myself too. I came to India broken, and I left whole, although still a work in progress, like all of us! What is your why and your story?

224

CHAPTER XVII

Mother India

India shaped my mind, anchored my identity, influenced my beliefs, and made me who I am. … India matters to me and I would like to matter to India.

—Shashi Tharoor

India is not, as people keep calling it, an underdeveloped country, but rather, in the context of its history and cultural heritage, a highly developed one in an advanced state of decay.

—Shashi Tharoor

There are some parts of the world that, once visited, get into your heart and won't go. For me, India is such a place. When I first visited, I was struck by the richness of the land, by its lush beauty and exotic architecture, by its ability to overload the senses with pure, concentrated intensity of its colors, smells, tastes, and sounds. It was as if all my life I'd been seeing the world in black and white and, when brought face-to-face with India, experienced everything re-rendered in brilliant technicolor.

—Keith Bellows, travel writer

Trying to reflect on India after six months living in Kolkata is about the same as someone trying to describe the US after living a similar amount of time in New York City. Both are unsatisfying because the two countries are incredibly large and complex. So, recognizing this, I know my short reflection is incomplete and perhaps superficial. Nevertheless, it documents my personal experiences of the country. The things that irritated me about India in February, still irritated me when I left in June. At the same time, I hardly heard the incessant beeping of vehicle horns after a while, although it was surely loud and constant. I'd learned better ways to hold on as I rode the buses so that I didn't fall as they bumped along the streets. Drivers will probably always play "chicken" with pedestrians throughout India. I got better at crossing the streets, which helped. I learned to be both more aggressive and more confident. A taxi driver tried to play chicken with me before I left and backed me up toward the curb twice. Aggravating! I gave him a good version of the Indian head waggle. The waggle can mean yes, no, bless your heart, or oh, no you didn't. I might have given this driver the last version, along with a gesture to clarify my feelings.

The trash in India still breaks my heart because it doesn't have to be like that. Every day I saw shopowners cleaning in front of their stores, so I know that change is possible. The government has run a serious ad campaign to encourage cleanliness, but there is not meaningful follow-up. Other street behaviors like public urination and endless spitting can be stopped as well. I have seen Indian men peeing right next to signs saying "Do Not Urinate Here."

On a sillier note, I got used to drinking minuscule cups of tea without chugging, but rather lingering over the hot beverage. And demonetization problems improved as India remonetized. By May, we could get 500-rupee notes from ATMs, which was a relief because no businesses were happy when asked to change 2000-rupee notes for a small purchase.

I still struggle with the relationships between men and women. Most of the men I knew in India were very nice, but guys in "packs" could be very aggressive. Several young volunteers shared stories with me about being groped on the streets. I too was uncomfortable with the sometimes-aggressive male attention on AJC Bose Street in the late afternoon and evening. It didn't matter how old you were, or how young they were, it was just maddening. Every day the papers contain unsavory stories about attacks on women throughout the country. While the government is working hard to change this, it will take a long time. Of course, it would be hypocritical of me to talk about rape and domination culture without noting the serious problem we have in the US. When you work at a college or university, you hear many horrible stories, and the "Me Too" movement has highlighted the universal issues around rape and sexual assault. Note: While writing this book, I saw a new Reuters report about the ten most dangerous countries in the world for women. It didn't surprise me to see that India was at the top of the list, followed by countries that one might expect to be named. What I did not expect was that the United States would come in at number ten. We have a lot of work to do!

If there is one thing that honestly pisses me off about India, it is the unbelievable bureaucracy and perhaps greed that prevails. It shouldn't take three days for your new phone to be set up because two different inspectors must come to your house for "proof of address." It shouldn't take weeks for your mail to be held up in Customs despite your assurances that you are not running an import/export business. For crying out loud, I was waiting for my new debit card. It shouldn't take every employee in a store to look at the imperfection in the cloth to decide whether to give you a discount. When you know your debit card is FINE and there is money in your account, you shouldn't have to listen to five waitstaff members telling you that cash is better. When you say no cash, the card reader is suddenly okay — imagine that! You shouldn't have to fight with a taxi driver over the meter (which is on) and what he would like you to pay. At least once a week I ran into such hassles. At first, they really bothered me, but then I just realized that I needed to get used to it, and I did.

I could tell you that within a mile of my house in Kolkata there were churches and other places of worship. There was an Assembly of God church just steps from my apartment, while a Seventh Day Adventist church and the Bishop of Kolkata's house were two blocks away. There were two mosques on the way to the Mother House, and I passed the Kali Temple (Hindu) on my way to Kalighat every day. If I didn't know better, I might have been tempted to think that there is religious harmony in India, but that would not be the whole story. There is a huge issue throughout the country related to the slaughter of cattle. This doesn't have as much to do with beef, which Muslims sell and eat and Hindus regard as sacred, as it does with religious differences. The government is now trying to ban cattle slaughter, which will ultimately affect cattle farmers. I could say that nothing like this happens in the US, that there is no religious disharmony, but I would be so very wrong. In a developing, related story, there is a crackdown on foreign faith-based NGO's and aid organizations throughout India. Compassion International shut its doors in March 2017 after 48 years in the country. The organization has been accused of engaging in religious conversions, and the government believes this is "detrimental to the national interest." Since Prime Minister Modi took office in 2014, more than 11,000 NGO's have lost their licenses to accept foreign funds. Compassion International works with and through 500 Indian partner organizations that may also have to shut down.

Approximately 194.6 million people are undernourished in India, which accounts for the highest number of people suffering from hunger in any single country in 2015 (1:4 malnourished people in the world live in India). I passed hungry people every day, sitting outside of restaurants or anywhere nearby where they could find even a little shade. I could be outraged by this fact (which I am), but if it would mean nothing if I failed to acknowledge that I live in a beautiful city (Winston-Salem, NC) that not too many years ago was the MSA (Metropolitan Statistical Area) with the greatest food insufficiency for children in the US.

One of my volunteer friends said to me that she thinks people either love India or hate it, with little in between. I've thought about that, and my take is that I love India enough to also acknowledge that there are things I hate about it! It sounds like a Facebook relationship status, but all I can say is, "It's complicated." To say that I will miss India is an understatement!

CHAPTER XVIII

Mother (Saint) Teresa

If you judge people, you have no time to love them.

If we have no peace, it is because we have forgotten that we belong to each other.

I have found the paradox that if I love until it hurts, there is no hurt, but only more love.

If you can't feed 100 people, then just feed 1.

Being unwanted, unloved, uncared for, forgotten by every-body, I think that is a much greater hunger, a much greater poverty, than the person who has nothing to eat.

From the first time I heard about Mother Teresa, sometime in the 1980's, I admired her remarkable work in Calcutta with the poorest of the poor. When Wake Forest conducted its first international service trip to Calcutta (The City of Joy) in 1994-95, I so wanted to be there. When the students returned, I went to every presentation they made, soaking up their stories. My interest grew over the next few years, and I was invited to serve as the faculty advisor for the 1998-99 trip. Although Mother Teresa had died the year before, I still wanted to go, to see, and to serve.

During my six months in India in 2017, I had many opportunities to talk with Missionaries of Charity (MC) sisters in groups and alone. Every story, every anecdote they told me, only confirmed my admiration. Mother Teresa lived her faith. I have always loved the phrase - "Preach the Gospel at all times and if necessary, use words," sometimes attributed to St. Francis. That is how Mother Teresa lived her life. What a legacy she left for us to follow.

I find it both interesting and instructive that Mother Teresa felt disconnected from God. Such times require us to remain faithful and trust, which she did. In *Come Be My Light*, we see a window into her agony over her relationship with God. She suffered a decades-long "dark night of the soul," even while ministering to the poorest of the poor. To me, this makes her more human and reminds me that feeling separated from God and being separated from God are two very different things.

While I was preparing to leave for Kolkata, I read some very negative opinions about Mother Teresa's life and legacy. I did not come to Kolkata to write an exposé, and I didn't give these stories too much credence. That said, I remained watchful and open. One complaint was that Mother Teresa encouraged members of her order to secretly baptize dying patients, whether they were Christians or not. I don't know what had happened in the past, but I can say that, sitting by the bedsides of sick and dying women, I NEVER saw any attempt to baptize or convert. When women died, their own religious practice determined what happened to them and where their physical bodies were taken. Another criticism was built around her relationships with some seedy characters including politicians, an embezzler, and others. Okay, we all know that Jesus hung out at the country club, right? In other words, I heard the complaint, but I didn't give it much credence.

Others say that, because the homes run by the Missionaries of Charity are small, the organization isn't helping that many poor people, using funds for conversion activities instead. The homes ARE fairly small except for Prem Dan, which has approximately 300 residents. I learned that the sisters help many poor families in Kolkata and around the world, in addition to the men, women, and children served in the homes.

Throughout the years there has been criticism of the medical care provided in the homes. I can only say this — for six months I worked alongside the sisters, and I saw conscientious wound care, no reuse of needles (usually taken from sealed packages), blood draws from a local lab, and residents going to the hospital for doctor visits on a regular basis. Sister A, who is responsible for the women's ward at Nirmal Hriday, is a nurse, and she is awesome. Some women were sent to the hospital when their conditions were too serious to be treated at Kalighat, and I watched Sister A give numerous injections. There are physical therapists who work at Kalighat 5-6 days a week, and I saw significant improvement in women who could not move certain muscles or limbs previously. Most women took individualized medicines in the morning and evening, and all of this was charted carefully. Nirmal Hriday was not meant to be the Mayo Clinic. Most of the women served didn't have anywhere else to go or anyone to care for them. Suffering is NOT, I repeat NOT, glorified at Nirmal Hriday.

After nearly six months in India, my admiration for Mother Teresa had grown enormously. What she started has continued and flourished since her death twenty years ago. As Jim Wallis noted in *America's Original Sin: Racism, White Privilege, and the Bridge to a New America*, "How we treat the poorest and most vulnerable, Jesus instructs us in that Gospel passage (Matthew 25), is how we treat him: 'Just as you did it to one of the least of these, you did it to me.'" Mother Teresa said something very similar, again using Matthew 25. "He has told us that he is the hungry one. He is the naked one. He is the thirsty one. Each one is Jesus in his distressing disguise (of the poor)." Many mornings we sang a simple song when we arrived at Kalighat: "Whatsoever you do to the least of my brothers, that you do unto me." Of course, I always wanted to make the language more inclusive, but the message was our mandate to follow.

CHAPTER XIX

The Missionaries of Charity

The Missionaries of Charity are the real deal. I am not Catholic, and serving as a sister is not my calling, but I admired the sisters I knew and worked with frequently. Sure, they had their own quirks, but they lived out their faith and their vows every day. I was so impressed by Sister A's MacGyver-like skills. If what she needed to help a resident wasn't available, she made something else work. When Aisha went home the first time, Sister A said to me, "Look at what your love did." That was a bit heavy for me to take on, and I told her that I thought it was the love we all gave and HER medical skills. She replied to me, "Jesus works through me, it is Him, not me." She was always this humble, and it was no act. On another day, she was very frustrated with one of our residents who was incredibly sick but fighting off our assistance. She said to me, "It is not important that she likes me, what is important is that I allow God's love to flow from me to her." I think of another day when she was doing chest compressions on a resident who was barely breathing. I am a bit ashamed to say that I wondered why she was trying so hard to save this one life. Would it have been more charitable to let her die? Yet that woman was still alive and doing well when I left India. I will think of Sister A for years to come — her smile, her caring spirit, her dedication to the women in our care, and her deep desire to do God's work every day. I appreciated the fact that she always took the time to explain her actions to volunteers.

There were many other sisters at Kalighat, and I was in awe of each one of them. We had young women working alongside us who had not yet taken their vows, but who were being trained daily. I regret that I did not get to know all their stories to discover what led them to the Missionaries of Charity. I am also indebted to Sister MM (American) and Sister M (Korean) for allowing me to work beside them at registration and orientation for new volunteers. They never wasted ANYTHING — not one thing. I finally had to start bringing my notebook to registration to write down anything I needed to tell them. White-out lives!! Also, they had been using the same notebook to write down the names and end dates for volunteers in each home for months or even years. With the constant erasing as volunteers left, the paper was sure to crumble eventually. I teased other volunteers saying that I couldn't imagine what would happen then. On a side note: There was a series of very large "official" books with the names, passport numbers, and countries of all volunteers in chronological order. I loved the way that Sister MM took the time to meet and greet each new volunteer. When it was decided where they would serve, she thanked them in their own language. During the time I worked at registration, we had three Vietnamese volunteers and she was delighted to learn from me how to properly thank them. That may have been the only language she did not know! I took with me the primer that the sisters provided to me during my tenure here — kindness, faith, frugality, and LOVE!!

CHAPTER XX

Love Letters to the Women of Kalighat

I can say without hesitation that the hardest part of saying goodbye to India was leaving the beautiful women of Kalighat. They were my teachers and mentors throughout my stay in India. Here's what I'd like each of them to know.

Tanvi — I really missed spending time with you after you were sent to a different home. For months, you were my emotional barometer, projecting the day's mood. Most days the first thing I saw when I came down the stairs was your sweet smile. But oh, my goodness, on other days I knew we might be in for trouble. I loved talking with you, in part because you couldn't hear a word I said, and I couldn't understand a word you said, but we always got our points across. You thought that your daily medicine might be poison, so you finally stopped taking it. You were always so feisty!

Diya — You were my first "family member" at Kalighat. It must have been frustrating to have so many caretakers who could not speak or understand your language (Hindi). We did a good job of learning about each other, though! I know that others wondered why you needed your water bottle and bedpan next to you when you were resting, but I quickly learned from you that they were more "comfort" items than anything else. I loved our laughing sessions over crazy things that happened at Kalighat and your awesome forehead smacks just because... I hurt with and for you the day that you were sent to a different home (with more Hindi speakers). I miss you, Diya.

Farha — You will always be Mary Poppins to me. Every time I saw your impish grin, I thought to myself that you must have been the best "real life" nanny EVER. How difficult it must have been for you after your fall down the stairs that resulted in such serious injuries? I love that you love sweets, and I imagine you sneaking them to the children you looked after. I will miss the kisses we blew to each other every day, but I will always remember the day when the chair I was pushing you on collapsed, sending us both to the floor. I didn't care about myself, but I was undone and afraid that you were hurt. I would have understood if you didn't want to be around me for a few days, but you insisted that I be the one to put you in bed and blew me the sweetest kisses of all that day.

Kavya — I could never have enough of your bright, beautiful eyes. When you came to Kalighat, you had several leg wounds. On days when your dressings were changed, I could see that you were nervous. Afterward you would show me your bandages, and I would kiss your boo-boos. We laughed about that. You also gave the best chin squishes with air kisses I've ever received.

Banhi — We were not close, but you taught me some valuable lessons. By observing you as I got to know the women of Kalighat, I realized that you don't like to be touched. When we first me, you reminded me of a turtle — you were sitting on a chair with your legs tucked under you and the back of your gown over your head. I learned to speak to you first to let you know I was near and then to move very slowly. You really challenged my assumption that we all both need and want human touch. It was great to see your physical therapy sessions with other volunteers!

Ananya and Pari — You left Kalighat not too long after I arrived. You two were my go-to's when I needed help and direction during those first weeks of volunteering. You taught me how to fold gauze bandages to your very exacting standards, and I did get the hang of it. Ananya — I saw the ones you snuck out of the pile to "re-do." I'm so glad that you were each feeling well enough to leave our care. I hope that you have finished your recoveries and are doing well now.

Bhakti — I didn't pay much attention to you when I first arrived at Kalighat because you always seemed to be sleeping/resting. One day after lunch I was putting you in bed with another volunteer, and somehow, we got tangled up. You ended up having a very hard landing, which made you so mad that you pulled my hair — HARD! I had to walk away because I could feel myself tearing up. When I came back a few minutes later to tell you I was sorry, you gave me a kiss and let me know all was well. When you were sick, I mashed bananas in my hands and fed you, despite how uncomfortable that made me (Mashed bananas are even worse than whole bananas). I miss your smiles every day!

Bhavna — It was usually hard to know what you see and hear. I do know that you love to have your hair stroked and knew it was time to eat when I put on your bib. I loved the way that you stop rocking when someone touched you gently.

Aama — The first time I saw you, I was stunned by your incredibly regal posture and the shawl wrapped around you just so. I quickly learned what you wanted and needed. Most of all, you loved to have your arm and leg scratched HARD. Not sweetly, but HARD. When I scratched you, I absolutely loved watching your face for the nods that let me know you were satisfied. Although I know it hurt, I was very proud of you for working so hard at physical therapy. After I'd been at Kalighat for a few months, I began to see your personality more deeply. I really appreciated your nods that acknowledged your understanding when I was taking care of other women and couldn't get back to you immediately. Most of all, I loved your laughter and your growing friendship with Lasya. When the two of you sat together and talked, it made me so happy.

Geetha — You were the most critically ill woman when I arrived at Kalighat. I couldn't have imagined then that you would stay with us until the week after Easter. You made me think a lot about the limits of care. When we pushed you to eat or to sit up, you would say in your small voice, "I'm a dying woman and I don't want to eat/do that." I was reminded of visiting my dad a week and a half before he died. I went with him to his scheduled physical therapy, and when the therapist left to take care of other business, I asked dad if he wanted to stay. He said no and, feeling that the end was near, I agreed with him and told the therapist that he was not going to continue. I refused to force food down your throat and checked on you often. I am glad that you are now free of pain; watching your face when you were hurting was difficult.

Ekta — You were with us such a short time, but you made quite an impression on me. The truth is that sometimes you'd open your eyes, but even then, I don't know if you were completely aware of our presence. Know that I saw you and cared about you!

Prisha — Whether you were here the first time I volunteered or not, I feel like I've known you for a long time. You are truly the "big boss" of Kalighat. I enjoyed watching you interact with other residents; you were certainly not afraid to be in someone's face if they were not "towing the line." I also appreciated the way you folded gauze bandages every day and read the newspaper. I think about you often.

Anushka — When you sat in your chair at Kalighat, you looked like a big, round Buddha (smiling). It was a bit hard to know what you saw and understood, but you had so many ways of letting us know when you did or didn't want something. When you were very impatient for lunch and your bib was already on, but we were slow in delivering your food, you would start pounding on the table. We ALL got the message. When your gown was wet or you were tired of it, you could get it off in seconds flat. I once made the mistake of bringing you a new gown with a hole in it. I didn't see the hole, but you FELT it and that was enough. Bye-bye to that dress and on with yet another new one!

Vanya — I was gutted when I learned that you had died while I was in Darjeeling. I ignored you for most of my first two months in Kolkata. Eventually, you held a mirror up to my face and made me realize that I had not been offering unconditional love. If I could have put a picture next to "unlovable" in the dictionary, that picture would have been of you. Your face was perpetually locked in a scowl, and you didn't seem to want any human contact. The day when I was rubbing oil into your scalp and massaging your head, and you pulled me into a big hug while sobbing, changed me. I felt called out and that was a tremendous gift from you. I began to rethink what unconditional love from the depths of my heart would look like. I miss you and think of you often....

Ruchika — For the entire week after you arrived at Kalighat, I know I stared at you a lot. I didn't know what to make of a woman who could down a complete meal in three bites and who refused to sleep on a bed, choosing the floor instead. When you didn't like the meal you were served, you'd throw it on the floor. I later learned that you had parasites and realized that you always FELT like you were starving. I will always remember the day that I came to say good night to you, and you said, "I saw you. I saw you walking. I want to walk again." I told you that it would take time and you'd have to work hard — and you did. I also loved the day when you spelled your entire name for me, as if to say, "Here I am, see me!!" I did see you and hated to see you leave Kalighat for another home.

Karima — Also known to me as "Princess Karima." I think that I didn't pay much attention to you when I got to Kalighat. I honestly didn't know how much you absorbed what was happening around you. Duh, for me. The reality is that you are funny, see EVERYTHING, and are very clear about your needs and wants. Keep on exercising, although I know you don't like it. Remember that you are strong and beautiful!

Shivani — You left early on, and it was hard to see you go. I think it was a good choice to send you to a place where you hopefully have more women to talk with. Talking is one of your favorite things, and I loved it when you would pat your bed several times and say, "Oh, Auntie, oh, Auntie," which was the cue to sit down with you for a while and just talk. Your compassion for other women who were hurting was a wonderful thing to see.

Adra — I will forever miss your luminous face and the joy you felt when one of the social workers brought you a book of native costumes and you saw YOUR OWN. It was hard to see you go, but I hope that you are enjoying the place where you have been staying and that you are getting closer to finding your family.

Darpana — Your baleful resting face made me think that you wanted nothing to do with Kalighat, but that changed when Maya came for the first time. When she came to us, she could not eat even a small amount of food without throwing up. For some reason, it seemed like all the new and very sick residents ended up in the bed next to yours. You were watching Sister A work on Maya, and you said to me, "How will she get well if she doesn't eat?" I was stunned to realize that you are quite fluent in English, as demonstrated by our subsequent talks. I hope that you are happy in your new home where there are (hopefully) more women with whom you can have interesting conversations.

Upasna — You were my little "wood sprite," just like a Shakespearean character. Every time you coughed or sneezed, I worried about the effect on your teeny, tiny body. I will forever remember and smile at the little self-soothing noises you made so often. Now you are in Heaven, and I imagine you with gossamer wings.

Lasya — You are the winner of the Kalighat "Good Samaritan" award. You ALWAYS looked out for others and seldom asked for anything for yourself. You made sure your neighbors had blankets, water, back rubs, or whatever else was needed. I so loved the day when you called to me and rested your head on my shoulder for the longest time. It meant SO much to me to be able to be there for you!

Parul — I miss you so much! It took a while for you to finally greet me, but I loved the day when you started reaching for my hand when I passed by. I'm not sure how old you are (I was told late 80's to mid-90's), but you have a grip that anyone would be proud of. And that arm of yours is like a heat-seeking missile, especially when it is hunting for food. You enjoyed biting my finger, but only when you thought (hoped) that it was actually FOOD. You would scrunch up your nose as if to say that this food tastes lousy. Do you remember the day that you pulled my hair and then proceeded to eat it? Kavita had to pull me away, and it's a good thing that she did, or you might have eaten a much bigger chunk. I loved feeding you and putting you to bed. You ate more than I do every single day!!

Deepika — The first day that I walked into the women's ward at Kalighat you shocked me. I saw you, but I also saw Ben in your eyes. Seriously, there was something about you that let me know that he was there with me. Your eyes were SO similar — big and brown. It broke my heart that most of our conversations were about your desperate longing to go home. When I talked with the social workers and learned that you didn't have a home to go to, I was beyond sad. The social workers continued to tell you that they were looking so that you didn't give up hope. I was shocked on the Friday morning I came in and realized that you were not there. I was happy to learn that your neighbors came and said that they would care for you, but beyond disappointed that I could not say goodbye to you. It was then when I realized that many pieces (chunks) of my heart were going to be left in India.

Zoya — You weren't with us for very long, but I loved your spirit and your smile. I also loved your ankle bracelets that you refused to take off (they were welded together and would have to be destroyed in order to be removed) because they were a gift from your late husband.

Jayanti — I missed you from the day that you left Kalighat for a more age-appropriate setting. I'm not sure exactly what happened to you, but given that it involved a group of young men, I have a pretty good idea. I was stunned the day you hit me, but I realized that you were very angry (at the world), and that you were afraid to have people get too close to you. I knew you needed a mama, and I was happy to play that role for you when you needed it. I know it was frustrating to the social workers when they couldn't find the addresses that you gave them for "home." I hope that someday, if you have a mom, the two of you can be reunited. We knew you needed more stimulation the week that you kept trying to escape. Fortunately, one of the massies chased you down the street and caught you on one of those days... You were the first "wanderer" while I was at Kalighat.

Maya — I miss you so much. To remember you, I close my eyes and do my best impressions of my favorite looks of yours. We had such an interesting history together. The first time you came to Kalighat, no one expected you to live for very long. You couldn't keep even the tiniest bit of food down. Sister A gave you an IV drip to help re-hydrate your system. But stubborn you — you pulled it out, so sister tied your arms down. She put the IV back in and left. Oh yes, oh no — if you couldn't pull it out, you could KICK it out with one of your feet. Oh, Maya! You ended up going to the hospital, and when you returned to us, you wanted to eat EVERYTHING. Even on my last two days, the first thing you asked me about in the morning was when snacks would be served. I loved the way that you answered all my questions. My guess is that you know some English, even if you won't speak it! Don't wander too far and make the volunteers chase you over in the men's ward. Promise?

Anjali/Rathi — How many times did you tell me that you were very old (83) and very tired/weary and that you wanted to sleep in your own (dry) bed? Even so, I never thought that you would leave Kalighat before me. I was stunned when you died just days after catching pneumonia. I think often of the day that changed everything for us. I accidentally spilled water on you and you started off on a massive temper tantrum/rant. It was so bad that I had to walk away and recover a bit. When I came back and said I was sorry, you said, "God sees everything. He is almighty and powerful." WHAT? I was stunned. That was the beginning of our many conversations

244

in English. I learned about your brothers: Benjamin, Yousef, and Reuben. I learned that your husband was a pastor, and that you were a teacher. The two of you never had any children. When you called me your dear daughter and told me that you loved me very, very much, I was moved beyond words. Of course, you did note that you also loved Sylvie, and apparently, from what we gathered, thought we were sisters (despite our thirty-year age difference), although you did call me the elder and her the younger. You loved to pray for Kalighat volunteers, and it amazed me to watch you put your hand on their heads and then start praying and praying in Hindi, followed by a big AMEN. I had to laugh over your refusal to bless me in May when it was so hot, and I was sweaty — until I wiped my forehead off. Once I did, all was well again. Some days you would tell me that they didn't feed you at Kalighat, so I got into the habit of reminding you each day before I left what you'd had for lunch. Some days you were incredulous — "Really, I ate that?" "Yes, really!" When you died the day before I left Kalighat, I knew that my time there was finished. I think about you every day with tears in my eyes. I love you still and always.

Aisha — You are a walking miracle. You were brought to Kalighat by the MC Brothers basically to have a comfortable place to die. Your family was planning your funeral. I had never seen anyone as "sunken" as you were then. You reminded me of those horrible pictures of people caught in famines and starving to death. I now know for sure what "skin and bones" looks like, and it's not pretty. You cried/screamed for a solid week, upsetting most of the Kalighat residents. The first time I sat with you in the dressings room, I was blown away by your bed sores that were so deep, I could see muscle and bone. I didn't know how one survived that. I also realized that the sisters had to clean them daily and cut away all the dead skin. I'm sure it hurt like crazy, but their diligent care kept you alive. Your screams as they did this kept everyone else awake — and sad. I'll never forget the days the phlebotomist came to take your blood; there was NO WAY that he could find a vein that was big enough or that had enough blood to draw. Eventually Sister A was able to find a small vein that worked. Everything changed the day that your husband and children came to visit. After they left, you were crying and crying, and we assumed that you just wanted to go home with them. Instead, you shared that you felt guilty eating well at Kalighat while they had little or no food. That day we realized that you really did want to get stronger to go home to your husband and babies (girl age 5 and boy age 2). Eventually, sister sent you to the hospital for a blood transfusion. You WALKED back into Kalighat a few days later to love and applause. We were all thrilled when you got to go home, and disappointed for you when you had to return to Kalighat. I'm so glad that you are back at home, but now you need to decide how to live your life. This is a critical crossroad, and my thoughts and prayers are always with you. You taught me more than I could ever tell you, and I am so very grateful.

To the women not mentioned in these pages — I love you too. Some of you I did not get to spend as much time with, and others of you were relatively new to Kalighat when I left. Each one of you is a magnificent human. I once described you as beautiful souls with difficult back stories. And isn't that what we all are?

CHAPTER XXI

What about Short-Term International Service?

I was very involved in short term international service experiences for college students for many years. Such programs can provide great opportunities for students to challenge their assumptions, help others, and learn about new cultures. Yet, critics wonder if the community impact is significant enough to truly make a difference. They further question whether communities may be inadvertently harmed by such programs. In part, volunteering with the Missionaries of Charity is a different animal. The organization welcomes and relies on international volunteers, but it is difficult to assess the impact of one individual or group on the overall population. That said, individual volunteers often experience incredible personal transformation that manifests through various service organizations and activities. So, do I still believe that short-term service is valuable for both participants and those served? My response is a conditional yes.

First, I must again discuss what I call drive-by compassion. I was very frustrated with groups touring Kalighat, especially those who looked with pity on the beautiful women in our care. As it turns out, there is a variation of that makes me CRAZY. One day a group of American tourists, primarily young women, came through as we were putting women in bed. One woman in the group went to sit with a resident, patting her on the back and looking at her lovingly. What that woman did not see was the woman whose back she was patting gently rolling her eyes at me. Our resident understood more than this young woman did how meaningless this gesture really was. Another young woman in the same group was tightly holding on to a woman who was walking to her bed. We were busy and let it go, but what I wanted to say to her was, "What you are doing is NOT helping. She does not like to walk, but she needs to do so in order to exercise her muscles." Ugh — I just wonder how these visitors discuss what they saw on their social media sites. Thankfully, they are not allowed to take photographs inside! For a snarky, spot-on commentary about humanitarian aid, I highly recommend the brilliant site barbiesavior.com (and Instagram).

I worked with many short-term (a month or less) volunteers at Kalighat. I think that most of them had positive experiences AND made contributions to life at Nirmal Hriday. However, I don't know how their service affected them after they returned home. Did they become more altruistic, compassionate, and/or kind? Did they decide to continue volunteering, or were they happy to have interesting stories to tell their friends? How did they compare their travel versus their volunteering?

For me, everything changed after two months. I wanted — NEEDED — to know the names of every woman in my care. I realized that I loved each one of them. I began to have fun with them, and we started to laugh together. We had conversations. We got mad at each other but could also say we were sorry. These women weren't stereotypes, losers of the caste system, or humans unworthy of attention from the greater society. They were part of my India family — and I was part of theirs. I realized that the sisters, massies, and women grew to trust me. But trust takes time and attention.

So, back to short-term volunteering. I think it still has value, but it needs to be properly structured, with appropriate preparation, community input, and critical reflection. I do know that the longer I volunteered at Kalighat, the more I learned about the back channels of support provided by the social workers and local hospitals. I also learned why the sisters do certain things, which can sometimes seem confusing to volunteers. When I wanted to know more about residents, I knew who to ask.

It is clear to me that language can make a real difference. While I always worked hard to understand what residents wanted or needed from me, I know that better command of Bengali would have increased my effectiveness. So, I'll keep on studying the language until I go back again.

CHAPTER XXII

Reentry

Reentry has been full of expected and unexpected challenges. I've come home from various parts of the world many times, but usually after just a few weeks away. Here are some of the things that have truly surprised me since my return from India.

Make no mistake — 117° F ("feels like," with high humidity) is a lot hotter than 85 or 90 degrees here in NC. I am slowly beginning to feel appropriately hot in Winston-Salem. For the first week I was home, I slept with the air conditioning off and wrapped in a blanket, and I was cold as could be.

I'm stunned at the prices of everything in the supermarket! I had a salad at dinner one night, and it was $18. My first "sticker shock" came at Sam's Club a few days after I returned. My cart wasn't even full, but I spent over $400. I just about fainted. After living on less than $100/week, this was tough to swallow. When I think of friends in Kolkata who were lucky to be making just over $100/month, I cringe at the difference.

By the time I left India, I was "done" with Indian bureaucracy, so I had to laugh when I ran into similar problems at home. I had multiple issues with my debit card not being accepted when I was trying to buy things. When Wells Fargo had to send me a new card due to a VISA data breach, they changed my permanent address to 7 Rawdon Court in Kolkata. So, when I used my home address in North Carolina, my addresses didn't "match." When I tried to make the final payment on a beach house rental for a family vacation, my card was declined. The sales representative and I tried to run the card four times. I told her I would call the bank, see what was going on, and get back to her the next day. Before I could call Wells Fargo, they called me to alert me to possible fraud associated with my card. Turns out that those four declined payments all went through. It is now fixed, but what the heck? My Harris-Teeter VIP account was closed due to inactivity, along with my CVS customer card. I went to pick up prescriptions at Walgreens, and there were issues with my account. Turns out that there is a lot of bureaucracy here too!

When I was in India, I had beautiful dreams about the foods I missed the most. BEEF, BEEF, BEEF, salad, salad, salad. It took a long time after I returned home for American food to taste right. Nothing I ate was as good as it tasted in my mind. So, not long after I returned home, I went off to my favorite Indian restaurant near home, and it was just right! It took me a few months, but I did make the adjustment back to eating and enjoying the food I have eaten all my life. I also will cook more Indian food when I have the chance. The best of both worlds…

CHAPTER XXIII

Love

All you need is love...

- The Beatles

We can do no great things. We can only do small things with great love.

-Mother Teresa, the Saint of Calcutta

From the day I returned home, I've missed my Kolkata life. At the same time, I'm happy to be home. I'm still adjusting, particularly with food. Things I've loved all my life just don't taste the same. I keep thinking that my Kolkata friends would be in shock at the orderly way in which we drive in America and at the quiet of my neighborhood.

When I was preparing to leave for Kolkata, several of my friends teased me, saying that perhaps this would be my own Eat, Pray, Love experience. I laughed along, of course, but never expected that to happen for so many reasons. Another wise friend and spiritual mentor told me that I needed to spend some time in India learning to love myself again. I chaffed at the comment, but now realize just how right she was.

The truth — My India experience was indeed all about love, just not in the way that my friends were suggesting. I relearned how to love myself, give myself grace and compassion for my shortcomings, and to celebrate my strengths, even through vulnerability. It was hard to admit on those scorching hot days in May, that the heat nearly flattened me. But everyone

I reached out to helped me. Even on the day that I passed out on the sidewalk, volunteer friends were right there caring for me.

I finally understand what Mother Teresa meant when she said "We can do no great things. We can only do small things with great love." I am someone who has always longed to do the "big thing," whatever that might be. I knew that my service in India wouldn't change the world, but I also know that I made the most of it. The highest compliments I have ever received came from fellow volunteers and from sisters — "You love so well, and I would love to have your compassion." I came to India, far from home, and worked hard to understand the culture. I came to Kalighat both eager and afraid that I might not be able to form bonds with the women or that the work might be too hard. As it turned out, the work was joyful. I realized that Kalighat is so much more than a place for the "dying destitute." It is a home that is very much alive with love and laughter. So many pieces of my heart remain in India, with the beautiful women I had the opportunity to serve. I went broken in spirit (and body too) and returned home whole. I went exhausted and came back energized. I went hoping to create a bridge from my career to my retirement. If I'm being honest, I must confess that I've never thought or said, "Gee, I wish I were back at work. I've worked some in the Gig economy and on projects that feed my soul, in addition to caring for my grandson during the week. Even though my service in India is like a drop in the big ocean of need, I believe I left a mark on the people I met. Oh, India – I will never forget you.

Epilogue

May 2020

As I write this epilogue, it is three years since I volunteered in Kolkata. Sometimes it seems like years and years ago, but at other times it feels like yesterday. I've acclimated back to American life, but India is never far from my mind. If I close my eyes, I can travel back to Nirmal Hriday and see the faces of those I loved. I miss them terribly. Yet, my longing for them reminds me that wherever I am, I need to be present in that place. If I pine for India while here, and think endlessly about home when I am away, I'm cheating myself out of the beautiful now. Sadly, in the midst of the coronavirus, all of the homes were closed to volunteers and visitors. There is a private volunteer Facebook page, so I can check in with friends to learn more about what is happening there.

In India, I challenged myself physically, mentally, spiritually, and emotionally. After volunteering at Nirmal Hriday for a while, I began to realize that stripped of all artifice, we are exposed at our very core. I didn't know what I would find inside. It meant so much to me that my degrees and titles meant nothing at Nirmal Hriday. Like other female volunteers, and a few guys, I wore headbands every day that covered most of my hair for lice prevention. Sometimes when I looked in the mirror, I saw a stranger looking back at me, but the longer I looked, I saw myself clearly. The only thing that mattered was who I was in my deep core. And when I looked there, I discovered a deep well of love that I had nearly forgotten.

During volunteer registration and orientation, Sister MM said something that really resonated with me. When asked by new volunteers what they should do in the homes, she told them to think about their own relatives and how they would care for them at home. After lovingly tending to the women of Kalighat, I came home realizing that I also wanted to serve my family in the same way. As it turned out, my realization that I had a short window in which to fulfill this dream was prescient. Shortly after my return from India, my mom had a cascading series of medical problems, and I was grateful that I had the freedom to spend time with her every month. Following the installation of a pacemaker in October 2017, she began to feel much better. I've been to Virginia to stay with her many times. During the past nine months, she has experienced excruciating back pain and been hospitalized several times after falls.

My daughter announced her first pregnancy in October 2017, and I was home in time for my sweet grandson Oliver to be born in June 2018. I've cared for him during the week since he was three months old. He is a character, and I love watching him learn. He'll turn two in a few weeks and is already displaying two-year-old stubbornness! Grandparenting is such a gift. I think that in large part this is because we know what new parents do not – this precious time flies by much too quickly! Oliver will have a sibling in October 2020 and I know I'll love the new baby too.

In March 2018 and 2019, I had the opportunity to attend the Commission on the Status of Women and NGO Forum at the United Nations (CSW62) in New York City. Over ten thousand women from around the world attended the meetings, and it remains a very powerful experience. Listening to panels and stories each year, I've been reassured that committed, caring people around the world are working toward creating meaningful change. After I returned in 2018, I accepted a leadership position with the International Human Rights Consortium (IHRC). In this capacity, I will continue to explore ways to create and sustain social change. I am involved in a number of activities that focus on international travel and humanitarian work.

Soulful travel is an integral part of who I am. After I returned from Kolkata, my brother, sister-in-law, and friends from their church embarked on a river cruise from Prague to Budapest. It was an incredible journey of discovery. In 2018, my son and I spent two weeks in Scotland and Ireland, exploring part of our heritage there. I also got hooked on *Outlander* while there. In October 2019, Jordan and I headed out again to Spain and Portugal. We don't know when or where we'll travel next, but we are looking forward to future travel together.

My heart and hands are full these days. I know that I will always feel called to serve, but I'm listening and discerning more. Mindful practices that I developed before I left for India and strengthened while there continue to sustain me in the ambiguity of life.

I realize, as others discovered before me, that India is a great teacher. The women of Kalighat were my mentors and mirrors. The gifts they gave me are some of the most precious I've ever received. Now I realize more fully how aptly I titled this book. Yes, I left pieces of my heart in India. But the truth is this – with every piece of my heart that I gave away, my capacity to love expanded.

Namaste!

Gratitude

I am so grateful to the people who made my experience in India possible and extraordinary. I began this journey to fulfill a promise to myself when I left India. More importantly, I wanted to honor Ben, who was the most giving person I've ever known, by continuing his legacy of service to others. In the last months of his illness, we were fortunate to have a team of hospice workers who were with us at some point every day. I appreciated their gentleness, honesty, and compassion, and I knew that I wanted to honor their service too.

I was thankful that my mom understood the call that I felt so strongly, despite natural "mom worries." From the time that I first shared my plans with my children, siblings, nieces, and nephews, I appreciated their love and support as well.

I had an incredible group of "prayer warriors" who held my travel, health, and overall experience in the light. They also prayed for the women of Kalighat daily, and when there were special needs and concerns.

I had the privilege of working with an incredible group of colleagues at Wake Forest University. I appreciated their lovely "send-off" care package just when I needed it, and their notes and emails of support.

I feel blessed to have great friends in Winston-Salem, and around the world. Once again, their support meant so much to me, as did their Facetime calls, care packages, blog comments, and more.

I didn't anticipate that I would be so enriched by the many, many volunteers I met. I hesitate to list names because I don't want to forget anyone. If we worked together and I did not mention your name, please know that my poor memory is to blame. In the text, I used pseudonyms, but here I am using actual names: Caroline, Ani, Ana, Ana Paola, Paula, Ines (2), Etienne, Michael, Father David, Brother Parker, Father Dominic, Kolleen, Dernsta, Kim, Nina, Stephanie, Megan, Barb, Lauren, Macie, Hilda, Francisco, Betty, Giovanni, Carlos, Anna, Julie, Sofia, Josette, Ine, Teckla, Tetsuya, Brja, Ngoc, Trini, Ariane, Brother Paul, Richard, Judit, Kristin, Katherine/Kathryn, Nick, Jules, Karen, Fabio, Jeannette, Ombline, Shamim, Keven, and so many more.....

Every MC sister I met was generous with her time and attention. The sisters at Kalighat were kind, compassionate, serious, and dedicated. I gained so much wisdom from my time with them. What a perfect school for "love." I miss the massies I worked with, the social workers, physical therapists, and every support person at Kalighat.

I miss my Indian "family" — Visakha, Brindaban, Sukumar, Sunaina, Catherine, and Imran Zaki. I doubt I will ever find a cup of chai that tasted better than those made by my housekeepers. They were a joy. I loved watching TV together (cartoons, cooking shows, movies, and the Discovery Channel) and just spending time at home.

It does take a village. THANK YOU, THANK YOU, THANK YOU!

About the Author

 Mary Gerardy worked in higher education for over 40 years, including 31 years at Wake Forest University, before her retirement in 2016. Her last position was Associate Vice President for Campus Life. During her career, one of her favorite activities was traveling with students on international service trips to Vietnam (nearly 20 times), Rwanda, Belize, St. Lucia, Cambodia, the Dominican Republic, and India. Since her return from India in 2017 she has accepted the position of CEO and President of the International Human Rights Consortium. In addition, she blogs, reads, paints, travels, and enjoys spending time with friends and family.

Discussion

1. Was there a place – either real or fictional – that captured your attention as a child? Where was it? If real, have you been able to visit that place as an adult? Did reality match your expectations? Why or why not?

2. The author writes about "hearing the call" to a place or a kind of service. Have you ever heard the "call in the night"? Were you compelled to answer the call, or did you let it go?

3. Have you engaged in volunteer service locally, domestically, or globally? What has been your favorite service experience?

4. Has there been a time or experience when you realized that you were braver, smarter, or stronger than you might have imagined? What was it?

5. Would you like to live as an expatriate (expat); that is, outside of the United States for a while? Why or why not?

6. What is your favorite book? What resonates the most with you?

7. Has there been a time, after a loss of some kind, that you experienced a sense of being "out of step" with the world?

8. What have you done that scares you? Would you do it again?

9. Have you thought of your life as a story? What are the key themes that you would emphasize?

10. Have you cared for family members in your home? What were some of the surprises you experienced? What were some of the frustrations or difficulties?

11. The author talked about the different kinds of love in her life. What kinds of love are present in your life?

12. Have you thought about the bridge from work to retirement? What will you do with the post-work chapter of your life?

13. Have you had frustrating travel experiences? Share your best and worst travel stories.

14. Have you ever visited a place that took you by surprise or that felt magical?

15. Have you made mistakes when you first visited or interacted with a culture that was not your own?

Made in the USA
Monee, IL
10 November 2020